Contents

Acknowledgements v

Introduction vi

Working in Health and Social Care vi

What is an NVQ? vii

How do I gain an NVQ? viii

Your portfolio x

How this book can help you xi

NVQ/SVQ and differences between England, Scotland, Wales and Northern Ireland xii

Evidence of knowledge xiv

Meeting individual needs xvi

Units

HSC 21   Communicate with and complete records for individuals   3
   21a   Work with individuals and others to identify the best forms of communication   4
   21b   Listen and respond to individuals' questions and concerns   20
   21c   Communicate with individuals   32
   21d   Access and update records and reports   44

HSC 22   Support the health and safety of yourself and individuals   55
   22a   Carry out health and safety checks before you begin work activities   56
   22b   Ensure your actions support health and safety in the place you work   68
   22c   Take action to deal with emergencies   80

HSC 23   Develop your knowledge and practice   93
   23a   Evaluate (assess) your work   94
   23b   Use new and improved skills and knowledge in your work   108

HSC 24   Ensure your own actions support the care, protection and well-being of individuals   121
   24a   Relate to and support individuals in the way they choose   122
   24b   Treat people with respect and dignity   134
   24c   Assist in the protection of individuals   148

Contents

HSC 214   Help individuals to eat and drink   159

     214a   Make preparations to support individuals to eat and drink   160

     214b   Support individuals to get ready to eat and drink   176

     214c   Help individuals to eat and drink   186

HSC 218   Support individuals with their personal care needs   199

     218a   Support individuals to go to the toilet   200

     218b   Enable individuals to maintain their personal hygiene   214

     218c   Support individuals in personal grooming and dressing   230

HSC 215   Help individuals to maintain mobility   243

     215a   Support individuals to keep mobile   244

     215b   Observe changes in mobility and provide feedback   270

HSC 223   Contribute to moving and handling individuals   283

     223a   Prepare individuals, environments and equipment for moving and handling   284

     223b   Enable individuals to move from one position to another   306

Links to City & Guilds Certificate in Health and Social Care Level 2   324

Summary of Acts within the care sector   325

Glossary   329

Resources   334

Index   337

Acknowledgements

The authors would particularly like to thank the following people for their support:

Colette Burgess	Husband Robert and daughters Holly and Megan for their patience and support while writing this book
Nicki Pritchatt	Graham for his tireless patience and understanding
	Hannah Salter, Bournville College Assessment Centre, colleague and friend, for her continual advice and support
Colin Shaw	Tracey and Matt for their patience and continued support while writing this book

The authors and publishers would also like to thank:

Dr Ann Williams and staff of the West Suffolk College, Bury St Edmunds, Suffolk, particularly Jess Scotford for her shared experiences of real-life situations

Karen Krabbendam of the Grange Residential Home, Bury St Edmunds, Suffolk

Management, residents and staff of Oaken Holt Care Ltd, Farmoor, Oxford, particularly Training Manager, Mandy Vettraino

Risby Park Nursing Home, Risby, Bury St Edmunds, Suffolk

The West Suffolk Disability Resource Centre, by permission of the Papworth Trust and Suffolk County Council

Pauline Sisley and Elaine Maclennan for reviewing and commenting on this publication

Models: Megan Burgess, Oliver Coote, Janet Hance, Christian Hough, Jessica Scotford, Colin Shaw

Jan Wood, Helen Alexander, Pen Gresford and Kathy Peltan for their continued advice and support.

Welcome to *ProActive Level 2 Health and Social Care*!

You have made some good decisions:

○ You have chosen a rewarding career in Health and Social Care
○ You are working towards a nationally recognised qualification – a Level 2 S/NVQ and possibly the Level 2 Technical Certificate and some Key Skills as well if you are on a Modern Apprenticeship scheme
○ You are using a book which will help you achieve your qualification as quickly and easily as possible.

ProActive Level 2 Health and Social Care covers the four core units plus four of the most popular option units for the Level 2 S/NVQ award. It also covers the knowledge required for the Level 2 Technical Certificate in Health and Social Care. You can use this book as a reference for any areas which you do not fully understand.

The book will also help you understand what you need to do to collect evidence for your S/NVQ. It contains lots of ideas for preparing work that could be assessed and used as evidence. You can work with your assessor to decide which of these are appropriate for you.

Working in Health and Social Care

A career in Health and Social Care can be very rewarding. There are many roles to choose from and different care sectors or environments in which to work. The skills and knowledge you will develop while working towards your qualification will be put to good use, and you will be able to deliver a high level of care.

Your exact job title and tasks will depend on which part of the care sector you are working in. The table on page vii shows some job roles that you could perform with a Level 2 S/NVQ qualification, and the sort of functions or tasks you may carry out.

When deciding which part of the sector you would like to work in, you need to take into account the different roles and functions, the hours of work and terms and conditions.

Sector	Job title	Role	Core functions
Health	Health care support	To provide support to qualified health care professionals, such as nurses, therapists and doctors	To carry out a range of duties to support the needs of patients, such as helping with: ○ personal care ○ mobility ○ eating and drinking ○ recording and reporting any changes in an individual's condition ○ clinical investigations.
Social Care	Social care worker	To support individuals, for example in their own homes or in care homes	To carry out a range of duties to support individuals, such as helping with: ○ personal care ○ mobility ○ preparing meals ○ administering medications ○ eating and drinking ○ recording and reporting any changes in an individual's condition.

What is an S/NVQ?

An S/NVQ assesses a person's ability to perform a job. It can also form part of a Modern Apprenticeship. The assessment is continual, but you will only be assessed when you are able or competent to complete the task properly. S/NVQs are divided into units. In order to be assessed as competent in a unit, you need to fulfil various requirements.

○ **Performance Criteria** – gives details of the actions you must carry out to pass the unit.

○ **Scope** – is the range of situations, knowledge and understanding you must show that you understand in your current work role.

○ **Evidence requirements** – explain how much needs to be assessed by observation, and how much can be covered by other methods of assessment.

How do I gain an S/NVQ?

The flowchart below summarises the process of gaining an S/NVQ. Each stage is discussed in more detail on the next page.

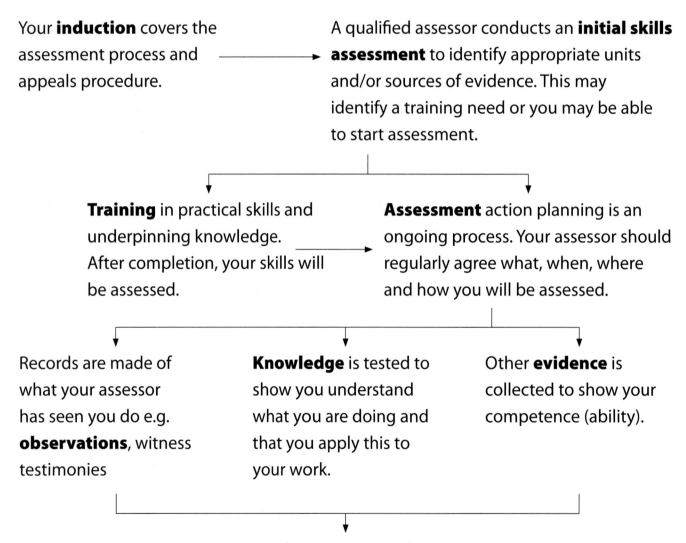

Your **induction** covers the assessment process and appeals procedure.

A qualified assessor conducts an **initial skills assessment** to identify appropriate units and/or sources of evidence. This may identify a training need or you may be able to start assessment.

Training in practical skills and underpinning knowledge. After completion, your skills will be assessed.

Assessment action planning is an ongoing process. Your assessor should regularly agree what, when, where and how you will be assessed.

Records are made of what your assessor has seen you do e.g. **observations**, witness testimonies

Knowledge is tested to show you understand what you are doing and that you apply this to your work.

Other **evidence** is collected to show your competence (ability).

Quality assurance – a qualified internal verifier checks the quality of the assessment you have received by regularly sampling your assessor's work.

Induction

You should receive an induction as soon as you start your S/NVQ. This should include an overview of the assessment process and a detailed explanation of the appeals procedures that you can follow should you have a complaint or want to make an appeal.

Initial skills assessment

When you start your qualification you should have an initial assessment with your assessor. Together you will work through the units you have selected to do in order to identify how much knowledge and/or skills you may already have. Your assessor may have a special form to record an assessment plan, so that you are very clear about what needs to happen next. You may be surprised at how many skills you already have.

Training

If your initial assessment identified a training need, you will receive training in practical skills, and the knowledge to support them before your skills are assessed.

Assessment

Your assessment will be ongoing, with your assessor. It will include:

Observation

Your assessor will regularly observe (watch) you carrying out tasks. Records of the observation will go into your portfolio.

Knowledge evidence

You will need to show your assessor that you understand why you do tasks the way you do. Your assessor may be able to infer some knowledge through your performance or you may have to do this by answering written, oral (spoken) or online (on the computer) questions.

Other evidence

It may also be possible to collect other evidence including:

- witness testimonies from colleagues or managers at your place of work, or from other agencies or professionals

- assessment of prior learning or experience required by the S/NVQ, such as induction or a food hygiene certificate
- work products (naturally occurring evidence) such as incident reports, appraisals.

Your assessor will work with you to decide on the best method of collecting evidence for each unit.

Your portfolio

All evidence should be placed into your portfolio and will need to be referenced to the S/NVQ standards. You will receive a paper copy of these standards, and a copy on CD, from City and Guilds when you start your S/NVQ. There are different styles of log books, depending upon which awarding body you are registered with. Alternatively you may be using an e-portfolio. Your assessor will advise you on whether to use a logbook or an e-portfolio.

Who checks my portfolio?

Your assessor will make decisions on your competence and work with you to help you build a portfolio of sufficient evidence of competence.

In order to ensure fairness and to monitor the quality of the assessment, an internal verifier (quality manager) will check the assessor's work regularly. This may be by observing them assessing you or by sampling evidence already collected and logged in your portfolio.

Shortly after you start your S/NVQ you will be registered with an awarding body, such as City & Guilds. The awarding body is responsible for checking the quality of the assessment and internal verification. The awarding body appoints an external verifier who may carry out checks before certification.

Modern Apprentices

If you are doing a Modern Apprenticeship then you will be working towards other qualifications alongside your S/NVQ, in particular:

- Key Skills Communication Level 2
- Key Skills Application of Number Level 1

o   A Technical Certificate in Health and Social Care Level 2

Some of the activities in this book could contribute evidence for Key Skills. Your assessor will help you to identify these opportunities.

The City & Guilds Level 2 Technical Certificate is assessed by assignments which are marked by your assessor. This book covers the knowledge required for the Technical Certificate. Some of the tasks in the book could also contribute towards parts of a Technical Certificate assignment. As always, you should plan your assessments with your assessor.

How this book can help you

Look out for the following special features as you work through the book.

Evidence

PC 3; KS 9   TC 003_B1

TC 003_B1

There are various ideas about activities that might be undertaken and could provide evidence of your competence and/or knowledge for your S/NVQ. Your assessor will discuss possible opportunities for evidence collection which are unique to you and your work setting and draw up a plan with you. These may include observations which demonstrate your skills and that you can apply your knowledge to what you do.

The evidence sections in this book are linked to performance criteria and knowledge statements which may help when considering your collection of evidence.

In the same way, there is also clear cross referencing which indicates how the content can be related to the Health and Social Care Technical Certificate (TC), which may help when considering what evidence you might provide for this qualification as well.

In the workplace:

Real-life case studies about working in health and social care that will help you to check your own level of understanding. You can find the answers to questions in these boxes on the CD-ROM

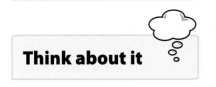

Think about it

A chance to think about how or why you do something

Have a go

Opportunities to put the learning into practice

definition   Clear definitions of words you need to know

Remember   Important reminders of health and safety tips

Scotland   Refers to laws relating to Scotland.

At the end of each unit:

What I have learned   Questions to test your knowledge. The answers to these questions are on the CD-ROM

Any questions?   Issues or problems that you may come across

Case Studies   To help you think about putting into practice what has been discussed in the unit. The answers to these questions are on the CD-ROM

At the back of the book you will find a CD-ROM which contains a number of Word documents that you can save and print out as necessary:

○ All the S/NVQ Evidence tasks in the book
○ All of the assessments for the City & Guilds Level 2 Technical Certificate
○ Answers to the 'In the workplace', 'What have I learned?' and 'Case study' features in the book.

NVQ/SVQ and differences between England, Scotland, Wales and Northern Ireland

Standards of conduct and practice in your work are regulated in the four different countries by four different Care Councils. However, they all work to ensure that individuals receive the highest level of care and support from you, your colleagues and your employers. You should be aware of these organisations. The websites are given on page xiii so that you can download the Code of Practice for your country.

Country	Code of Practice	Web address
England	The General Social Care Council	www.gscc.org.uk
Scotland	The Scottish Social Services Council	www.sssc.uk.com
Wales	The Care Council for Wales	www.ccwales.org.uk
Northern Ireland	The Northern Ireland Social Care Council	www.niscc.info

This book will make general reference to the Care Councils of the UK, and to the general Code of Practice for Social Care Workers. However, you should always check the specific requirements of the Care Council of the country in which you work.

Specific differences within Scotland

○ **Structure of the SVQ:** To achieve the SVQ Level 2, candidates are required to complete six units. These six units must include two core units and two optional units. The two remaining units can be taken from either the core or the optional sections.

○ **Unit numbers/codes are different for Scotland:** The SQA puts a six-digit number before the national occupations code. You can see these at http://www.sqa.org.uk/files_ccc/SVQ_HealthSocialCare_InfoSheet_level2.doc

○ Information and evidence gathering forms are different in layout for SVQ. See www.sqa.org.uk. The Health and Social care page provides blank examples of documents, information sheets, unit downloads, assessment strategy and guidance.

There is a very useful book called *Social Care and the Law in Scotland* which might be a useful reference for you to use.

Other specific differences concerning Scotland will be mentioned within the book and in the Summary of Acts section.

In your S/NVQ Standards the knowledge evidence is divided into three parts:

- values
- legislation and policy
- theories and practice.

All of the knowledge you need under these headings is related to your job role at work.

Values

Values or value base is the term used to describe the way everyone in health and social care should behave towards individuals using the service. We all have different values or attitudes, but at work we have to put our own values to one side and follow those described in our Care Council's Code of Practice.

Legislation and policy

There is an enormous amount of legislation in health and social care. You do not need to know every piece of legislation, or have to know the detail and all the dates, but you do need to know which major pieces of legislation are relevant to the way you work.

For example, you should know that the Health and Safety at Work Act places a duty on you to work safely and help your employer to keep the workplace safe. You also need to know that there is legislation in place which means that unfair discrimination is unlawful.

In addition your workplace will have developed a range of policies and procedures to help you work safely within the law. Your line manager or assessor will be able to tell you which pieces of legislation are most important to your work.

Theories and practice

Policies, procedures and processes are there to help us work safely and respond appropriately. Many of them are developed from theories based on research. Some people will talk about 'evidence based practice' which is the same thing. It means we use techniques which have been 'tried and tested'.

Theories were developed when it was realised that we all show certain similar patterns of behaviour or development, for example factors that impact on important stages of someone's development in early life may affect the way that person forms relationships or copes with every day pressures in later years.

In health and social care we use theories to help us understand social relationships and to provide explanations for the way someone may react to a situation. Being aware of theories can also prevent us from responding to a situation inappropriately.

Everyone is different – and each time you help an individual with their care, you need to think about their **holistic** needs. If you are looking after someone with a broken leg, it is easy to think about their physical needs and not consider other needs, for example, their emotional needs.

holistic
treating the whole person not just the disease

An easy way to consider a service user's holistic needs is to think about their Physical, Intellectual, Emotional and Social needs.

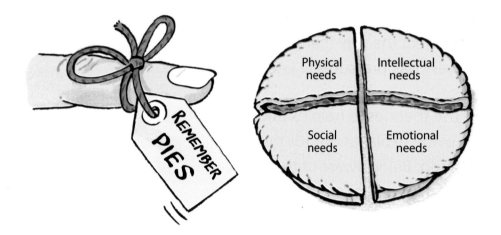

REMEMBER PIES

Physical needs | Intellectual needs

Social needs | Emotional needs

Physical needs such as food, drink, warmth, shelter and security.

Intellectual needs are about keeping the brain stimulated by getting involved in new and challenging activities.

Emotional needs are the needs we all have to be liked and loved.

Social needs are met through relationships with other people. They help people feel included and valued.

Have a go

Think about a service user that you care for and describe how you meet their holistic needs. Use the PIES diagram to make sure that you consider all of their needs.

In the workplace: A typical day

Sammy has learning disabilities and lives in a house in the community. Tara is Sammy's support worker and helps him to be independent.

Today is Saturday and there is a karaoke night in the local pub tonight. Sammy is very excited because he loves to sing.

Sammy asked if he could ring his mum to let her know the songs that he was hoping to sing. Tara helped him to use his new mobile phone to ring her.

Tara reminds Sammy to shower and shave ready for tonight. He has a waistcoat that he likes to wear for special occasions.

Tara helps him to work out how much money he will need. When they arrive, Sammy buys a drink at the bar and checks that he has been given the correct change. (Tara is there to help him if necessary).

Sammy joined in with the karaoke and had a wonderful night.

Look at the PIES diagram. What needs did Tara consider when caring for Sammy? Explain how.

HSC21

Communicate with and complete records for individuals

This unit is a core unit, which means it is one of the four units that you must complete as part of the NVQ award. You should cover this unit alongside the other units you have chosen.

Communication plays a very important role in your work because communication is how we give and receive information. You cannot complete any task in health and social care without some form of communication taking place. In this unit you will cover all the main ways of communicating. These include speaking and body language, as well as using signs, symbols, pictures or writing.

How you will be assessed:

For this unit your assessor will observe, or watch, you while you work to cover the Performance Criteria. The knowledge can be covered by discussion with your assessor or by answering questions from your assessor.

This unit covers the following elements:

- **21a** Work with individuals and others to identify the best forms of communication

- **21b** Listen and respond to individuals' questions and concerns

- **21c** Communicate with individuals

- **21d** Access and update records and reports.

This unit maps to Technical Certificate Unit 003: Communicating with, and completing records for individuals in a health and social care setting.

Work with individuals and others to identify the best forms of communication

Communication is used in different ways within every activity you do. We all have our own ways of communicating. You will need to find out how the people you care for prefer to communicate. This element looks at how you identify, or find out about, the best way to communicate with the individuals you work with.

To get evidence for this element, you will usually work with **individuals** you are meeting for the first time. However, even when you know how an individual **communicates**, this can change. It may change because their physical or mental state has changed. You should **assess** the individual's method and level of communication regularly.

individual
a single human being as distinct from a group
communicate
show or tell someone what you mean
assess
look at and judge

In this element you will cover:

o Ways of communicating
o How physical and mental health factors affect communication
o How personality, culture and beliefs affect communication
o Seeking information
o Reviewing your own communication skills
o Seeking extra support
o Sharing your findings.

Getting to know someone is a big part of successful communication

We all communicate in different ways, depending on where we are and who we are communicating with. Communication can be **verbal**, such as talking and shouting, or it can be as simple as just nodding your head. Laughing and a smiling expression on your face can communicate how you are feeling. The tone of your voice also tells the other person how you are feeling. People can also communicate through touch.

What do you think is the most used form of communication – speaking or facial expressions? If you answered 'speaking' you may be surprised to know that this is not correct. Facial expressions are a very important form of **non-verbal communication**. In fact, non-verbal communication accounts for 90 per cent of our communication.

TC 003_B1_a

verbal
spoken

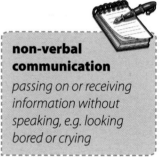

non-verbal communication
passing on or receiving information without speaking, e.g. looking bored or crying

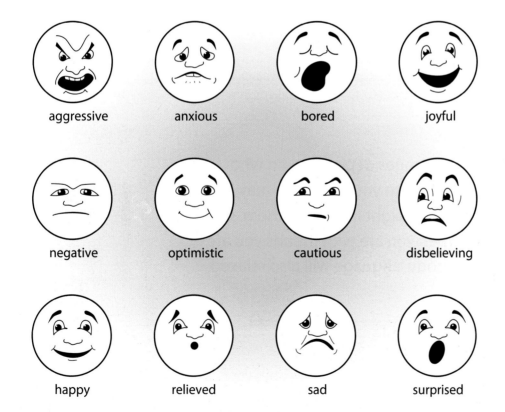

aggressive	anxious	bored	joyful
negative	optimistic	cautious	disbelieving
happy	relieved	sad	surprised

Facial expressions can say many things

Environments

The environment, or where you are, can affect the way you communicate. If you were in a library you would whisper or talk very quietly because you must not be noisy. If you were on a crowded bus with a friend, you would probably talk quietly because you would not want everyone to hear what you were saying. In a nightclub you would need to talk loudly so that you could be heard over the music. When you are in any of these environments you will use a lot of facial expressions and **body language** when you are talking.

body language
movements of the body communicating how someone feels

Have a go

Next time you are in a public place, try watching people's body language. Look at how they are sitting, moving their hands or using facial expressions. Try to work out what you think they are communicating.

Who you communicate with

The way you communicate also changes depending on who you are communicating with. Talking to your manager may make you nervous. You may sit up straight in front of them and you are probably very polite. When you are with friends you are more relaxed. Your speech and body language will also relaxed.

Think about it

Think of the different places where you talk to people. How does your communication change?

What facial expressions and body language do you use in different places, and why?

Think about it

Think about all the different people you communicate with in your life – everyone from the bus driver to your family to your manager at work. Try to think how your communication changes, depending on who you are communicating with. Do you communicate differently at work from the way you do at home? Why do you think this is?

Try watching people's body language and working out what you think they are communicating

In the workplace: Jake likes to joke

Jake works in the community with young people and their families. He enjoys a laugh and a joke with the individuals he provides care for. He finds it is a good way to communicate with young people.

1   *Do you think he should always be like this with the young people he works with?*

2   *Can you think of occasions when he might have to be more serious?*

3   *How should Jake speak to his manager?*

Key points

o   Everyone communicates in some way.

o   Talking and shouting are forms of verbal communication.

o   Non-verbal communication, such as facial expressions and body language, communicate more than verbal communication.

o   Where you are can affect your communication.

o   Who you are communicating with can change the way you communicate.

■ How physical and mental health factors affect communication *KS 7, 8*

No matter what their age or **ability**, everyone communicates in one form or another. A newborn baby cannot talk, but it lets everyone know how it feels by crying or moving its arms and legs. Just because someone cannot speak does not mean they cannot communicate.

TC 003_B1_b

Some people's communication **skills** and abilities may be affected by their mental or physical health. The table below shows problems that can arise from some disabilities.

ability
being able to do something

skills
something that you can do

How some disabilities can affect communication

Type of disability	Example	Possible problems
Learning disabilities	autism	Poor social skills, does not speak, poor eye contact, interested in objects more than people, easily distracted, poor concentration skills.
Mental health issues	dementia	Short-term memory loss, long-term memory loss, difficulty recognising people or things, poor concentration, poor motivation.
Physical disabilities	sight loss	Unable to see, unable to read written words.

In the workplace: Facial expressions

Nancy is working with an older man in his own home. He can hear, but he cannot speak. When Nancy asks him a question, she looks at his face to see what his answer is. She has taken the time to learn the way he uses his face to say 'yes', 'no', 'I don't know', 'I'm happy', 'I'm sad', 'I'm confused' or 'I'm angry'.

1   *Describe the ways you think he uses his face to say these things.*

2   *If you were a new carer coming in when Nancy was on holiday, do you think you could communicate with him?*

Some mental or physical health conditions mean a person may not be able to communicate very well verbally. Their speech may be very slow, or it may be difficult to understand when you first meet them. However, after you have worked with the person for a while, you may start to understand what they are saying much better.

If a service user cannot see, they also cannot see your body language or the expression on your face. We said earlier that these account for 90 per cent of communication. This could mean that someone who is blind only receives 10 per cent of what we are trying to communicate to them.

Think about it

Imagine you cannot see, how do you think you would feel? How do you think it would affect your communication?

Evidence

KS 7, 8   TC 003_B1

Choose one of the conditions in the table on page 8. Write more about how this condition may affect an individual's communication. Show your account to your assessor.

Learning to communicate with each service user may take time

Key points

o Everyone communicates in some way.

o An individual's physical or mental disability can affect the way they communicate.

o Once you get to know an individual, you can often communicate with them better.

■ How personality, culture and beliefs affect communication *KS 7, 8*

An individual's personality, **culture** and beliefs make them the person that they are. The individual's personality, culture or beliefs may also have an affect on their communication.

culture
customs, ideas and behaviour of a group of people

Personality

If an individual is shy or has a very quiet personality they may be very withdrawn. This means they may give very little eye contact, be quietly spoken or may not want to speak. Some individuals, however, have a strong personality. This type of person is not at all shy. They are often very friendly, and will speak to anyone. An individual's personality can affect the way they communicate, not just through speech, but also through their body language.

Think about it

Think about the individuals you provide care for, how does their personality affect their communication?

Culture and beliefs

If an individual has been raised in a different culture, they may use a different language. You may not speak their language, or they may not speak yours. There are other cultural differences, too. In some cultures it is wrong or impolite to look another person in the eye when talking. But someone from another culture might think that person was being rude for not maintaining eye contact. Some cultures have strict rules about how men and women should behave towards each other.

The way someone has been raised by their family can affect how they communicate with others. You may have been told as a youngster not to speak until you are spoken to, or never to speak to strangers.

Remember

Never assume how an individual communicates by the way they look.

This may have affected how you communicate with others now. You may wait for people to start talking to you before you talk to them. Or you may find it difficult talking to a person you do not know. Remember this when you are working with individuals. You may not know how they have been raised as a child. Their upbringing could have affected the way they communicate now.

In the workplace: Is she just shy?

Asia is a young Muslim woman. She is refusing to talk to a male support worker, and is turning her head away from him. What is she communicating and why?

Evidence *KS 7, 8*

Think of a time when you have had difficulty communicating with a service user or a **colleague** because of their personality, beliefs or cultural differences. Write an account of the difficulties you had. Show your account to your assessor.

colleague
person you work with

Key points

o Someone who is quiet and shy communicates differently to someone who is outgoing and has a strong personality.

o An individual's culture and beliefs can affect the way they communicate.

o In some cultures there are strict rules about how men and women behave towards one another.

o The way an individual was raised can affect the way they communicate.

You can find out information on an individual's communication method or needs in a numbers of ways, including:

TC 003_A1_ai,aii

- from the individual themselves, by **observing**, listening and talking to them
- from colleagues, by asking them questions, and by watching how they work with the individual
- asking the advice and opinions of the **professional** people involved in a service user's care
- asking the individual's family and friends how they communicate with the individual
- reading the individual's care plan, case notes and records.

Before you begin looking for information on an individual's communication needs or method you need to be aware of the Data Protection Act 1998 and the Access to Medical Records Act. Part of the Data Protection Act deals with **confidentiality** concerning the service user's records. You need to find out how this affects you. You also need to know your organisation's policy on who can look at records and reports. You can find more information on this in the last element of this unit.

observe
watch

professional
specialists such as doctors, speech therapists, occupational therapists

confidentiality
keeping information secret

People do not always have to speak to say how they feel

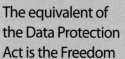

Scotland

The equivalent of the Data Protection Act is the Freedom of Information Act

Think about it

TC 003_A1a

What questions do you need to ask people to help you find out how an individual communicates? You may want to ask:

o Can they speak; is their speech clear?

o Can they hear me and understand me?

o Can they see me?

o Do they use **sign language**, and if so, which one?

o Do they have their own signs they use? If so, what are they, and what do they mean?

sign language
using your hands to make signs, e.g. British Sign Language or Makaton

Evidence *PC 1; KS 8*

TC 003_A1_a

Speak to a service user, a colleague or a service user's family members to find out some information on the way the service user communicates. This should be a service user that you do not know very well. You could use the questions from the Think about it box. Ask your assessor to observe you finding out the information.

In the workplace: Stephanie's new job

Stephanie is a new member of staff in a care home. She works with four service users who have learning disabilities. She has not worked with people with learning disabilities before.

How can Stephanie find out how each of the individuals communicates?

Key points

o You can speak to the individual, their family, your colleagues or professionals to find out how an individual communicates.

o Read the individual's case notes, care plan and records.

o Be aware of the Data Protection Act, the Access to Medical Records Act, confidentiality and your organisation's policy on accessing records.

o Always get permission before accessing records.

Remember

Always ask for permission from your manager before reading an individual's case notes.

When you meet and work with an individual for the first time you may find that you cannot understand the way they communicate. If you find yourself in this position, you need to change. You must try to find a way that you can communicate. You need to make sure that this person can understand you, and that you can understand them. Communication is a skill and it needs to be practised carefully to get it right.

What skills do you need?

There are many skills you need to communicate well with people. For example, you need to be able to watch, listen, remember and be patient. You also need to be understanding, and to **respond** to the other person. You should make sure you accept the individual's differences and don't **discriminate** against them in any way. Use the table on page 15 to help you review, or look at, the skills you have and the skills you need to develop.

Remember

Never act just on what you think a person wants. Always confirm with them first to make sure you have understood correctly.

respond
answer or communicate back to someone

discriminate
treat unfairly, e.g. because of age, race or gender

Think about it

Have you ever been on holiday in another country where people do not speak your language? How did you feel when people could not understand what you were saying? What did you find most helpful?

Skills needed to communicate well

TC 003_A1_aiii

Observe or watch an individual so that you can understand what they are communicating. Watch their body language and facial expressions. Check with them what you think they are communicating by repeating it back to them.

Listen for any sounds an individual makes, such as humming, smacking their lips or clicking their tongue. These sounds could be how the individual communicates.

Find out what these sounds mean so you can **understand** them. For example, if someone smacks their lips when offered a drink, it could mean 'yes'. A clicking sound could mean 'no'. Everyone has the right to communicate in their own way.

Remember the way an individual communicates so that you do not have to find out again. Remember the sounds they make for different words, or the facial expressions they use.

You may need to be very **patient** with some individuals, especially if they speak very slowly or have difficulty in saying certain words. Never say the word for an individual if they are having difficulty getting it out. Give them time and encouragement to speak for themselves. This is known as active support.

Respond to the individual in a way they will understand. There is no point in just nodding your head when you answer a question from an individual who is blind. They will not be able to see you.

Do not **discriminate** against anyone. This means working in a way that does not favour one individual over another. You should communicate with individuals using their preferred method of communication. Not using an individual's preferred method of communication is a form of discrimination.

Evidence *PC 3; KS 3*

Look at your communication skills. Do you think you have the right skills to communicate with the individuals you work with? Do you have other skills that are not in the table that you feel help you to communicate? Talk to your assessor about the skills you have and how they meet the needs of service users.

Key points

o   You need patience and understanding to communicate well.

o   In order to review your own communication skills, you need to find out what communication skills you have.

o   Ask yourself if your skills help you to communicate well with individuals.

o   Identify what other skills you need to meet the communication needs of the individuals you work with.

There will be times when you will not have the right skills to communicate with certain individuals. You should not feel uncomfortable if an individual speaks a different language from you. It can take many years to learn a new language. The important thing to remember when you have difficulty in communicating with someone is to seek extra support. You should not just walk away or expect someone else to do it for you. It is your **responsibility** to get help for yourself. There are a lot of people who can help you.

responsibility
*something it is your
duty to do*

Where can you get extra support?

Extra support can come from many people including:

○ colleagues – other members of staff who may have known the individual you are trying to communicate with longer than you have

○ interpreters – people who support the communication between two people who do not share the same language, for example, Urdu to English or spoken English to British Sign Language

○ translators – people who help communication by changing the written word into an easier to read format for the individual, for example, into Braille for a blind person.

TC 003_B3_b

Have a go

Find out the names, addresses and telephone numbers of organisations or people who can help you. This could be a translator or interpreter. You may need to ask your manager or supervisor for help to find out how you can contact these people in your area.

Why might I need extra support?

If you do not have the skills needed to communicate with an individual, you will not be able to find out what their views, needs or wishes are. You would not be able to understand the individual and they would not be able to understand you. This is not fair on the individual. As human beings we all have the **right** to communicate in our preferred and chosen way. This is a legal requirement under the Human Rights Act 1998. You can find more information on this Act in the book *Health & Social Care Level 2* by Yvonne Nolan.

right
something an individual is legally able to do

Evidence *PC 4, KS 2, 3, 8*

Tell your assessor where you can get help to communicate with an individual who:

1. speaks a different language to you
2. is blind
3. is deaf.

Give your assessor their contact details including names, addresses, emails and telephone numbers.

Scotland

For more information, see the book *Social Care and the Law in Scotland* in the Resources section.

Key points

o   Do not feel embarrassed about asking for help.

o   It is important to seek extra support if you need it.

o   Extra support can come from colleagues, translators and interpreters.

o   Support helps you to meet the views, needs and wishes of individuals.

o   It supports the rights of individuals under the Human Rights Act 1998.

You have searched through the individual's case notes. You have spoken with the individual and their family. You have observed the individual to learn their body language and facial expressions. You have worked very hard to identify the best way to communicate with someone. Now you should really share your findings with others. You cannot keep this important information to yourself. You need to share it so that everyone else knows how that individual communicates. Sharing information can save the individual repeating the same information to others.

How do I share my findings?

The best way to share your findings on an individual's communication needs and method is by a written report. Your report should detail how the individual communicates, by what method, and any particular meanings of body language or facial expressions that you have found.

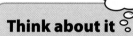

Think about it

Imagine if no one ever shared the information they had found. Professionals would be queuing up all asking the same sorts of questions. The individual would soon get very fed up!

Name Ivan Jenkins   **DOB** 17.01.68

Address 30 Quarry Road, Cardiff

Comments

Ivan has no verbal speech, but is able to show his likes and dislikes and his needs and wishes through facial expressions and body language.

Facial expression/body language	Meaning
Two blinks of the eyes	Yes
One blink of the eyes	No
Smacking his lips	I want a drink
Clicking his tongue	I want some food
Rocking body side to side	I want the toilet
Closing eyes tightly	I am in pain

Signed *Kabul Sable*   **Date** 3 August 2007

An example of how you could write a report on how an individual communicates

Making a written report in an individual's case notes ensures there is a permanent record, one that cannot be forgotten. For more information on record keeping, please look at the last element of this unit, on page 50.

Another way of sharing your findings can be through a team meeting. But the problem with verbal information is that it can be forgotten, so it is important you make a written record as well to avoid all your hard work going to waste.

By verbally passing on the information, your colleagues can ask you questions to make sure they have understood the information correctly

In the workplace: Sharing information

Maria has worked in Peart Place for four weeks. She has worked hard at identifying the communication needs of individual service users, but has not shared her findings with anyone.

What problems could this cause the other staff and the service users?

Evidence *PC 5, KS 14*   TC 003_B1

Using the information from the Evidence activity on page 13, share your findings of an individual's communication needs, wishes and preferences at a team meeting. Ask your manager if you can invite your assessor to the meeting, so that he or she can observe you sharing information.

Key points

o   You cannot keep information to yourself.

o   You should share your findings by writing a report for others to read.

o   You can share your findings in a team meeting.

Listen and respond to individuals' questions and concerns

This element looks at how you listen to an individual's communication and how you respond to their questions and concerns. For this element, you need to show that you know the individual well enough to have identified their preferred method of communication.

Listening plays a very important role in communication. If you do not listen properly, you will not be able to respond to what an individual wants. Apart from listening with your ears, you also need to show that you are listening, and that you are interested in what the individual is communicating.

In element 21a, on page 6, we mentioned that body language is very important in communication. One part of body language is how we **position** ourselves when we are communicating.

position
the way we sit or stand

In this element you will cover:

- Positioning yourself correctly
- Showing that you are listening
- Responding appropriately
- Seeking additional advice and support.

Active listening shows that you are interested in what is being communicated

Imagine sitting next to someone who has their back to you. You are trying to talk to them, but you find it difficult because you do not know if they are listening or not. How you sit or stand when communicating is very important. A positive (good) position, such as leaning forward, can show respect and understanding. A negative (bad) position, such as turning your body away or not looking at the person, shows disrespect and that you are not interested in what they have to say.

Get into position

To be in the right position you must:

○ Face the person you are talking to, so that you can see each other's body language and facial expressions clearly. This will help you both to understand what is being communicated.

○ Be at the same height. If a service user is sitting down or in a wheelchair, you should sit down near to them, or bend your knees so that your face is at the same level as theirs. If you stand over someone you can make them feel uncomfortable.

○ Have good eye contact, so that you can look at the person's eyes. This will show that you are listening to them and what they have to say.

○ Be at a suitable distance for the communication. Sitting too close to someone can make them feel uncomfortable.

Think about it

If you were in a wheelchair and a sales assistant stood over you to ask you questions, how do you think it would make you feel?

Do not look down at individuals when communicating. Make sure you are at the same height

Have a go

Look at how the care worker in this photograph is positioned. Is he in the correct position to communicate with the service user?

| Intimate zone (touching) | Personal zone (less than 1 metre) | Social zone (1–2 metres) | Public zone (2 metres +) |

Think about your daily work and when you would use these positions

Evidence *PC 2, KS 9*   TC 003_B2

Think about a time when you positioned yourself correctly when communicating with an individual. Write an account of the position you took and state how you felt it helped you to understand what the individual was saying.

Barriers

Tables and desks can be **barriers** to good communication. If you are sitting behind a desk, how can you see all of the individual's body language? Always position the chair to the side of the desk when communicating with individuals. This will let you see the individual's body language and you will be able to listen to them properly.

barrier
something that gets in the way

TC 003_B2_b

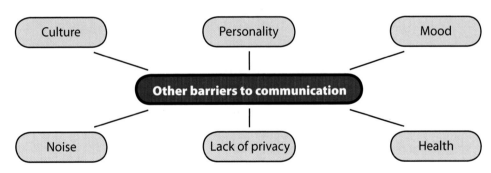

Barriers need not be physical, like tables or chairs

When you select or create an environment suitable for communication you should also consider the individual's choice and preference, and their comfort.

Key points

- o   Take care to position yourself correctly when communicating with someone.
- o   Face the other person, and maintain good eye contact.
- o   Be at the same height.
- o   Do not sit too close.
- o   Avoid barriers such as desks or tables whenever possible.

Sometimes people appear to hear what someone is saying, but they are not really listening. To listen properly you need to **focus** on the individual so that you hear what they say and how they say it. You then need to think about what the individual said, and act upon it in the right way.

Listening is a skill which needs to be practised. You can see when someone is listening by his or her body language, facial expressions, the sounds they make and the eye contact they have. This is known as active listening.

Body language

We mentioned body language earlier, and we have just talked about being in the correct position to listen. There are several other ways in which your body language can show that you are listening. For example, your body and head will face towards the other person. If you are sitting down, you may be leaning forward towards them. Your head may lean to one side, and you may nod in agreement where **appropriate**. Your facial expressions should match the information that is being communicated.

Use appropriate sounds

As well as nodding your head and using facial expressions, making appropriate sounds can also show that you are listening. Sounds such as 'mmm', 'oh' and 'ahhh' all show that that you are listening. You can also repeat back part of what someone has said to you, but you should not do this all the time as it could become very annoying to the individual.

focus
pay full attention to

Think about it

If someone told you that they were in pain, you would have a concerned facial expression. You would not smile if someone told you their cat had just died.

appropriate
suitable for the occasion or use

Remember

Make sure you are really listening when you are nodding your head to what someone is communicating; it may not always be appropriate.

Have a go

Have another look at the facial expressions on page 5. Which of them, if any, would you use for the following? Which wouldn't you use?

o   An older lady tells you her husband died a month ago.

o   A young man tells you he won some money on the lottery last week.

o   An older man talks to you about how he enjoyed his army days.

o   A young man is crying.

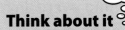

Think about it

If you use appropriate body language, facial expressions, sounds and eye contact, it will encourage the individual to communicate with you more. They are then more likely to tell you if there is a problem.

Why should you show that you are listening?

Have you ever tried to talk to someone who was not really listening? Did you carry on talking to them, or did you give up? When someone listens to you and shows that they are interested in what you have to say, it encourages you to continue talking. It is the same for the service users you work with.

Evidence *KS 2, 9*

TC 003_B2

Write a short statement on why active listening is important. Explain how to focus on the individual, and how to use appropriate body language, eye contact and facial expressions when communicating with them.

Key points

o   Use appropriate body language to show you are actively listening.

o   Make appropriate sounds.

o   Occasionally repeat what has been said.

o   Maintain eye contact.

When a service user asks you a question, you need to listen very carefully to make sure you respond in the right way. You should also ask yourself whether you have the right information or level of experience to give the correct answer. You should always be fully aware of how you respond to an individual's questions and concerns. Take a moment to think first, to prevent an **inappropriate** response.

inappropriate
not suitable for the occasion

Appropriate responses

The appropriate response very much depends on the question or concern raised. It also depends on the experience or ability of the person responding. Here are some general rules you should follow:

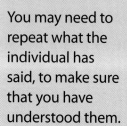

Remember

You may need to repeat what the individual has said, to make sure that you have understood them.

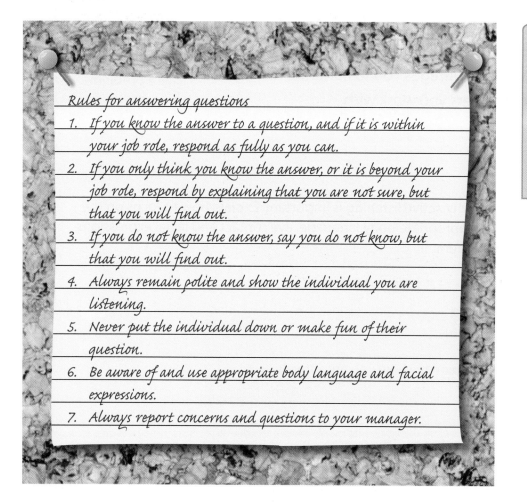

Rules for answering questions

1. *If you know the answer to a question, and if it is within your job role, respond as fully as you can.*
2. *If you only think you know the answer, or it is beyond your job role, respond by explaining that you are not sure, but that you will find out.*
3. *If you do not know the answer, say you do not know, but that you will find out.*
4. *Always remain polite and show the individual you are listening.*
5. *Never put the individual down or make fun of their question.*
6. *Be aware of and use appropriate body language and facial expressions.*
7. *Always report concerns and questions to your manager.*

Inappropriate responses

Many inappropriate responses are a result of the stresses of the job and inexperience. For example, a service user might ask a busy nurse, 'What time is the newspaper being delivered?' If the nurse responds by shrugging her shoulders and raising her hands, saying, 'I dunno', this is an inappropriate response. Even if you are very busy, it is not an excuse to respond inappropriately.

It can take some individuals a lot of courage to ask a question or raise a concern so it is important that you respond appropriately. If you respond the wrong way they may not want to ask any more questions or voice any concerns, which could be harmful to their health.

Some individuals ask questions as a way of getting attention. Even though working in a care environment can be very busy, you still need to make time to sit and listen to individuals. Never rush your response to questions. If you are in the middle of something, explain this, and say you will come back to them, but you must make sure you do.

Remember

If you say you will come back with an answer, make sure you do!

Remember

Make sure the service user cannot hear any irritation in your voice when you reply to them.

Think about it

Think about how you would feel if you were in the same position as the individual who is asking you the question. How would you want someone to respond to you?

Questions and concerns

Question or concern	Response	Given by
'I have a pain in my leg.'	'Don't worry, I'll get you a tablet.'	housekeeper
'When can I go home?'	'I'll speak to the manager and let you know.'	senior care worker
'I'm scared of walking to the bathroom by myself.'	'Don't be silly, you can do it.'	support worker
'I know I'm diabetic, but can I have just a little more chocolate?'	'Oh go on then, it shouldn't hurt.'	senior care worker
'I don't need my tablets tonight; I'm feeling much better.'	'Oh good, I'm so pleased you're better; you won't need your medication.'	senior care worker
'I can't get to sleep.'	'Is there anything worrying you?'	support worker
'What time is the care worker coming to take me to bingo?'	'I don't know, could be any time.'	support worker
'He looks rough. I bet he's been taking drugs.'	'Yes. He does look a bit pale and thin doesn't he? Just like those druggies.'	support worker
'I can't eat this, I'm a vegetarian.'	'Bad luck, that's all there is on the menu tonight.'	housekeeper

Evidence *PC 2, 3, 4, 5, 6; KS 2, 3, 9*

Write a detailed account of when an individual asked you questions. Say how and why you positioned yourself and actively listened. Describe how you gave them sufficient time and responded appropriately.

Support workers must have excellent active listening skills

Key points

To be able to respond appropriately you should:

- listen carefully to the question or concern
- follow the general rule – 'If you don't know, say so'
- always remain polite and be aware of your body language
- give individuals time to ask questions
- think about your answer before you respond.

When you are communicating with individuals and **key people** there may be times when they ask you a question or raise a concern that you cannot help with. In the previous topic you looked at how you respond to an individual's questions. Now you will look at why you respond in a certain way when you are asked something that you are not able to deal with.

key people
people who are important in an individual's life, such as parents, friends, carers, relatives

Roles and responsibilities

Everyone within the care sector has his or her own job role and responsibilities. They are able to do their job because of their **qualifications, knowledge** and experience. You are working as a care worker because of your knowledge and experience. It takes a certain type of person and many months of practice to learn how to be a good care worker. For some areas of work, it takes even more time to develop the knowledge and practical skills required. For example, becoming a qualified nurse, doctor or speech therapist takes many years of study.

qualifications
exams a person has passed

knowledge
something you know and understand

Who can you seek advice and support from?

Your colleagues, managers or supervisors may be able to help you with general questions or concerns that individuals or key people put to you if you cannot deal with them yourself. For more complicated queries, you may need to talk to other professionals for their advice and support.

Remember

You should not deal with any question or area of concern that you are not trained or qualified in.

Dietician – can be contacted to deal with any questions or concerns raised by a service user about their diet. If the service user is on a special diet for **diabetes** or another condition, you should pass their questions to the dietician. Dieticians can also help with eating problems, for example, if a service user needs foods that are easy to swallow. They can help the individual to lose weight or gain weight safely and can give advice on **allergies** to certain foods.

diabetes
a serious medical condition affecting the levels of sugar in the blood

allergy
a bad reaction by the body to a substance

Physiotherapist – can be contacted to deal with any questions or concerns about a service user's **mobility**, exercise, or if they need supported seating. A physiotherapist has trained for many years and has a good understanding of how human bones and **muscles** work.

Doctor – can be contacted to answer any questions or concerns about the service user's health problems or medication.

mobility
ability to move around, or from one position to another

muscles
strong, fibrous tissues which shorten to give the body movement

---

In the workplace: Christy's classes

Christy has been asked by the residents of the care home to set up an exercise class. Who do you think she should talk to before she sets up the activities, and why?

Think about it

What could happen if you gave advice to an individual who had diabetes on how to lose weight?

Evidence *PC 7, KS 4*

Think of a time when you asked for advice and support to deal with a service user's questions or concerns. Write an account of the concerns. Say who you got help from, and why.

Key points

o Only respond to questions or concerns that are within your job description and level of qualifications.

o Always seek additional advice and support on questions or concerns that you cannot deal with.

o You can seek advice and support from your colleagues, manager or other professionals, such as dieticians, doctors and physiotherapists.

The first element in this unit covered the preparation you need to do before you are able to communicate with individuals. The second element looked at positioning, and the listening and responding skills you need. This element will help you to put all of this information together. It also gives you more skills so that you can support people to communicate the way they want to.

You have already learned that communication is more than just talking. You have also learned that individuals can communicate in a variety of ways. These include verbal communication (using speech) and non-verbal communication, such as facial expressions, body language and sign language.

In this element you will also look at how you should communicate with individuals while respecting their **individuality** and their rights.

individuality
being treated according to your own likes and dislikes

In this element you will cover:

o Means of communication
o Rights to communication
o Supporting individuals to use their preferred means of communication
o Adapting your communication.

The multicultural society we live in has many different cultures and languages, so not everyone communicates in the same way that you do. The way we communicate is part of our identity.

Every person is unique. However busy you are, it is very important to remember that all the people you come into contact with are individuals. They may have different needs, values, backgrounds and personalities from your own. They may have different levels of understanding or ability. This may affect how they communicate. You must try to avoid judging people because of their sex, age, race or background, or this could affect how you communicate with an individual.

We live in a diverse community, but everyone has the right to communicate in the way that is appropriate for them

Types of support for communication

TC 003_B2_a,b,c

Verbal speech There are nearly 7,000 recognised languages in the world including 55 different languages in the UK. How many different languages do you speak? In addition, some regions of the UK have different dialects or forms of language. For example, the word 'yes' is pronounced 'aye' in Lancashire, 'ah' in Warwickshire and 'ar' in the Black Country (central England).

Wait

Touch For example, putting your hand on the shoulder of an individual who is blind to let them know you are there. Some people with learning difficulties communicate a lot through touch.

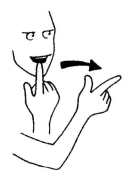

Tell/Say

Sign language British Sign Language is used to communicate with individuals who have a hearing loss.

Makaton A form of simple signing, used to support speech.

Body language For example, nodding your head for 'yes', facial expression or changing the position of the body.

Go to see
Some useful examples of British Sign Language

Technical aids Electronic equipment that can change written text to the spoken word. It is often used by people who have problems with their sight. People who cannot speak can use computers and other electronic equipment to communicate.

TC 003_B3_a

Human aids Translators, interpreters or **advocates**.

advocate
someone who represents, or speaks, for someone else

Visual aids Using picture boards, pen and paper or other means to write instead of speak.

tap
twice

The man   is eating   an orange.

Makaton is a simple form of sign language

Makaton was developed to help people with learning difficulties to communicate. Because it is much easier to learn than British Sign Language, it is also a useful means of communication for an individual who has had a stroke or a head injury.

Think about it

How would you like to communicate if you could not speak? How would you want to be treated?

Evidence *KS 8*   TC 003_A1_a, B1

Find out about the different ways the individuals you work with communicate. Explain these ways to your assessor.

Key points

o Everyone is an individual.

o The way an individual communicates will depend on their level of ability, and their culture.

o Technical and visual aids can be used as a means of communicating.

o Human aids to communication include translators, interpreters and advocates.

Try to imagine not being able to communicate and having no one to help or give you support. What would this mean for you? You may not be able to live where you want, or even eat what you want. You may not be able to go out where you want, or do what you want. This would not be fair and would mean you were not being treated equally.

Communication rights

Communication is just one of the basic human rights all individuals have and it is your responsibility to ensure these rights are met. The table below looks at communication rights, based on the Care Council's Code of Practice.

Scotland

For communication rights, refer to the Scottish Social Services Council or their website: www.sssc.uk.com.

Communication rights of individuals

Rights of individuals	Effect when communcation needs are not met
The right to diversity, or to be different	The individual will not be able to express their own identity or culture
The right to equality	The individual will not be treated equally if they are unable to communicate their views or opinions
The right to control their own life	The individual will not be able to make choices regarding their life
The right to dignity	The individual is not being treated with respect by denying them their right to communication
The right to effective communication	The individual will not be able to communicate effectively
The right to safety and security	The individual will not be able to express their safety concerns or report acts of abuse
The right to take risks	The individual will not be able to choose the risks that they take

Other rights to communication include:

○ The Human Rights Act 1998. This states that all individuals have the right to freedom of expression. This means people should be able to express their views.

○ National Minimum Standards. These say all individuals receiving care should be helped to access appropriate aids to communication and have their communication needs met. The National Minimum Standards are part of the Care Standards Act. This Act tells people working in care how they should treat individuals in their care.

The organisation you work for should have policies and procedures on communication, which you should be aware of. Ask your manager or supervisor for your organisation's policy on communication.

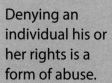

Remember

Denying an individual his or her rights is a form of abuse.

Evidence KS 5

Read your organisation's policy on communication and explain the contents. You may need your manager or supervisor to go through it with you to make sure you fully understand it. Then explain it in your own words to your assessor.

Scotland

The Care Commission uses National Care Standards to ensure that care does not fall below a minimum standard.

Key points

○ Everyone has the right to communicate.
○ It is your responsibility to ensure individuals' rights are met.
○ Denying an individual his or her rights could be seen as a form of abuse.

The amount of support an individual needs to communicate will depend on the method of communication they use. If the individual speaks a different language, or uses sign language, they may need an interpreter. If the individual uses a different written language, such as Braille, a translator can help.

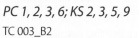

TC 003_B2_c

You can learn to communicate in many different ways

Evidence

PC 1, 2, 3, 6; KS 2, 3, 5, 9
TC 003_B2

Write an account of how and why you have supported an individual's communication and show it to your assessor.

When communicating using an interpreter or translator, make sure that you focus on the service user. You are communicating with the service user, not the interpreter. This is the same for any individual with a disability who has someone else with them. Imagine that the interpreter or carer is not there. Look at the individual when you ask them a question, even though they may not understand you. Continue looking at the individual when the interpreter is giving their reply. This shows equality, dignity and respect to the individual. Always use a reliable translator or interpreter who will be able to explain and respond accurately.

Remember

It is not good practice to ask family members or friends to interpret for individuals.

General support

Always communicate at a speed the individual can follow. Don't rush, and always give them time to answer any questions. If you speak too fast, the individual may not be able to understand everything you say.

Be aware of the individual's level of understanding. Check that they have understood you. You can do this by simply asking, 'Do you understand?' and by watching the individual's facial expressions. If they look confused, you should repeat what you have said, but in a slightly different way.

Support can be given by simply reassuring the individual during the communication. Reassurance can be given verbally, by smiling or by a gentle touch of the hand to show the individual you are there if they need you.

Always make sure that the individual has what they need to communicate. If they use pen and paper, make sure the pen works and that they have enough paper. If the individual communicates using a technical aid, ensure that the batteries have been fully charged and that the equipment is working.

Key points

- The amount of support individuals need for communication varies.
- Be careful to focus on the individual if using an interpreter or translator.
- Always communicate at a pace the individual can follow.
- Check that the individual has understood you.
- Always make sure that the individual has everything they need to communicate.

You will need to communicate with many different individuals and key people on a daily basis. It is important that you are able to communicate well with everyone and that what you say is understood. If you are having difficulties making yourself understood, then you will need to **adapt** the way you communicate. You might also need to adapt the way you communicate in different circumstances.

adapt
change

How can you adapt your communication?

As we have already discussed, if an individual communicates through signs and gestures then you will need to change the way you normally communicate to use and understand their signs and gestures.

Some individuals, such as those with learning disabilities or **dementia**, can become very confused if you use too many words at a time. In this case you will need to change your communication to just using simple words or very short sentences. If the person has a visual disability you should say who you are before you start talking to them. This can help the person to identify you and stops them becoming startled by your voice.

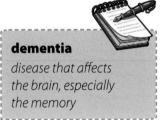

dementia
disease that affects the brain, especially the memory

Changes in an individual's communication

Some individuals' means of communicating may change because of a change in their health. A person who has had a stroke may have difficulty speaking at first, but with support their speech may become clearer. You can support this change in their communication with picture cards showing items they want or need.

Remember

You may think that what you are saying to an individual is clear and easy to understand. Just because you understand what you are saying does not mean everyone will.

Food   Fruit

Bed   Drink

Picture cards can help people with speech difficulties to communicate

If you notice any change in the way an individual communicates, whether they are communicating more easily or their communication has become worse, it is important that you report this to your manager or supervisor. It may mean that there is a medical condition that needs attention.

Communicating with colleagues and other professionals

When you are communicating with colleagues or other professionals, you should communicate in a professional manner. This means you should express yourself clearly and politely. You should keep to the point and only say what needs to be said.

You would not go up to a doctor and slap him on the back saying 'All right, mate?'. You may do this with your family and friends, but you should not do this in the workplace.

You should be a little more formal and polite when you are talking to professional people, or when discussing service users in meetings. You may have friendly, relaxed relationships with many of your colleagues, but you should always be polite to the colleagues you are friends with as well.

In the workplace: Shirley's speech has changed

Paul has worked with Shirley for a few months at a care home for older people but this morning he noticed that her speech had become **slurred** and was difficult for him to understand.

1 *What should Paul do and why?*

2 *Speak to your supervisor or manager to find out the possible reasons why Shirley's speech had become slurred.*

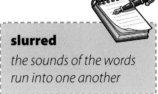

slurred
the sounds of the words run into one another

Think about it

Think of all the different people you communicate with at work. You should be able to identify quite a lot of people. Think about the different ways you communicate with them and the ways you have to adapt your communication from one person to another.

'Yo dude, how's it going?'

Everyone has a different way of communicating

Communicating information clearly

If you are passing on information, it is important that the facts are given clearly and are understood. For example, if you were to give directions to a key person on how to get to the visitors' lounge and they received the wrong information they could end up in the wrong place and might become very annoyed and upset. It is even more important if you are discussing a service user's condition or needs.

If necessary, you can check that the person you are communicating with has understood what you have said. You can ask them to repeat it back to you.

Evidence *PC 5, 6, 7; KS 3, 9*

Think of a time when an individual or key person had difficulty understanding you. How did you know they were having difficulty? How did you adapt your communication? Did it make a difference? If so, how did you know? Write an account, or tell your assessor about this.

Key points

You may have to adapt your communication:

o   to ensure an individual understands you

o   to meet the needs of the individual, especially if they change

o   between colleagues, professionals, individuals and friends

o   to ensure the correct information is given and received.

In the first element of this unit we looked briefly at records and reports. This element will look at this in more detail.

Accessing and updating records and reports is a big responsibility. All the information about the individual you provide care for is kept in different records and reports. You may not be able to access all the individual's records, but you should be able to access the ones relevant to the care you provide.

access
to get to

In this element you will cover:

○ Confidentiality
○ How to access records and reports
○ How to complete records and reports.

You may need a password to access some information

We have all made promises to family or friends that we have not been able to keep. Breaking these promises may have caused some trouble. Confidentiality of information is a 'promise' not to let others see that information or overhear verbal reports. Breaking this could get you into a lot of trouble.

Confidentiality is a legal requirement under the Data Protection Act 1998. It is also the right of the individual to have their information kept confidential. All records on individuals should have the word 'confidential' on the front. This is to make sure care workers know that the information needs to be looked after properly.

TC 002_B1,B2
TC 003_C2

Confidential report writing must be done in a private place

In the workplace: George is in a hurry

George works in the community with older people. He has gone into the head office to look at one of the service users' files. The filing cabinet is not locked so he takes the file he needs to read and sits at an empty desk. George's manager asks him to go an emergency visit. George is in a hurry so he leaves the file on the desk.

What problems with confidentiality are there here?

Keeping records confidential

Some records may be kept in a filing cabinet in the office where you work. The filing cabinet should be locked to stop other people seeing the records. Other records, especially older or unused records, may be kept in a large storage room, designed to keep the records safe. Many care organisations today have computers that contain confidential information relating to the individuals. The computer should have a secret password to prevent **unauthorised people** from accessing the information. Some people are skilled at accessing information from computers, so it is very important to keep them secure.

unauthorised people
those that do not have permission

Think about it

What sort of information would you not want people to know about you? How would you feel if they found out this information?

Why is confidentiality important?

If you broke a promise to a friend, they probably would not trust you again. It is similar in the care sector where you work. Service users, and also the wider community, would lose trust in you and the organisation if you did not keep confidential information safe. Service users are vulnerable and their personal details are private and often of a sensitive nature. The individual might become very embarrassed, upset or even depressed if others found out their private details.

Think about it

What could happen if the home address of an individual staying in a care home fell into the wrong hands?

Evidence *KS 4, 13*

TC 003_C2,C3a

Write down the sort of information that you have looked up in a service user's file. Explain to your assessor how and why you should keep this information confidential.

Key points

o Confidentiality is a legal requirement under the Data Protection Act 1998. It is an individual's right to have personal information protected.
o Unauthorised people should not see confidential information.
o Confidential information should be stored safely.

You have learned how to keep information safe and confidential by storing it correctly. What if you needed to look at that information? How would you read a file kept in a locked filing cabinet, or get into a computer which is secured by a password? The answer is that you need to seek permission.

Why should you seek permission?

Because records are confidential, they should be kept under some type of security. This could be a key which only one person has, or a password, which needs to be put into the computer. If everyone had keys or knew the password, the information would not stay confidential for very long.

Whom would you ask for permission?

You would need to seek permission from the appropriate person. In your organisation this could be your manager. In larger organisations you may need to seek permission from the Medical Records Officer. This is the person who is responsible for looking after patients' or service users' records. You should also ask the individual for their permission to look at their records.

How would you get permission?

If you work in a large organisation you may have to write or send an email to the Medical Records Officer. You may need to explain why you want to access the records. Simply wanting to have a look would not be a good enough reason to get permission. In smaller organisations you may just need to speak to the appropriate person, again giving them a valid reason.

Have a go

Find out who you should seek permission from to access records where you work.

Maintaining confidentiality

When you do have records or reports, you must make sure no one else can take them from you or read them without proper permission. Do not leave confidential records lying around. When reading the records, make sure no one else can see what is written.

When you access records on the computer make sure that no one else can read them from the screen. If you need to leave the computer, make sure you close down the records to stop anyone else accessing them.

When you access records on the computer, make sure that no one else can read them from the screen

Evidence *KS 5, 11, 13*

TC 003_C2

Write down what you have to do to access service users' records where you work (but don't include any passwords!). Include who you have to ask or write to and any problems you have had getting permission.

Key points

o Seek permission from the appropriate person in order to access records.
o Seek permission from the individual they relate to.
o Give a valid reason for wanting to access records and reports.
o Make sure unauthorised people don't see the records when you are using a computer.
o Never leave confidential records lying around.

Records and reports are a way of keeping information together. They are legal documents and need to be completed by following the proper legal and organisational policies and procedures.

TC 003_A1_bii
TC 003_C3_b

Under the Data Protection Act 1998, all records completed by you must be:

o   fairly and lawfully obtained and processed

o   held, used, disclosed and processed for limited purposes

o   accurate, adequate, relevant and not excessive

o   not kept for longer than necessary

o   processed in accordance with the subject's rights

o   kept secure

o   not transferred to other countries without adequate protection

o   made known and available to data subjects on request without excessive delay or expense, and corrected or erased where necessary.

How to complete records

When you write in individuals' records you must make sure that you write:

✓   clearly – people will need to be able to read and understand your handwriting

✓   accurately – what you write should be factual (only the facts), based on what you see or hear, not your opinion (what you think or feel)

✓   precisely – your writing needs to be to the point; do not write more than you need to

✓   completely – writing in records and reports should be finished with your signature and the date

✓   relevantly – do they really need to know?

> **Have a go**
>
> **Speak to your manager, supervisor or colleagues and ask them to explain what the terms from the Data Protection Act mean.**

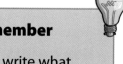

> **Remember**
>
> Only write what you are happy to show the service user today, tomorrow, next week or next year.

When you write in a report you should use black **indelible ink** to stop it from being erased or rubbed out. Black ink is also better for photocopying.

indelible ink
ink that cannot be rubbed out

Have a go

Which of the following are factual statements, based on what can be seen or heard by the care worker, if any? Which are opinions (what you think or feel), if any? Are there any that should be given by someone else (such as a doctor)?

1   *Mrs T said she had a headache.*

2   *Mrs B has a stomach upset.*

3   *Mr L has had a bath this morning.*

4   *Mrs H looks a bit down this morning.*

5   *Mr D is constipated.*

---

19 June 2007

Isabella has been speaking very clearly today. She would like her brother to visit some time this week – the brother has been informed. Isabella is due to see the speech therapist tomorrow at 11.30.

Brenda King
Senior Care Worker

When you write in individuals' records you must make sure that you write clearly, accurately, precisely, completely and relevantly

Evidence
PC 2, 3   TC 003_A1_b

If your job role allows, write a report on an individual in their records, making sure you follow your organisation's policies and procedures. Show the report to your assessor.

Key points

o   Follow the Data Protection Act 1998 when completing records and reports.

o   Write clearly, accurately, precisely, completely and relevantly.

What have I learned?

1 State three factors that can affect communication.

2 How can you find out how a person communicates?

3 Name three skills you need to communicate well.

4 What does a 'barrier to communication' mean?

5 How can you show that you are listening?

6 Describe three ways of communicating.

7 What does confidentiality mean?

8 How can you keep confidential information safe?

9 What is the Data Protection Act?

10 How should you write records?

Any questions?

Q *I know the individuals I work with very well. We do not have any new individuals and no one has any difficulties communicating. How can I get evidence for Unit 21a?*

A If you work with an individual who has dementia, this can help you provide evidence. Individuals with dementia can communicate in different ways, depending on their mental state. Individuals who are very forgetful can also be good evidence. You may need to find out what they have forgotten and remind them. If you do not work with individuals who have these difficulties, and you are not expecting any new individuals, you may have to speak with your manager. Ask your manager if you could spend a short time working on a different unit or in a place where you will meet individuals for the first time.

Q *I am new to the care home I work in and the way the individuals communicate has already been recorded in their case notes. What is the point in doing it again?*

A You need to show that you are capable of identifying and recording individuals' communication methods and needs. If you observe the individual for yourself, you may find that the way they communicate has changed since it was last recorded. Making the records up to date will help the individual, you and your colleagues communicate better.

Q *I work in the individual's own home and do not complete any records or reports. How can I get evidence for Unit 21d?*

A Speak with your manager and ask if you can work in the office for a short time to access the records and reports kept there. See if the individuals you work with should have reports kept on them. If so, discuss how this can be set up.

Case study

TC 003_A1,B1,B2,C2,C3

Miriam

Miriam is a young girl who has mild learning disabilities and cerebral palsy. She started having respite care at Ackers Care Unit for the first time this week. She has had a couple of visits to the unit but you were not on duty and so you have never met her before.

Julian, the unit manager, was always on duty when Miriam came to visit, so he has started to get to know her. Julian introduces you to Miriam and you put out your hand to greet her. Miriam lets out a high-pitched screech and throws herself back in her wheelchair. You are quite startled by this, and step back from her. Julian leans forward and talks to Miriam gently. She soon relaxes back into her wheelchair. Miriam says a word, but you cannot understand what she is saying.

1   *How can you find out about the different ways Miriam communicates?*

2   *How could you get permission to access Miriam's records?*

3   *Why should you get permission?*

4   *When reading Miriam's records, how can you ensure they remain confidential?*

You have worked with Miriam on quite a few occasions now. You have a good understanding of how and what she is communicating.

A new staff member, David, has just started working on the unit, so you take him to meet Miriam. When she sees David, Miriam lets out a high-pitched screech and throws herself back in her wheelchair, just as she did with you. You talk to Miriam to calm her down and introduce her to David. Miriam asks David a question, but he cannot understand her. Because you know Miriam well you understood that she asked, 'Are you married?' and you tell him this. David's face goes red and he does not answer. Miriam starts to bite her hand. You have never seen Miriam do this before and you ask her what is wrong. Miriam tells you she is upset because David ignored her question.

5   *Describe the important things you would do when communicating with Miriam, such as your position and how you listen, and state why these are important.*

6   *You have realised that Miriam bites her hand when she becomes upset. What should you do with this information and why?*

7   *Why should you complete Miriam's records accurately, legibly and completely?*

HSC22

Support the health and safety of yourself and individuals

This is a core unit, which means it is one that you have to do. You will need to show that you can work safely. It is very important that you know about the laws relating to health and safety. You also need to be aware of hazards and risks. Infection control is also important. You will need to show that you are able to protect yourself and others from the spread of infection. Emergencies can happen at work, so your assessor will need to know that you can deal with these in a calm, safe manner.

Records relating to health and safety may need to be completed. You will need to show that you can fill these in properly, and pass them on to the right person. Moving and handling procedures relating to health and safety will be covered separately in Unit 223.

How you will be assessed:

Your assessor will need to observe you for each element. He or she may also ask you to collect other types of evidence, for example witness testimonies and self-reflective accounts.

This unit covers the following elements:

- **22a** Carry out health and safety checks before you begin work activities

- **22b** Ensure your actions support health and safety in the place you work

- **22c** Take action to deal with emergencies.

This unit maps to Technical Certificate Unit 004: Understanding health and safety practice in a health and social care setting.

A care worker's job can be a risky one. There is a danger that you could hurt yourself, and others could be hurt too. In this element we will look at the importance of being aware of the dangers and hazards before starting any work activity. We will also look at laws and regulations that you need to know about relating to health and safety.

In this element we will cover:

○ What are the hazards?
○ What are the risks?
○ Completing health and safety records
○ Laws and policies relating to health and safety.

A clean, tidy room which is free from clutter will create a safer environment for everyone

There are **hazards** all around us, all of the time. There can be several hazards in the workplace. Before starting any work activity, check around. Is there anything that could cause harm to you or to the service users? Remove anything you can, and always report hazards to your supervisor.

You may be working with individuals who are **vulnerable**. For example, if you are working with someone who has learning disabilities, or with children, they may not be able to protect themselves. They may not be aware of the hazards, and so are more at risk of hurting themselves. Your job is to help keep the service users and others safe.

hazard
anything that can cause harm, e.g. chemicals, body fluids, slippery floors

vulnerable
at risk of harm or abuse

TC 004_A1_a

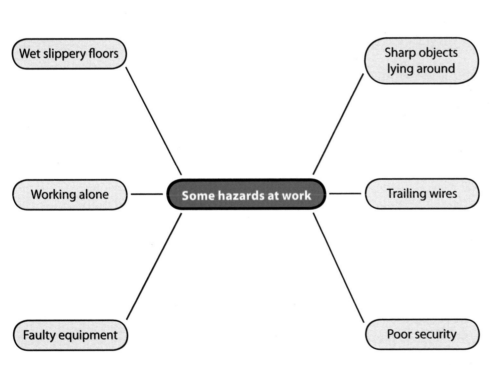

With a little thought many hazards can be avoided

Your responsibilities

Under the Health and Safety at Work Act 1974 you have a responsibility to look out for hazards at work. Remove them if you can, or report them to your supervisor if you cannot remove them yourself.

Have a go

Look around the area you are in now. Are there any hazards, for example, trailing wires or fires without guards?

In the workplace: Bridie's poor sight

Bridie is 85 years old and lives alone. Until recently she managed to care for herself. Her sight is very poor and is gradually getting worse.

Bridie lives in a small terraced house and sleeps upstairs. Over the years she has collected a lot of furniture and other items - she does not like to throw things away!

She has a pet cat which sometimes brings home mice and small birds and is often sick after eating them.

A care worker visits Bridie in the morning to help her with personal care and to prepare lunch. Bridie's sight is now so poor that she cannot read the labels on food cans. Recently the care worker cleaned out the fridge and threw away some food that was 2 months past its 'use by' date. Bridie also has trouble telling what is the cat's food and what is hers.

1   *List some hazards that you think might harm Bridie.*

2   *What are the dangers to Bridie in relation to the hazards you have listed?*

3   *How could the care worker make the area safer for Bridie?*

Evidence *PC 2, 5, 6; KS 15*

TC 004_A1a

Walk around your workplace with your supervisor and point out all the hazards that you can see and, if possible, remove them. If you cannot remove them, report them to the correct person. Ask your supervisor for a witness testimony.

Remember

Always check equipment before you start work and report anything faulty to your supervisor.

In the workplace: The Briars

The Briars is a care home for young people with learning disabilities. Some of the service users have scars, as they have self-harmed in the past by cutting themselves. A little while ago Robbie needed to be taken to hospital because he drank some bleach.

The care workers do not want the residents to get bored so they often organise activities. James likes to cook. Sarah is very tidy and likes to make sure that everywhere is clean and neat. Leroy loves to do craft activities, such as woodwork and model making.

1 *List some hazards that might be found at The Briars that could cause harm.*

2 *What might happen if the care staff are not aware of the hazards?*

3 *What should the care workers do about the hazards?*

Key points

o We are surrounded by hazards.

o Before starting any work activity, always check for anything that could cause harm.

o Remove hazards to keep service users and others safe.

o Report hazards to your supervisor.

Your employer must think about **risks**, and make the workplace as safe as possible for you and others. The managers will have written down the possible risks and said what should be done to make the area safer. This is called a **risk assessment**.

You already make a risk assessment before you do many things. For example, when you cross the road you ask yourself, 'Is there a car coming? Will the lights on the crossing change? Will a car drive around the corner?'. You assess the risks before you decide whether you will cross the road or not.

You must work with your employer by making sure that you know what the risks are and what to do to avoid harm to yourself and others. Before you start any task, you need to do a risk assessment. Ask yourself the following questions:

o   Are there any hazards?

o   Is it safe to carry on?

o   Will it be too risky?

o   Do I need to do anything to make it safer?

risk
the chance that somebody will be harmed by a hazard

risk assessment
a report that shows likelihood of harm

Have a go   TC 004_A1b

In the last topic you were asked to look for hazards. For each hazard that you found, suggest what can be done to reduce the risk of harm.

Think about it

The Health and Safety at Work Act 1974 says that your employer must look after the Health and Safety of their employees. Think of ways that your employer does this.

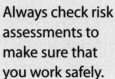

In the workplace: Ethel's change of character

Ethel lives in a care home called Loch View. Most of the residents are able to look after themselves, but some need a little help with daily activities. Ethel had a stroke last year and made an excellent recovery. She managed to look after herself fully until last week, when she caught a stomach bug which made her very weak. She has been vomiting and has diarrhoea. Because she is so weak she cannot get herself out of bed to go to the toilet. However, Ethel has also become very unpredictable in her moods and behaviour and will sometimes struggle and hit staff when they try to help her.

1 *What are the hazards?*

2 *What could be done to reduce the risks?*

3 *Who could you go to for advice?*

Remember

Always check risk assessments to make sure that you work safely.

Remember

Check risk assessments regularly because hazards can change.

Evidence *PC 1, 2; KS 12, 15*

Spend some time working with your supervisor. Show him or her how you make sure that it is safe before starting any work activity. For example, you could show what you do before washing someone or moving and handling them. Point out any potential hazards and explain what you would do to reduce the risks of harm.

Key points

o Your employer must think about risks.

o Your employer will have written down the possible risks in the workplace.

o You will need to know what the risks are at work.

o Before you start any job you need to do a risk assessment.

You may need to keep records relating to health and safety. For example, you may have to make sure that visitors sign in the visitors' book. You may need to complete or update risk assessment forms. If you have witnessed an accident at work, you may be asked to fill in an accident form. (This is covered in more detail in Unit 22c.) If there are changes in an individual's health or well being you may need to update their care plan.

TC 004_B2

There may be other forms that you need to fill in, depending on where you work.

In the workplace: Safety first

Sharon works in a unit with individuals with behavioural problems. Some can be violent towards others or damage property. It is not safe for some service users to be left without a member of staff nearby.

Knives and other cutlery used to prepare meals are counted as they are replaced back into a drawer that is locked. Plastic cutlery is used by the service users.

1   *What records may need to be completed by Sharon?*

2   *Why do you think these records should be kept?*

Have a go

List all the records that you need to look at or fill in relating to health and safety.

Show the list to your supervisor. Have you have found them all or did you miss any?

Always ask visitors to sign in – and remind them to sign out. If there was a fire you would need to know who was in the building

In the workplace: Checking equipment

Molly works in a doctor's surgery where she helps the registered nurse with some patient care. There is a lot of electrical and technical equipment in the surgery. It includes a glucometer for checking blood sugar levels, resuscitation equipment and blood pressure monitoring equipment, to name just a few. Molly checks these regularly and signs a book to say that she has done it.

The nurse feels confident that if Molly found a piece of equipment which was not working properly then Molly would tell her.

1   *Why does Molly sign to say that the equipment has been checked?*

2   *What should she do if she finds that some equipment is not working properly?*

Remember

Make sure that you know about and complete the health and safety records where you work.

Some equipment, for example, hoists and electric beds, needs to be checked and serviced regularly. Other electrical items such as kettles and televisions should be checked too. They should each have a label showing the date it was tested and when the next test is due. Do not use any item that has not been tested, or that has an overdue test date. Remove it if possible and report it to your supervisor.

Remember

Inspection teams will check to see that health and safety records are completed properly.

Evidence *PC 6*

Show your assessor a health and safety record that you have filled in. Explain what you did with the record after completing it.

Key points

o   You may need to keep records relating to health and safety.

o   You need to know what records you must fill in where you work.

o   Inspection teams will check health and safety records.

o   It is very serious if health and safety records are not filled in properly.

There are many laws and regulations relating to health and safety to help prevent individuals from being hurt. Your workplace will be guided by the Health and Safety at Work Act 1974, which has many regulations. You do not need to know them in great detail, but you must know your responsibilities. Some of the regulations that may affect you in the care sector are shown below.

TC 004_C1

Workplaces should display important information to their workers about Health and Safety Law

Have a go

Look around your workplace. Can you see any posters or documents that mention Health and Safety Law?

Working together to be safe	
What your employer or manager must do to make it safe for you to work	**What you must do to stay safe at work**
Make sure that equipment is safe	Take care of yourself and others
Provide health and safety training for you	Cooperate with your employer
Make sure that no one is put at risk	Not interfere with, or misuse, any health and safety equipment
Make sure there is a health and safety policy	Understand what you have to do to help your employer keep the workplace safe
Make sure that the workplace is kept in good condition	Do your bit to keep the workplace risk free and report any dangerous situations to your manager
Provide Personal Protective Equipment free of charge	Always use the Personal Protective Equipment provided

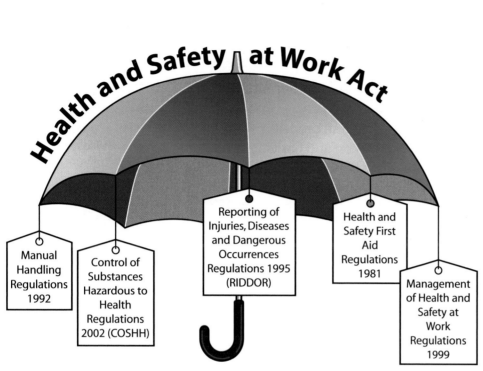

The Health and Safety at Work Act is like an umbrella

Reporting of Injuries, Diseases and Dangerous Occurrences Regulations 1995 (RIDDOR)

Employers must report accidents, diseases and dangerous occurrences to a government department called the Health and Safety Executive (HSE). The HSE uses this information to do risk assessments. This means that the workplace must have an incident reporting **procedure** in place. This will include a form to complete that will give all the information that is needed about any incident. A detailed account of the incident may prevent another similar event from happening again. (Information is given in Unit 22c about how to complete forms properly.)

procedure
the proper, official way to do something

In the workplace: A near miss

TC 004_C1

Martyn has been admitted to a busy general hospital, because the doctors think that he has **appendicitis**. Martyn has agreed to have an operation and he is taken to the ward. The staff prepare him for theatre. They make sure that he has his gown on and has clean bed linen. They also check that he has two name bands to make sure everyone knows who he is.

Martyn has an **anaesthetic** and is taken to the operating theatre. The surgeon is just about to start operating, when a nurse notices that Martyn has not signed the consent form, giving his permission for the operation. The surgeon does not operate on Martyn.

1 *Why do you think that the surgeon did not continue?*

2 *What form will need to be filled in?*

3 *What could be done to prevent the same thing happening again?*

4 *Who has access to this information?*

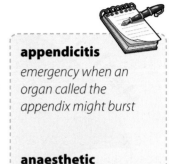

appendicitis
emergency when an organ called the appendix might burst

anaesthetic
drug that puts someone into a deep sleep for an operation

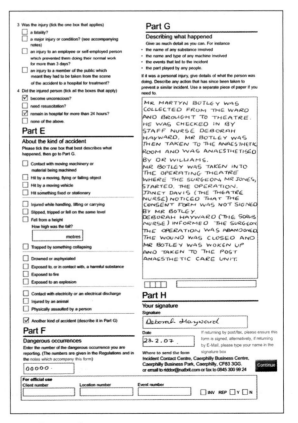

Near misses must be reported as well as actual accidents

Control of Substances Hazardous to Health (COSHH) Regulations 2002

TC 004_C1

These regulations are in place to make sure that employers control exposure to hazardous substances. In a care setting, hazardous substances could include cleaning solutions, bleach, disinfectants and body products, such as blood and urine. There should be a member of staff who makes sure that the COSHH guidelines are followed. These are two of the guidelines:

- Chemicals should be stored safely
- Hazardous substances should be properly labelled.

Evidence KS 4, 7, 8, 10, 11

Look around your workplace and note down the hazardous substances that you can find. Where are they stored?
Who is responsible for making sure that the COSHH guidelines are followed?

Harmful

Toxic

Irritant

Flammable

Corrosive

Dangerous for environment

Make sure you understand what these warning symbols mean

Key points

- There are several laws and regulations relating to health and safety.
- At work you will be guided by the Health and Safety at Work Act 1974.
- You do not need to know the Act and regulations in detail, but you will need to know your responsibilities.
- Your employer must make sure that the workplace is safe.
- There should be a member of staff who makes sure that regulations about dangerous substances are followed.

In your job, you may have to deal with spills and you may have to **dispose** of waste. Some of this waste could be a risk to you and the service users you work with. It is important that you deal with this waste correctly to make sure that you and others are kept safe.

> **dispose**
> *get rid of*

Washing your hands properly is the key to controlling the spread of infection. You will need to know how to do this in the correct way. It is not just the health and hygiene of the service users that matters – yours does too!

In this element you will cover:

- Dealing with spillages and safe disposal of waste
- Hand washing and controlling the spread of infection
- Your health and hygiene.

This care worker makes sure that the area is clean and tidy before serving food

Always clear up spillages quickly because they can spread infection and they could cause someone to slip and hurt themselves. Body fluids and waste such as urine, **vomit**, **sputum** and **faeces** should be flushed down the sluice drain, and the area should be disinfected well. Body waste is a source of infection, so you need to protect yourself by wearing gloves and washing your hands when you take the gloves off.

vomit
what is brought up when someone is sick

sputum
coughed-up saliva or phlegm

faeces
waste matter discharged from the bowels

Think about it

It is important that waste is properly disposed of to keep people safe. Other people have to deal with the waste after you have put it into a bag or container.

Red bag (with inner dissolvable liner) – Dirty and soiled sheets and linen should go in this bag

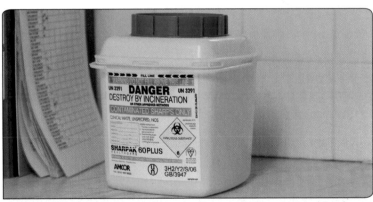

Yellow sharps box – Put needles, syringes, glass in here

Yellow bag – Used for clinical waste such as pads, nappies, wound dressings, used gloves

Most workplaces use the same system of coloured bins and bags for disposing of waste. Some workplaces also use special bags labelled 'confidential'. Confidential documents that are no longer needed should be put in these bags so they can be shredded. Large black or clear plastic bags are usually only used for household waste. Make sure you know which bags to use for different types of waste where you work. Not all workplaces have exactly the same systems for confidential documents and ordinary household waste.

Look around the place where you work. How do you safely dispose of waste? Do you have different coloured bags?

Remember

Make sure that you protect yourself and others by wearing gloves.

Remember

Poor handling of dirty laundry can increase the risk of the bacteria *Clostridium difficile*.

In the workplace: Shauna's slip up

TC 004_D

Shauna works in a care home for older people. She helps the service users to be independent, but some need help with their personal hygiene and to go to the toilet. Mrs Hamish had a stomach bug which gave her diarrhoea. She sometimes was not able to get to the toilet in time.

Shauna was helping Mrs Hamish, whose nightdress and sheets were soiled with faeces. Shauna put on an apron and gloves to help Mrs Hamish. She changed the bed for her and made her comfortable again. Then Shauna placed the soiled nightdress and sheets into a white bag.

Shauna washed her hands and placed her gloves in the waste paper bin in the room. She took the linen bag into the sluice ready to be sent to the laundry.

1   *What did Shauna do wrong?*

2   *What could happen because of her actions?*

3   *Explain how she should have disposed of the waste properly.*

Aprons

It is good practice to use different coloured aprons for different tasks. For example, one colour may be used for serving food and another colour when giving personal care. This will focus you on the task you are doing and remind you not to mix tasks. This will help to reduce the spread of infection.

Remember

Wear an apron when giving personal care, as this will protect your uniform and reduce the spread of infection too.

Evidence *PC 1, 6; KS 9, 10*   TC 004_D

Collect a witness testimony from your supervisor to show how you safely cleared up spillages and disposed of waste.

Key points

o   Always clear up spillages quickly.

o   Handling body waste can spread infection.

o   Dispose of waste properly because others have to deal with it when you have put it into the bag or container.

o   Protect yourself and others by wearing gloves and an apron.

o   Wash your hands when you take your gloves off.

The best way to control the spread of infection is by washing your hands properly.

Remember that germs can easily get under rings and nails. It is best not to wear rings when working, but if you do, make sure that you clean and dry under them properly. Even though you may be very busy, always make time to wash your hands thoroughly.

How to wash your hands properly

Wet hands and squirt liquid

Rub hands together and make a lather

Rub palm of one hand along the back of the other hand

Rub in between your fingers and thumbs of both hands

Rinse off soap with clean water

Dry hands thoroughly on a disposable towel

When should you wash your hands?

o before starting and finishing work

o after using the toilet

o after blowing your nose

o before and after touching someone

o before and after eating

o after handling dirty waste, such as laundry and waste bags

o before and after using gloves.

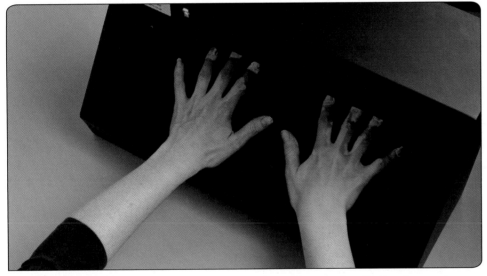

How well do you wash your hands? This ultraviolet light shows how germs can remain on your hands after washing. The blue areas show the parts that have not been washed properly

Alcohol hand rub

Alcohol hand rub can be very useful when your hands are quite clean already. These hand cleansers are available in small tubes that can be attached to the care worker's uniform so they are always available. They are particularly useful when you are not near soap and water. All wards in hospitals have hand cleansers mounted on walls for staff and visitors to use.

This care worker is wearing hand cleansing gel on his uniform

Rub the gel into your hands and use the same procedure as you would with soap and water. The hand rub should be rubbed in until the hands are completely dry. There are alcohol-free alternatives available as well, in case you have sensitive skin or an allergy to the alcohol.

Wearing gloves can also help control the spread of infection

When should you wear gloves?

○ when you are likely to have contact with any body fluids, for example, urine, faeces and sputum

○ if you need to handle used pads and other clinical waste

○ if you are about to have contact with the skin of someone who has a rash, wound, bleeding or broken skin

○ if you have a cut or broken skin, to protect yourself

○ when assisting with personal hygiene needs.

You do not need to wear gloves when you are not likely to be in contact with body fluids, for example, at meal times.

Some gloves are made out of latex which some people are allergic to. All workplaces should have latex-free gloves available.

Remember

Always check that gloves do not have any holes.

How to put on and take off gloves

Check the gloves for holes before putting on

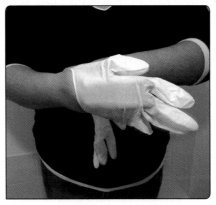

Pull the gloves on

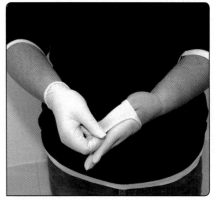

Take them off by pulling from the cuff

Pull off the second glove, while holding the first glove

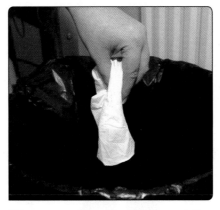

Dispose of both gloves while holding the first glove

Remember

To wash your hands after you take your gloves off.

Key points

o The best way to control the spread of infection is by washing your hands properly.

o Germs can easily get under nails and rings.

o Always make time to wash your hands properly.

o Alcohol hand rub is very useful when you are not near soap and water.

o Wear gloves whenever you are likely to be in contact with waste or body fluids.

You need to make sure that you look after your own health and hygiene so that it does not put anyone else at risk. Do your best for service users by keeping yourself fit and healthy.

Hair: Keep hair neat and tidy. Tie long hair up away from your face. If a service user was confused they could pull your hair.

Hands: Keep your hands and nails clean. It is best not to wear rings because you may hurt a service user and germs can get underneath them.

Clothes: Wear a clean uniform each day. Trousers are more practical for moving and handling. Wear a coat over your uniform when you travel to work.

Teeth: Prevent bad breath by cleaning your teeth. Remember that smoking can make your breath smell. Drink plenty of water to help keep your mouth fresh.

Jewellery: Keep jewellery to a minimum. Necklaces and dangly earrings are very dangerous because they can get caught in things.

Feet: You can be on your feet for several hours. Make sure that you have well-fitting, comfortable, flat shoes that grip well.

When moving heavy objects remember to:

o   keep load close to body

o   get a firm grip of the object

o   co-ordinate move

o   use equipment when possible

o   don't twist or jerk

o   place feet apart with leading leg forward.

Working long shifts can make you tired. Tiredness can make you more likely to have an accident, more prone to infection and can make you short tempered.

It is not just your physical health that you need to be aware of, your mental health is important too. Try to avoid stress by taking regular breaks. Employers have a responsibility to have an awareness of work related stress and reduce it as much as possible.

In the workplace: Emile smokes

TC 004_D

Emile works at The Sycamores, a residential school for younger people. He smokes quite heavily and his clothes smell of stale smoke. Emile has a bad cough most of the time.

Emile is a very good care worker and the young people like to be with him. He helps with school work and activities. He also gives some of his own time to plan outings for the young people.

At break times Emile stands in the courtyard with some other members of staff to have a cigarette. The head teacher warned one or two of the young boys about smoking when they were seen smoking by another teacher.

Some parents are complaining about Emile and the smell of smoke on him. One mother blames Emile's smoking for bringing on her son's asthma attack.

1   *What are the risks of smoking to Emile?*
2   *How is his smoking affecting his work?*
3   *Why are the parents concerned about Emile smoking?*

Remember

From July 2007 all four countries of the UK will have new legislation about smoking in the workplace and in public areas.

Remember

Never smoke in front of children.

Have a go

Use the links to the HSE (Health and Safety Executive) website to find out more about stress and work.

Think about it

If you needed to receive care, what standards of health and hygiene would you expect of the person who was looking after you?

Look after yourself so that you can look after others

Smoking: Give up if you can. Smoking is bad for your health. You will be more likely to get coughs and colds. It also makes your clothes and your breath smell.

Alcohol and drug abuse: Looking after people is a very responsible job. You need to be alert at all times and have a clear head. Alcohol and drugs affect how you think and act. Your work will not be as good the next day after a night out drinking alcohol.

Diet: Make sure that you eat a well-balanced diet and drink plenty of fluids. Don't be tempted to skip meals. You can find out about healthy eating in Unit 214, pages 161–167.

Exercise: Exercise is good for you; it will keep you in shape and can help you to relax. It can help to keep your body strong and fight infection.

Remember

You can still be affected by alcohol that you had the night before the next day.

Remember

You should not work unless you are 'fit' for work. Doing so puts service users at risk of inadequate care and could spread infection.

Don't forget to look after yourself by taking proper breaks and eating healthy snacks

In the workplace: Mary has the flu TC 004_D

Mary is a care worker in a busy surgical ward. She is very hard working and reliable. She often works extra shifts to help out when they are short staffed. She will also work on other wards if other shifts need to be covered.

Mary recently had the flu and was off work for only one day. She came in because she was keen to get back to work. She knew how busy the ward was, and she had heard that other people were also off with the flu. The ward sister has suggested that Mary does not come back to work until she has fully recovered.

1   *Was Mary right to come back to work when she did?*

2   *What are the risks to Mary if she comes back to work too soon?*

3   *What are the risks to the patients if she comes back to work too soon?*

Evidence *KS 14*

Explain to your assessor how it could harm the individuals you care for or work with if your health and hygiene were not good.

Key points

o   Looking after people is very tiring.

o   You need to look after your own health and hygiene so you don't put anyone else at risk.

o   Never smoke in front of children.

o   You may still be affected by the alcohol that you had the night before the next day.

o   If you have been off work ill, make sure that you are fully recovered before you return.

You may be faced with emergency situations from time to time at work, for example, if someone tries to break in, there is a fire or someone has a **seizure**. It is important that you know what to do. There will be procedures in your workplace to tell you what to do in the event of an emergency. Thinking about what you would do will give you confidence should an emergency ever occur. Other people can be affected by the emergency, so you will need to think about them too. You will need to fill in forms afterwards, so you will need to know how to do these properly.

seizure
a sudden attack of illness, e.g. a stroke or an epileptic fit

For this element you must have assessor observation.

In this element you will cover:

- Dealing with intruders and security issues
- What to do if you suspect a fire
- Health emergencies.

PRESS

Good security is crucial in a care setting

Service users are vulnerable; you need to protect them from people who may harm them or their property. Only authorised people should be allowed to enter the places where people are being cared for. Dealing with **intruders** is very worrying. The service users are at risk, but you need to be safe too.

TC 004_C2

intruders
people who break in

In the workplace: A broken window   TC 004_C2

Maria is a night care worker in a care home for older people. One night she is sitting in the office and a service user calls. She goes to Mr Hall, who says that he heard glass breaking and he is very anxious. Maria notices that a ground floor window is broken.

1   *What is the immediate danger?*

2   *Who should Maria inform?*

3   *What else should she do?*

Most workplaces have procedures in place to prevent unwanted visitors from entering the building. Some have a system where all visitors' right of entry is checked and they are asked to sign in a visitors' book. The people who work there may have to wear badges with their photos on. Special security key pads and swipe cards can also keep the building secure.

Remember

If you see an intruder, don't challenge them. Raise the alarm and/or ring the police.

Have a go

Find out your workplace policy for letting visitors in.

Don't let people follow you into the building unless you know who they are. If you work with individuals in their own home encourage them to be aware of security. Advise them to check the identification of visitors to their home, for example, workmen and meter readers. Suggest that they have security door chains and or viewers (peepholes) fitted. Strong locks on all doors as well as window locks should help to prevent intruders.

Think about it

What might happen if an intruder did get into your workplace?

Evidence *PC 1; KS 18*   TC 004_C2

Explain what you would need to do if you discovered that you had an intruder in the building.

Remember

People may look as if they have the right to enter, but always be on the safe side. Follow the correct procedure and check their identity.

Keeping bank and credit cards safe

Help service users to keep their bank and credit card information safe and secure to protect them from other people accessing their accounts and taking their money.

Advise them not to write down their PIN (Personal Identification Number) and not to tell anyone their number (not even you). When out shopping or at a bank make sure that no one can see the number they are entering.

In the workplace: Keeping information safe

Emlyn works in the community. He helps several service users. Emlyn has a book that he keeps in his work bag with information about individuals that he cares for. For example, he helps some people who are not mobile and are very weak. He has some information in this book about getting into some houses when the service user is unable to answer the door.

One night Emlyn left his work bag on the back seat of his car. The next morning he discovered that his car had been broken into and his work bag had been taken.

1   *Why are the service users that Emlyn visits at risk?*

2   *What could happen if information about the service users got into the wrong hands?*

3   *How could this have been avoided?*

Think about it

Your Care Council's Code of Practice says that you must protect service users from danger or harm and that you should follow Health and Safety procedures.

Key points

o   Knowing what to do will help you in an emergency situation.

o   You need to protect the service users from intruders.

o   People working for large organisations usually have badges with photographs to show who they are.

o   Make sure you know who is in the building; check all visitors' right of entry.

o   If you see an intruder, do not challenge them – raise the alarm.

o   Don't take chances – follow security procedures.

■ **What to do if you suspect a fire**

KS 2, 4, 7, 16, 18

The Fire Precautions (Workplace Regulations 1997) say that all places of work must have a fire risk assessment and that there must be an **evacuation** procedure. Your employer must provide regular fire training, which you must attend. There should be at least one fire drill each year so that everyone knows what to do if a real fire should happen. A fire can be caused if people smoke in places where they should not.

Remember, service users may have problems walking or understanding what is happening and what to do. It may be more difficult, and take longer, to help them to safety if there is a fire. Most workplaces have smoke alarms fitted; make sure that the batteries are checked regularly and that they are working properly.

evacuation
way to move people away from danger

TC 004_C1,C2

A 'ski pad' can be used to help evacuate people who cannot walk

Have a go

Look around your workplace to find out where all the fire fighting equipment is. Check on each extinguisher and make a note of what type of fire it should be used on. See if there are any special instructions for using each type of extinguisher.

Water with additive

For wood, paper, textiles, fabric and similar materials

Foam

For burning liquid fires

Powder

For electrical burning liquids and flammable liquid fires

CO_2 gas

Safe on all voltages, used on burning liquid and electrical fires and flammable liquids

Fire blanket

For kitchen fires

Non-electrical fires   **Electrical fires**

Different types of fire extinguishers

In the workplace: Is Henry smoking?

Sunny Court is a care home for older people which is now non-smoking inside the building. Henry is 84 years old and has been a resident there for several years. Until recently, he was able to smoke in a small downstairs room. Henry has smoked for nearly all of his adult life and does not wish to give up now. During the day Henry usually goes outside the building to have a cigarette, but he has started to be a little muddled at times and occasionally lights a cigarette in the lounge. The care workers remind him that he should not smoke inside.

Henry's room is upstairs at the far end of the building and he has asked not to be disturbed at night. The care workers suspect he is smoking in his room.

1   *What could make the care staff suspect Henry is smoking in his room?*

2   *Who is at risk if Henry is smoking in his room?*

3   *What could be done to prevent a fire?*

Evidence *PC 1, 2; KS 18*   TC 004_C2

Find and read your workplace procedure on what to do if there is a fire, and explain what you would do if there was a fire at work.

Remember

If you suspect a fire, don't delay – raise the alarm immediately.

Key points

o   All workplaces must have a fire risk assessment.

o   Your employer must provide fire training, which you must attend.

o   It may be more difficult to help service users to safety if they have problems walking or understanding.

o   Check that smoke alarms are working properly.

o   If you suspect a fire, raise the alarm immediately.

This book does not tell you what to do if you are faced with first aid emergencies. For this, you will need to attend a first aid course and be assessed by a specially trained first aid instructor. They will want to see that you can demonstrate some first aid procedures such as the recovery position and **resuscitation**.

First aid at work

Even if you are not qualified to give first aid, you should know who is. You should also find out where the first aid boxes are at work. All work places should have a first aid box ready to be used in the event of an emergency.

However, you must have first aid training to use the contents of the box. There must also be an appointed person who is responsible for restocking and checking the contents. Whenever anything from the box is used, it must be replaced.

How to help in an emergency

✓ Try to be **calm** and **don't panic** (even though you may feel like it!).

✓ **Protect yourself** – don't put yourself in any danger.

✓ **Call** for **help**.

✓ **Support** and **comfort** people who are involved.

✓ When the experts arrive, they may ask you to help them.

✓ **Comfort others** who are involved, for example, bystanders.

✓ **Report** and **record** the incident.

✓ You may need to **talk about your feelings** to someone afterwards, for example, your supervisor.

TC 004_C2

resuscitation
special techniques used for reviving people

Have a go

Check in your area for first aid courses. If you do go on a first aid course, remember that you will need to keep your skills up to date.

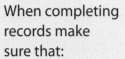

Filling in an accident form

If there is an accident or a near miss at work, this must be recorded. The law says that this must be done. When your workplace is inspected, for example, by the Commission of Social Care Inspectorate (CSCI) or the Health and Safety Executive (HSE), they will check accident reporting and other records. They will look closely to check that they are written properly.

Ten top tips for filling in forms well

1 Read through the form.
2 You may wish to write it in pencil first.
3 Use black ink.
4 Write it in a logical order; read the form headings carefully.
5 Do not use abbreviations or jargon.
6 Use formal language (use professional words, not slang).
7 Keep to the facts.
8 Make sure there is enough detail.
9 Check the spelling and grammar.
10 Sign and date the form.

In the workplace: Mrs Farr's table

Amy works in a care home for older people. One night, she was working in the office when she heard a service user shouting for help.

Amy went to the service user's room straight away. Mrs Farr was on the floor beside her bed. The bedside table was tipped over. Everything that had been on the table was on the floor, including a vase of flowers. Amy called for her supervisor.

Amy was asked to fill in an accident report form.

1 *Why does she have to write an accident report form?*

2 *What advice could you give her to help her to write it properly?*

Remember

When completing records make sure that:

o you write clearly
o you keep to the point
o the details are true
o your report is based on fact (not on what you think happened).

Remember

Ask your supervisor to check the form for you if you need to.

Evidence *PC 6*

TC 004_B2

Ask your manager's permission to show your assessor an incident or an accident form that you have filled in. If you have not filled one in, then you could ask your assessor to suggest an incident that you can write a report on.

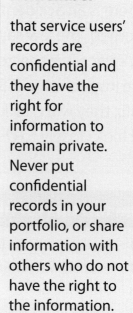

Remember

that service users' records are confidential and they have the right for information to remain private. Never put confidential records in your portfolio, or share information with others who do not have the right to the information.

What should go into a first aid box?

There is no set list of what a first aid kit must contain. It depends on where you work and the type of accidents that you are most likely to have. The Health and Safety Executive (HSE) suggests that the following would be useful:

- a leaflet giving general advice and guidance on first aid, for example the HSE leaflet, 'Basic advice on first aid at work'
- twenty individually wrapped sterile adhesive dressings (different sizes)
- two sterile eye pads
- four individually wrapped triangular bandages (preferably sterile)
- six safety pins
- six medium sized (approximately 12 cm × 12 cm) individually wrapped sterile unmedicated wound dressings
- two large sized (approximately 18 cm × 18 cm) individually wrapped sterile unmedicated wound dressings
- one pair of disposable gloves.

Protecting yourself

Be aware of your own safety at all times if you are involved with any emergency. In a health emergency, when in contact with blood and other body fluids, protect yourself from infection by wearing gloves. If you don't have gloves, you could use a plastic bag to create a barrier.

Remember

You should not keep tablets or medicines in a first aid box.

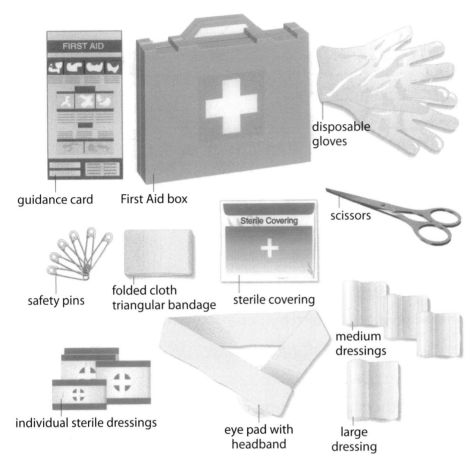

guidance card   First Aid box

disposable gloves

scissors

safety pins

folded cloth triangular bandage

sterile covering

medium dressings

individual sterile dressings

eye pad with headband

large dressing

Here are some items that should be in a first aid box

Being involved with health emergencies can be very upsetting. You may feel fine immediately after the event but you may suffer effects afterwards. Supervision is useful for you to discuss any issues or concerns that are worrying you.

Key points

o You should know who can give first aid where you work.

o Try to keep calm in an emergency and support others.

o You may need to talk to someone after you have been involved in an emergency.

o Accidents and incidents must be recorded. These records will be checked when your workplace is inspected.

o Service users' records are confidential so keep them private.

What have I learned?

1 List five hazards in your workplace.

2 Suggest five risks you may find in your workplace.

3 What is a risk assessment?

4 What records do you need to fill in relating to health and safety?

5 List three regulations under the Health and Safety at Work Act.

6 What are your responsibilities under Health and Safety Law?

7 What are your employer's responsibilities?

8 How can you control the spread of infection?

9 Explain the correct procedure for the disposal of different types of waste.

10 How can you make sure that your health and hygiene is of a high standard?

11 How can you protect service users from intruders?

12 What should you do in the event of a fire?

13 How can you help to support others in an emergency?

Any questions?

Q *I never have to deal with any emergencies; can we do a role play (simulate) what I would do to cover some of Unit 22c?*

A No, simulation is not allowed for this element – you must have some assessor observation.

Q *I completed a risk assessment form for one of the people that I care for when I arranged for her to go into town. Can I photocopy this and put it in my portfolio?*

A No, you must not put confidential information into your portfolio. Get permission to show your assessor the risk assessment form that you completed and make sure that you put it back in its proper place. He or she can then write a statement to say that they have seen it.

Q *I attended an infection control study day last week. Will this cover some Knowledge Specifications for Unit 22?*

A Well done, it is good that you are keeping up to date. Speak to your assessor about what you have learned and how you will put it into practice. A certificate of attendance on its own is not evidence – you could have been asleep at the back of the classroom! Write a reflective account of what you have learned, to show your assessor.

Case studies

Going swimming

Tom works in a residential school for younger people who have behavioural problems. He helps the young people with their personal and social care.

A group of boys have asked Tom if he can arrange for them to go swimming. Tom is very pleased with the way that the six young people have tried with their school work and behaviour recently, so he is keen to arrange a treat to take them swimming. They are aged between 12 and 15. The leisure centre is about five miles away. The school has a minibus.

1   *Who will Tom need to involve when arranging this outing?*

2   *What are the possible risks involved and what should be done to reduce them?*

3   *What records will need to be completed?*

4   *What is the correct procedure for taking service users on an outing?*

Staying at home

Valda lives in her own small bungalow. Over the years her rheumatoid arthritis has made her less able to get out of bed herself and to look after her own personal care needs.

Valda had an assessment of her needs and it was decided that she would have a carer who comes in to help her get out of bed in the morning and who returns later to help her get back into bed. As Valda is not able to stand on her own, a hoist has been organised for the carers to help her get in and out of bed.

Valda's bedroom is quite small and she has a lot of large antique furniture. There are many ornaments and lots of clutter in her bedroom. She does not want to get rid of any of her furniture or belongings.

It is difficult to get the hoist in and out of the room because of a narrow hall and doorway. Also, there are some small tables with more ornaments in the hall.

1   *What are the risks to Valda? What are the risks to the care workers?*

2   *How could you make the area safe, taking into account Valda's wishes?*

HSC23

Develop your knowledge and practice

This core unit asks you to look at the skills and knowledge you have already, and to ask for help to develop them even more. You also need to identify any new skills and knowledge needed for your job. Once you have gained these, you will need to use them in your job.

From time to time, the government creates new laws, policies and guidelines that workers need to follow. Care organisations and professional care workers have a 'duty of care' to service users to provide them with the best possible care. Remember that it is the service user's right to be treated properly. Under your country's Code of Practice, care workers must continually review and improve their practice to give service users a high standard of care.

How you will be assessed

For this unit, your assessor will want to observe you while you are working. Your assessor will want to see you receiving feedback from different people, and putting any new skills into practice.

Your assessor may also ask you to get some work products, such as a self-appraisal form or supervision record to support your performance. You should only use these documents for evidence if you are happy with them.

This unit covers the following elements:

o 23a   Evaluate (assess) your work

o 23b   Use new and improved skills and knowledge in your work.

This unit maps to Technical Certificate Unit 001: Developing own knowledge and practice in a health and social care setting

This element asks you to assess how well you do your job. As a professional care worker, it is important that you understand why you need to review your knowledge and skills on a regular basis. You also need to know how you can improve your practice through reflection.

To help you provide service users with the best standard of care possible, you need to be up to date in your own knowledge and skills. The Code of Practice of your Social Care Council says that you have to be responsible for the quality of your work. You also have to take responsibility for maintaining and improving your knowledge and skills.

In this element you will cover:

- The importance of feedback
- Reflection and the reflective cycle
- Being aware of your values and beliefs
- Assessing your knowledge and skills.

Remember

Ensure you know your responsibilities under the Code of Practice for your country.

Everybody has skills and qualities within a team and everybody will need to maintain these skills and develop new ones

Feedback from other people can be a very useful way for you to learn more about yourself and can help you to improve your practice. Feedback can be **formal** or **informal**. For example, your manager may give you formal feedback during a supervision or **appraisal**. Informal feedback often comes from friends and work colleagues, when you talk about work events while having a cup of tea or coffee, during a break, or over lunch.

Service users can also give you valuable feedback on how you have done a job for them. Your assessor will see you working with individuals as part of your NVQ, and will give you feedback on your performance. This feedback will most often be verbal (spoken), and then written on the assessment plan. If you use a computer to email your assessor, feedback may be given to you in an email.

feedback
communicating someone how well or badly they are doing

formal/informal
official/not official

appraisal
review of your work

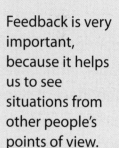

Remember

Feedback is very important, because it helps us to see situations from other people's points of view.

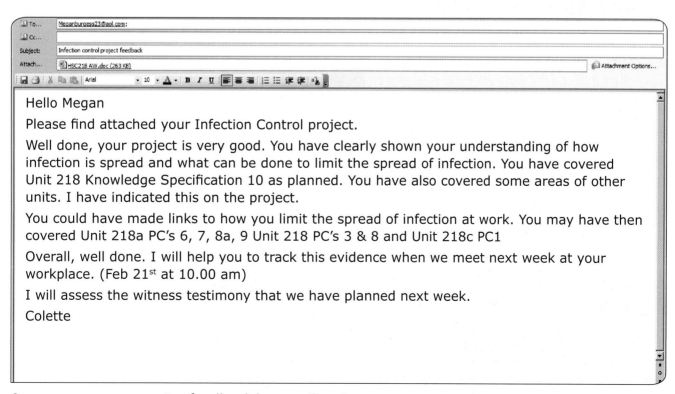

To...	Meganburgess23@aol.com;
Cc...	
Subject:	Infection control project feedback
Attach...	HSC218 AW.doc (263 KB)

Hello Megan

Please find attached your Infection Control project.

Well done, your project is very good. You have clearly shown your understanding of how infection is spread and what can be done to limit the spread of infection. You have covered Unit 218 Knowledge Specification 10 as planned. You have also covered some areas of other units. I have indicated this on the project.

You could have made links to how you limit the spread of infection at work. You may have then covered Unit 218a PC's 6, 7, 8a, 9 Unit 218 PC's 3 & 8 and Unit 218c PC1

Overall, well done. I will help you to track this evidence when we meet next week at your workplace. (Feb 21st at 10.00 am)

I will assess the witness testimony that we have planned next week.

Colette

Some assessors may give feedback by emailing it to you

You can receive feedback from different people, such as your manager, work colleagues or service users. From whoever gives you feedback, it is important for them to tell you what you have been doing well, as well as what you have not been doing well. This type of feedback is called **constructive feedback**. This means that the feedback can help you to see areas of your practice that you do well, and areas that need to be **developed**.

constructive feedback
feedback that helps you to improve your practice

developed
improved

Giving feedback

Sometimes you might need to give feedback to other members of staff on jobs that they have done. Therefore, you must be able to give constructive feedback, as well as receive it. When you give feedback to other people, it is important to make them feel **valued**. You can do this by starting with something positive, such as, 'I like the way you asked Mr Smith if he wanted a wash this morning.' You can then tell the person the area they need to develop: 'You could also have offered Mr Smith a bath or a shower, so perhaps next time you could ask if he would like a bath or a shower.' Finally, you can end on another positive point: 'Mr Smith said that you were very patient and he was pleased that you combed his hair.' Feedback given like this is known as the 'positive feedback sandwich'.

valued
of importance to other people

Another reason for using the positive feedback sandwich is because some people find it hard to receive feedback. It makes them feel they are being blamed for something, or that they are being picked on. The positive feedback sandwich should help stop this from happening, because you identify positive aspects of practice, not just areas for development.

You can use the positive feedback sandwich when giving people feedback

Evidence *PC 2, 5; KS 4, 12*

Now that you understand more about feedback, you can ask people to give you constructive feedback. Try asking for feedback on your performance from your manager, work colleagues or your NVQ assessor. You may want to arrange an appraisal or supervision with your manager. If you are happy for your assessor to see your supervision or appraisal, you can use it as evidence for your NVQ.

Key points

o   Feedback is important to help improve your practice.
o   Feedback can be formal or informal.
o   Feedback should be encouraged on a regular basis.
o   Feedback can be given as well as received.
o   Use the positive feedback sandwich when you give feedback.

One way you can improve your knowledge and skills is to look back on events at work. You can use what you learn from both good and bad experiences to improve your practice. Looking back like this, and thinking about a situation or event, is called reflection. Knowing how to use this type of reflection will help you to improve the quality of care that you give the individuals you care for.

Think about it

Practising reflection will help you to become a more independent worker. It will also help to put theories you hear or read about into practice. But always check with your manager first that these are appropriate for where you work.

The more you practise reflection, the more you will be able to put it into practice. In fact, you probably do some form of reflection already, without even realising it!

If you have said, 'I should have said this', then you have reflected on an experience

Reflection *on* action

When we talk about reflection, we are normally referring to 'reflection *on* action.' This is when we think back to an experience, whether it was good or bad. For example, if you have ever thought 'I could have done that better', then you have reflected *on* an experience. This is because you have thought about what has taken place, whether it was good or bad, and realised that you could have done something differently or better. If you cannot think what you would have done differently or better, you could ask your manager, college tutor or assessor for advice. They may be able to suggest how you could have done something differently.

Reflection *in* action

Reflection *in* action is when you think about the possible outcomes of your actions while you are actually doing a task. For example, at work you may have to help an individual to move from their bed to a chair. The individual's care plan may say to use a stand aid, but because you have done the task before, you may suggest to your manager that you use a hoist because you know that a hoist is the best method for moving this particular individual. By choosing the hoist you have reflected *in* action because you will have thought 'If I use the hoist, the move will be easier for the service user and myself. If I use the other equipment, the move will be difficult.'

If you think about the possible results of your actions while doing a task, you have reflected in action

Using a reflective cycle

The reflective cycle is a simple tool that will help you to improve your practice. It is very simple to use. You just follow the steps in the illustration below.

Following an incident or an experience, you and other people can reflect upon it, even if you were not directly involved. This means that you can learn from other people's practice, as well as your own. You can still use the steps in the reflective cycle, and just imagine that you were involved in the incident. How would you have felt? What would you have done differently?

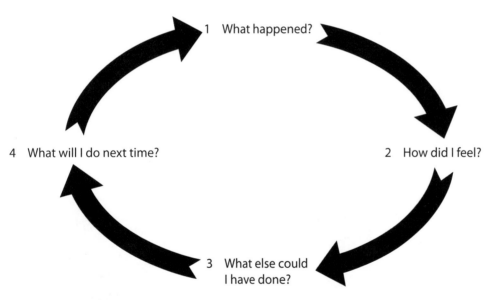

Using a reflective cycle can help improve practice

Self-reflective accounts

All the way through your NVQ, you will be encouraged by your assessor to write reflective accounts. These self-reflective accounts can be written using the reflective cycle titles described above.

Evidence

PC 4; KS 9

Using the reflective cycle, write a reflective account of a work-related incident, which you have been involved in over the past month. Try to explain what you have learned from this incident and how you plan to improve or change your practice.

Think about it

If you complete your reflective cycle in enough detail, your assessor may be able to cross-reference the reflective account into some of your other units.

In the workplace: 'Just a minute!'

Alex is a 24-year-old male carer, who has been working in a care home for one month. Yesterday, Alex was busy helping to care for a service user who was not feeling well. As Alex passed one of the other service users, they asked Alex if he would help them to walk to the toilet. Alex was busy at the time, so he told the service user to wait a minute and that he would be back as soon as he could.

When Alex returned later, he found the service user on the floor calling out in pain. Alex called for help and the service user was taken to hospital with a suspected broken hip. It was later discovered that the service user had tried to walk to the toilet on their own, because they could not wait for Alex. When Alex was told this information he felt very upset and felt that it was his fault that the service user had broken their hip.

1   *What could you suggest to Alex to help him look back on the incident?*

2   *Was the accident Alex's fault?*

3   *If you were his work colleague, what would you say to Alex?*

Have a go

Write a reflective account for Alex, using the reflective cycle.

Key points

o   Reflection can help to identify areas of poor practice.

o   We can reflect *on* action as well as *in* action.

o   Reflection can help to identify areas where you need to improve your knowledge and skills.

o   Other people can reflect on your actions.

o   You can use the reflective cycle to help you write a self-reflective account.

o   Reflective accounts can be used as evidence within your portfolio (but remember the importance of confidentiality).

Remember

To respect service users' confidentiality when collecting evidence for your portfolio.

All service users have rights that relate to how they are treated. You can read more about these in Unit 24, but they include the right to:

o   be respected and be treated as an individual
o   be treated equally, without discrimination
o   be cared for in a way that meets their needs
o   be protected from danger and harm.

We all have our own values and beliefs. Sometimes you may be caring for individuals with very different beliefs to your own. As a care worker you have to make sure that your beliefs do not affect how you care for the service users.

Remember

Respecting service users' rights will help you provide good quality care.

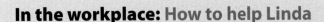

In the workplace: How to help Linda

Linda works in a care home for older people. Albert is in the early stages of dementia. One afternoon Albert became very aggressive and attacked Linda, leaving her very upset and shaken. After that, Linda avoided being involved in Albert's company in case he became aggressive again. Linda has never liked working with individuals with mental health problems because she finds them challenging.

Social Services have asked the manager to specialise more in caring for people with dementia. The manager discussed this with the staff at a team meeting, and said that they would need to attend dementia care training. Most staff were happy with this change, and to attend training. However, Linda was very unhappy with this decision.

1   *Why do you think Linda feels this way?*
2   *How is Linda's past experience affecting her work?*
3   *What could the manager do to help Linda?*

Remember

Do not let your own values and beliefs get in the way of the care that you give.

As a care worker, you also have the right to be respected and treated equally when it comes to opportunities for training to help you to do your job better. You should not be discriminated against. For example, if you work part-time or work night duty you should have the same access to training as those who work full-time and on day duty.

In the workplace: Training for all

Bryn Derwen is a care home for older people. There are 15 care workers. There are some training sessions that all staff must attend.

The manager and care workers usually discuss training opportunities and needs at the care worker's appraisal. For the past three years Ceri has asked for training in dementia care, because it would help her do her job better. Other members of staff have had a variety of other training that they have asked for. The manager tells Ceri that there is no money available for her to have the dementia care training that she has asked for.

She is the only member of staff who has not had any other training other than the **mandatory** training.

1   *Is Ceri being treated fairly, and if not, why?*

2   *How might Ceri feel about being treated this way?*

3   *What are Ceri's rights?*

mandatory
what workers must have

Have a go

Find your Care Council's Code of Practice and see what it says about your right to training.

Key points

o   Service users have the right to be treated fairly and to be well cared for.

o   You must not let your beliefs or values get in the way of how you care for individuals.

o   You also have rights, such as equal access to training.

We have already looked at the benefits of feedback from other people, and how you can use reflection to improve your practice. Now you need to discover the areas of your job that you need to develop. Before you can do this, you need to **identify** what skills and knowledge you have already. You will probably find that you actually have a number of skills.

identify
find out

Training

You can start by looking at the training you have received from your employer. Some training is formal, and you may have received a certificate for attending a course, such as first aid or moving and handling.

Just because you attended a training event doesn't mean you learned anything!

Evidence *KS 7*

Certificates can be used as evidence for your NVQ, but you must say how the training improved your practice. For each certificate that you have, you must write a small reflective account. You must also give the name of the organisation that provided the training. For example, was it a college or a private training provider? Say how you managed to get onto the training, and what you learned from it.

Informal training

TC 001_A1

Formal training is not the only way you can learn new skills and knowledge. In fact, many workplace skills are learned informally from working with colleagues and by work shadowing. You can also learn new information and knowledge by asking people questions, and through discussions with other learners, colleagues and your NVQ assessor. You may want to do your own research by reading books and using the Internet. Everyone has their own way of learning and it is important to identify a learning style that works for you.

Have a go

TC 001_A3,A4

Make a list of some of the training events you have been to so far in your current job role. Then for each training event state:

- whether the training was formal or informal
- what your input was. For example, did you ask any questions, or were you asked to take part in any practical activities?
- what you learned from the training
- how you used the new knowledge and skills to improve your practice.

SWOB assessments

This term may be new to you. SWOB stands for:

Strengths, **Weaknesses**, **Opportunities** and **Barriers**.
Doing a SWOB assessment means that you think about how each of these terms applies to you and your work. If you have done a skills scan or a skills audit as part of your NVQ, you will already have the information for the strengths section of the SWOB assessment.

strength
something you are good at

weakness
something you are not very good at

opportunity
having the chance to do something

barrier
something that stops you from doing something

Have a go

Part of your appraisal system should encourage you to assess your own ability and identify your strengths and weaknesses. You could use the headings in the following table to identify your strengths and weaknesses; this will help you to assess how well you do your job.

Strengths – what are you good at?	**Weaknesses** – what areas do you need to develop?
Opportunities – what opportunities are available for you to learn?	**Barriers** – what might stand in the way of your progression? What support do you need to achieve your goal?

Evidence PC 1

Complete a SWOB assessment, and list some things you need to do to improve your practice. Show this to your assessor, and ask for feedback.

In the workplace: The annual appraisal

Vera has been told by her manager that they will be doing her annual appraisal in three weeks' time. Vera's manager has given her a self-assessment form. She must complete the assessment form and return it to her manager a week before the appraisal. Vera has also been asked to think about the training she would like to complete over the next 12 months. She has to make a list of the training she wants so they can talk about training at her appraisal.

1   *What can Vera use to help her complete her self-assessment of her practice?*

2   *What can Vera use to help her identify the skills she already has and the training that she will need to help her improve her practice?*

An appraisal is an opportunity to take stock

TC 001_A2,A3,A4

Badgers Walk Care Home

Employee Self-Assessment form

Employee Name: Vera Smith	Date: 01/04/07
Job Title: Care Assistant	Department: Care
Return To: Frank Williamson	Return Date: 09/04/07

Your next appraisal / supervision is planned for Friday 13th April 2007. This self-appraisal form will help you to prepare for your appraisal and will help your manager to understand how you are feeling about your job. It is important to complete this form with as much detail as possible and to return it to Frank Williamson by Monday 9th April 2007.

Answer the following questions

Question	1 = Strongly Agree	2 = Agree	3 = Disagree	4 = Strongly Disagree
I enjoy coming to work		✓		
I am always on time for work	✓			
I like the people I work with	✓			
I am encouraged to use my initiative			✓	
I am a team player	✓			
I am up to date with my training		✓		
I have a good understanding of my job role	✓			
I would like to develop new skills	✓			
I have good communication skills		✓		

What are your strengths: I work well with other members of the team and am a team player. I have a good knowledge of care values and always help to promote the rights of the service users.

What would you like to improve: I would like to complete NVQ level 2, because I think this would help me to develop my knowledge and skills. I would also like to develop my written communication skills, so that I can write on the service users' care plans.

Self-appraisal forms can help you to identify gaps in your performance

Key points

o Training can be formal and informal.
o Informal training can be just as valuable as formal training.
o SWOB assessment helps to identify your strengths, weaknesses, opportunities and barriers.
o We need to use feedback, reflection and a skills assessment to help identify the gaps in our knowledge and skills.

This element builds on the assessment of your skills and knowledge carried out in Unit 23a. It looks at how you can get on to learning and training programmes that can help you to improve your working practice. This is an important part of any training and development planning. There is no point identifying your strengths and weaknesses unless you plan to improve the weaknesses that you identified.

In this element you will cover:

- How can I develop my knowledge and skills?
- Why is it important to develop my knowledge and skills?
- How can I put my new skills into practice?
- Reviewing practice.

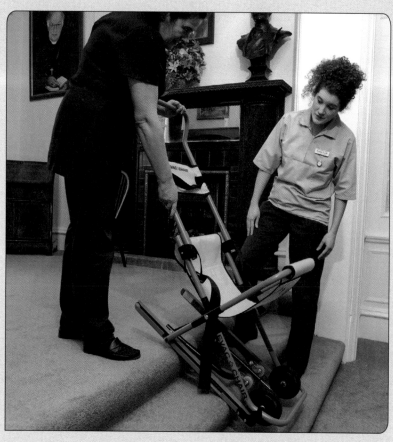

New equipment brings the need to learn new skills

In Unit 23a, you completed a SWOB assessment, which helped you to identify your strengths and weaknesses. Now you know your weaknesses, you need to do something to overcome them. You may also find that your line manager identified some of these weaknesses at your appraisal or supervision. They may have used this information to help set **objectives** on your Personal Development Plan (PDP), to help improve your practice.

objectives
goals or plans for the future

Personal Development Plan

Employee name: Molly Edwards	Date: 12/02/2007
Manager name: Justin Macdonald	Date: 12/02/2007

What are my strengths? Good communicator, knowledgeable about job role and very caring.

What are my weaknesses? Need more training with moving and handling.

How will I overcome my weaknesses? Complete a moving and handling course. I also think that completing the NVQ level two in health and social care would benefit me.

Who will help me overcome my weaknesses? My manager and work colleagues, as well as the moving and handling trainer.

What extra skills will I need to help me develop?

	Comments
Communication	I would like to get a level two in communication skills.
Working with others	I enjoy working with others and would like to do a team building day.
Problem solving	I am not very confident with solving problems and rely on other people to help me. I would find a team building event very useful.
Additional support needed	

Employee signature: Molly Edwards	Date: 12/02/2007
Manager signature: Justin Macdonald	Date: 12/02/2007

A completed Personal Development Plan (PDP)

As part of your PDP, your manager may have agreed that you need to go on formal learning or training programmes. These training programmes will give you the information you need to improve your knowledge and skills. Before starting your training, it is a good idea to talk to people who have information on the training that you need.

Think about it

Think about when you needed to find information out about your NVQ. Who gave you information? Who did you talk to?

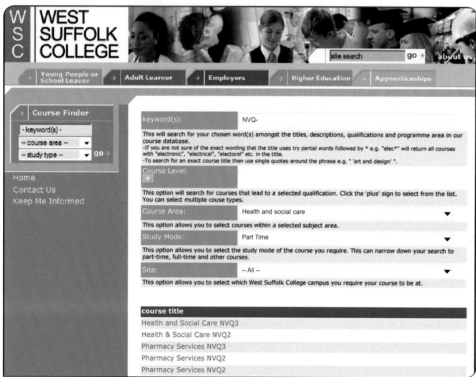

Training provider websites can be a good way of finding out information

In the workplace: Is experience enough?

Stella has worked in a small care home for people with learning disabilities for ten years and is very experienced. One of Stella's colleagues tells her that there is a study day about moving and handling. She asks Stella if she will be attending. Stella replies that she has worked in care for ten years and knows what she has to do. Stella says that the study day will be a waste of time and money.

1   *Is Stella right to think like this?*

2   *What risks does Stella's attitude pose to service users, colleagues and herself?*

What can you do?

Not all the weaknesses identified in your SWOB assessment mean that you need to go on formal training programmes. Courses like these can be very expensive. You also need to find out information for yourself, so that you keep up to date with changes in health and social care. It is no good always waiting for your manager to provide training for you, because learning is an ongoing process!

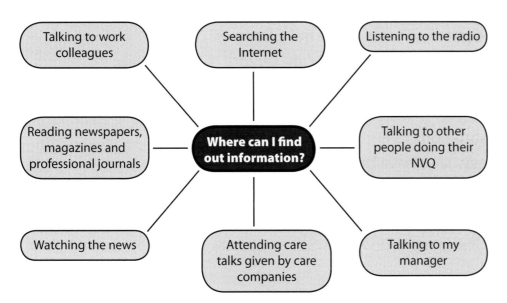

There are a number of ways you can keep yourself up to date

Key points

o   Once you have found your weaknesses or gaps in your knowledge, you need to do something about them.

o   Your manager can help you to set objectives as part of your Personal Development Plan (PDP).

o   You can get advice and information on training opportunities from a number of people and organisations.

o   You can keep yourself updated by finding information out for yourself.

There are many reasons why it is important to develop your knowledge and skills. Improving your skills and understanding will help you become better at what you do. This may help you to get a **promotion** in the future.

Protecting service users

Another reason why it is important to develop your knowledge and skills is to help protect service users from danger, harm or **abuse**.

It is a sad fact, but over the past few years, there have been a number of **failings** within the health and social care sector. These have led to service users being harmed or abused, and some have even died. Following these events the government set up enquiries and investigations to find out what went wrong. As a result, many new laws have been made to help protect service users. You must make sure that you know what these new laws are.

promotion
a better job, with more responsibility

abuse
physical harm or cruelty towards someone

failings
serious problems or weaknesses

A simple error could cause a service user serious harm

Remember

If you don't know the latest information on the equipment that you are using or on the latest moving and handling methods, you may be at risk of abusing service users.

It is also important to make sure that you have had the correct training before doing new tasks, such as giving service users their medication. Jobs like this may look easy, but you must not do something like this unless you have had the proper training.

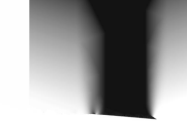

In the workplace: **What a pain**

Magda is a new carer for a care agency that helps to care for people in their own homes. She has been asked to visit Mr Lem, a 69-year-old man, and to help him to have some lunch. Mr Lem has just come out of hospital, following some tests for his stomach ulcer.

When Magda goes to see Mr Lem, he complains of a bad headache. Magda asks Mr Lem if he would like some pills for his headache, and gives him some of her own aspirin pills. Mr Lem says that he does not want any lunch today, because of his headache. Magda writes on the care plan that Mr Lem has refused lunch, but does not say that she has given Mr Lem some aspirin.

A few hours later, the care agency is called by Mr Lem's son, who is very upset. He tells the care agency manager that his dad had to go back into hospital because his stomach ulcer was bleeding.

1   *What has Magda done wrong?*

2   *What should Magda have done?*

Remember

Never give a service user medication that has not been prescribed by their own doctor.

Key points

o   Service users can be harmed if you do not keep your knowledge and skills up to date.

o   Care workers should not perform tasks when they haven't been properly trained to carry them out.

o   There are laws to protect people and you need to be aware of these laws and also any new ones.

It is very important to use any new skills and knowledge that you have learned from training or from carrying out your own research to improve your practice. It is easy to rely on old, familiar ways of doing things which you feel comfortable with. You may feel that you can do your job more quickly the old way, so you may need to make sure that you give yourself time to include the new information in your working practice.

TC 001_A2, A3, A4

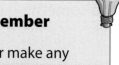

Discuss first

Before you try to include new skills, you need to discuss what you have learned and what you would like to change in your practice with your manager. It is very important that you talk to your manager first, because there may be reasons why you should not change your practice. For example, if you have learned how to apply dressings to wounds on a first aid course, you may now feel you should be allowed to do this for service users. However, this may not be part of your job role within your workplace.

Remember

Never make any changes to your practice without discussing them with your manager first.

Remember

Tasks such as changing dressings may be the role of another member of staff, such as a registered nurse.

Making an action plan

Once you and your manager have agreed what new knowledge and skills can be used within your job role, you can design an improvement action plan. This action plan should state how you will try to change your practice on a day-to-day basis. The action plan should also include how long it could take to make these changes. For example, it could take a month, three months, or even longer before all the new information you have learned has been put into practice.

Evidence *PC 3, 4, 5, 6*   TC 001_A2,A3,A4

Show your assessor your action plan. Ask if they noticed the changes in your practice.

Action Plan

Action	Review date
To complete NVQ level two in health and social care by September 2008, this will help with all aspects of the job role.	30/09/2008
To try and write a reflective account, using a reflective cycle, of an incident every fortnight to help me improve my practice.	30/06/2008
To use the slide sheets every time I have to turn service users.	31/05/2008

Action plan review comments:

Employee signature: Molly Edwards		Date: 12/02/2007	
Manager signature: Justin Macdonald		Date: 12/02/2007	

An Action Plan sets realistic targets

Including your colleagues

If your manager agrees that you can apply your new knowledge and skills, you can share them with your colleagues. For example, if you have just been on a moving and handling course and learned some new hoisting techniques, you could share this information with your colleagues the next time you have to use the hoist.

Key points

o   It is important that you use new skills you receive from training.
o   You must agree any changes to your practice with your manager.
o   Develop an improvement action plan to help you put your new skills into practice.
o   You may be able to share your new knowledge with your colleagues.

Have a go

TC 001_A2,A3,A4

Talk to your manager about any new skills you have that you would like to use where you work. Then develop an improvement action plan. Ask your manager to check it for you. Don't try to do too much in one go. Give yourself time – but make sure there is a fixed time to complete any changes to your practice.

Once you have put your improvement action plan into action, you need to review your progress on a regular basis. You could also ask your manager, work colleagues and service users if they have seen any improvements in the way you are working now. Your assessor may be able to give you some feedback too.

When you have achieved your improvement action plan, you could do another SWOB assessment, to see if your strengths and weaknesses have changed. Your second SWOB assessment may identify new strengths and weaknesses, or you may feel you are ready for more training. You can then make a new improvement action plan that shows what you plan to do next.

Reviewing your practice is not something you only do when you are working in care. It is something you do in your daily life. For example, if you have learned to drive, you would have reviewed your practice so that you could improve and pass your driving test. Reviewing your knowledge and skills is something you will do throughout your life.

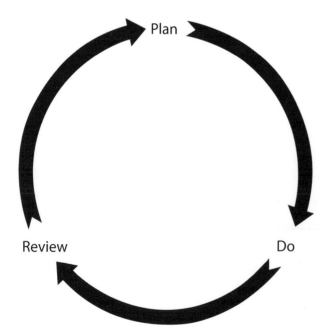

You should be continually planning and reviewing so that you are always thinking about what you are doing

In the workplace: Using new skills

A few weeks ago, Hassan attended a moving and handling training session. On the course Hassan learned how to use a slide sheet and realised they were not so difficult to use, after all. Hassan's colleagues had always said that they would not use a slide sheet because they would take too much time.

After the training session, Hassan's manager asked if he would use a slide sheet for a service user who needed turning regularly. Hassan was very nervous at first, but he followed the advice given at the training session, and it went well. Hassan decided to use an improvement action plan to increase the number of times he used the slide sheet. Within a month he was able to use the slide sheet easily.

However, when Hassan talked with his work colleagues, they still said they did not like using a slide sheet, because they said it was difficult to use. When Hassan asked, they had only actually tried to use a slide sheet once or twice since the training session.

1   *Why are Hassan's work colleagues finding it difficult to use a slide sheet?*

2   *What could Hassan suggest to his work colleagues to help them to develop the skill of using a slide sheet?*

Key points

o   Review your practice once you have implemented any new skills.

o   Ask your manager, work colleagues and NVQ assessor for feedback on your practice.

o   Identify your new strengths and weaknesses and develop a new plan to improve your weaknesses.

What have I learned?

1. What does your Care Council's Code of Practice say about your responsibilities for developing your knowledge and skills and improving your practice?

2. What is the purpose of your appraisal and supervision and how would you make arrangements for this?

3. How can you learn from the feedback that you receive from other people?

4. How can you assess your own values, skills and knowledge?

5. There are a number of organisations that can provide you with development opportunities. List the organisations that are available to help you to develop your knowledge and skills.

6. There are a range of activities you can use to find out new information and develop your skills and knowledge. List the activities you can do to improve your knowledge and skills.

7. How do you make sure that you keep your skills and knowledge up to date, so that you do not put service users at risk?

8. Why should you go on training programmes?

9. Who can help you identify the skills and knowledge that you need to do your job and to get on to the correct training programmes?

Any questions?

Q *Do I have to use my appraisal or supervision records as evidence in my portfolio?*

A *No, if you do not want to use your appraisal or supervision records then you don't have to. These are your private and confidential records, so it is up to you if you use them.*

Q *Do I have to do another course to show that I can access training and then implement the new skills?*

A *No, you should be able to show your assessor your training records and explain to them how you accessed training you have done before. You can also explain how you put the new skills into practice.*

Q *Does my assessor have to observe me?*

A *Yes, it is a requirement of this unit that you are observed.*

Case studies

Promoting independence

Zak is 21 and today is his first day working as a carer in a busy care home for young adults with learning disabilities. Before starting this new job, Zak used to work in a care home for older people, where he completed his NVQ level 2 in Health and Social Care.

Your manager has given Zak his Health and Safety induction and has asked you to look after Zak for the rest of the day. As you work with Zak, you notice that he does not offer the service users any choice at meal times. Also, he does not promote their independence, because he does everything for them. When you talk to Zak, it becomes clear that this is the practice he is used to. Zak is a kind person and you do not want to offend him, but his practice needs to be improved.

What should you do?

Back to school at my age!

Margaret is 55 and has been a care worker for 30 years. Most of her colleagues have done their NVQ level 2, but Margaret has always avoided doing hers. At her recent appraisal, her manager said that unless Margaret does her NVQ, she will not be able to work in health and social care.

Margaret became angry with her manager, saying, 'I have been doing this job for 30 years – why do I need a piece of paper to say I can do it?' The manager reminded Margaret that it is a requirement under the Care Standards Act for a certain proportion of staff to be trained to NVQ level 2.

When Margaret got home she reflected on her school days and the times when the teacher told her off and made her feel silly because of her poor spelling. Margaret reluctantly enrols on a college course.

1   *Why did Margaret's manager insist on her doing the NVQ?*
2   *What does your Care Council's Code of Practice say about developing your knowledge and skills?*
3   *Why do you think Margaret feels the way she does?*
4   *How could the college support Margaret?*

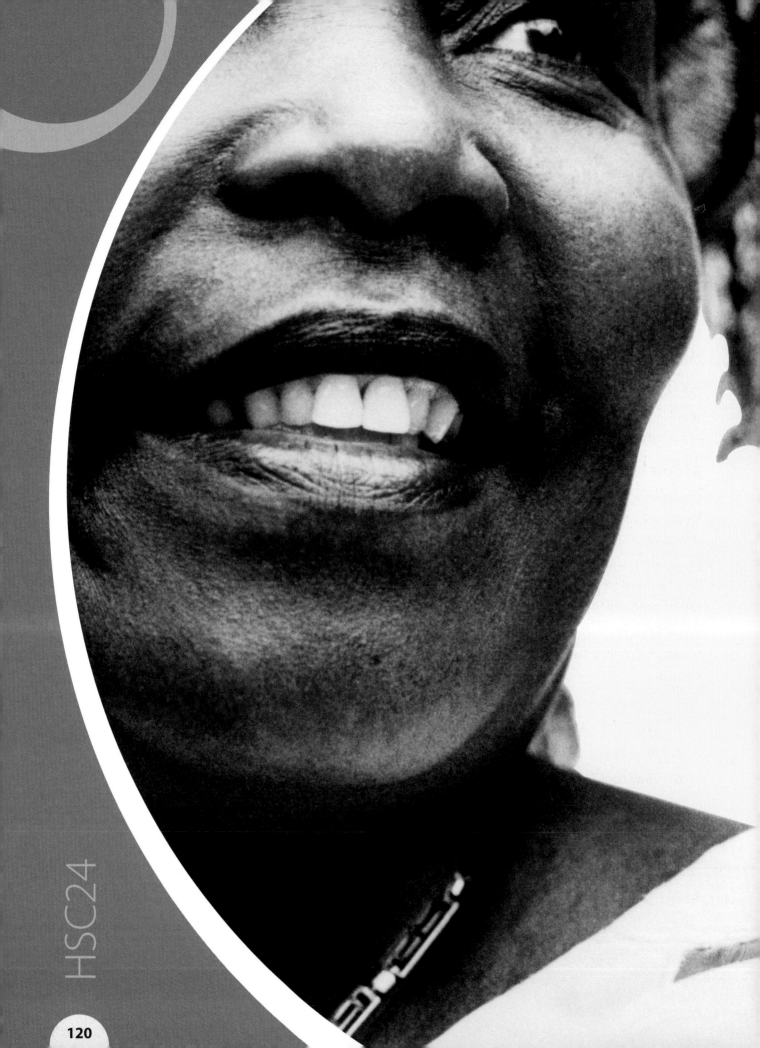

HSC24

Ensure your own actions support the care, protection and well-being of individuals

This is a core unit, which means you must complete this as part of your NVQ award. In this unit, you will need to show that you treat individuals with dignity and respect and that you value their differences. You will also need to show that you can protect them from danger, harm and abuse. In addition, you will need to show that you apply the same respect and protection to your fellow care workers and to yourself.

How you will be assessed

You will need assessor observation to cover some parts of each element in this unit. Your assessor may ask you to collect some self-reflective accounts and witness testimonies. The evidence that you collect for this unit must come from real work activities, which must fit in with your workplace policies and procedures. Simulation, or reproducing a situation, is not allowed.

This unit covers the following elements:

o **24a** Relate to and support individuals in the way they choose

o **24b** Treat people with respect and dignity

o **24c** Assist in the protection of individuals.

This unit maps to Technical Certificate Unit 002: Supporting the care, protection and well-being of individuals in a health and social care setting

Relate to and support individuals in the way they choose

The people you work with have rights and responsibilities. In order for you to help to support them, you need to know what these rights and responsibilities are. You will need to build a trusting relationship and deal effectively with conflicts.

In this element you will cover:

o The rights of service users
o Your and others' responsibilities
o Building a trusting relationship
o Conflicts or difficulties in care work.

Building a trusting relationship is important when working with individuals

Everyone has rights. It is important that you know about these, so that you can support the rights of service users. Many rights are protected by law. Workplace policies and procedures support them too. You also have a Code of Practice to work to, so you need to know about your responsibilities relating to rights.

The European Convention on Human Rights has made a list of rights. This was brought into UK law as the Human Rights Act 1998. This means that, if necessary, people can go to court to insist on their rights.

TC 002_B1_a,b,c

Remember

Laws do change from time to time, so make sure you keep up to date.

Think about it   TC 002_B1

How does the Human Rights Act affect service users and how you care for them? There is some information about the Human Rights Act on page 325 in the section that gives a summary of Acts relating to the care sector, or you can look up the Human Rights Act on the Internet.

Remember

For up-to-date laws in Scotland see the Regulation of Care (Scotland) Act 2001 and www.scotland.gov.uk. For Wales see www.csiw.wales.gov.uk.

Have a go   TC 002_B1

Unit 23 and your Care Council's Code of Practice say that you must keep your knowledge up to date. You can view up-to-date laws by visiting www.opsi.gov.uk. Ask your supervisor to help you if there is anything that you don't understand.

Care Standards Act 2000

The Care Standards Act protects the rights of service users. It has **regulated** standards of health and welfare services. The Act has set National Minimum Standards, which means that all the people working in care and the places that care for people have to provide a certain level of care. This makes sure that

regulated
made rules about

service users receive at least the minimum standard of care wherever they live. These rules apply to both adult and children's services.

Care establishments are inspected regularly, usually twice a year. One inspection is planned, and the other unplanned. The home manager will not know when the unplanned inspection will take place.

The Care Standards Act also says that employers must check that people who work with vulnerable people do not have a criminal record. (We will look more closely at this in Unit 24c and Unit 22).

Employers must also make sure that all their staff have proper training. As well as training, all staff should have regular appraisals and supervision. You can look back at Unit 23 to remind yourself about this.

How can care providers look after the rights and responsibilities of service users?

All care service providers will have a Statement of Purpose. The Statement of Purpose says what your workplace promises to provide for individuals. The service users will have been given a copy of this, usually before they use your service. There should be a copy displayed where everyone can see it and it should be presented in a way that everyone can understand it. For example, for younger service users, or those with learning disabilities, it may be in picture form. You should provide the same level of care in people's own homes. If you work in someone's home, you will usually be based at a central office. The office will have a Statement of Purpose that will apply to you.

Scotland

The Care Commission regulates and inspects all care services.

Remember

Children have special rights under the Children Act 2004, which has the broad strategy of improving children's lives.

Remember

It is very important that you understand your organisation's Statement of Purpose. You need to read it carefully. Ask your manager or supervisor if there is anything that you do not understand.

Evidence *KS 1, 7, 8, 11, 14*

Find the Statement of Purpose where you work. Use your own words to explain to your assessor what it promises to provide for the individuals you support.

Remember

Carers also have rights. The Carers Act 2004 supports carers in England and Wales.

In the workplace: Helping Maud with her rights

Maud is 82 years old. She is a private person who has no children, and who does not like socialising with other people. Until a year ago, she lived independently in her bungalow with no help or support. Then she fell and broke her hip. When Maud came out of hospital, she was admitted to a care home until she was able to walk properly again. She never intended staying in the care home for a long time and wants to move back into her bungalow.

Maud has become very **depressed**; she cannot walk on her own and she is very unhappy. She always says that she wants to die in her own home. She is desperate to get home. Her nephew says that she better off where she is.

1   *What are Maud's rights?*

2   *Why would her nephew feel that she is better staying where she is?*

3   *What might happen if she continues to be unhappy?*

4   *If you were her care worker, what would you do?*

depressed
feeling of great sadness and hopelessness

Key points

o   Everyone has rights. You need to make sure that the people that you care for know what their rights are.

o   Many rights are protected by laws such as the Human Rights Act and Care Standards Act.

o   Workplace policies and procedures support the rights laid down in law.

o   Care establishments are inspected regularly.

As well as having rights, you and the service users you work with also have responsibilities. There will be a contract explaining the care that your workplace will provide. It will also make clear the responsibilities of the service user, for example, how much the fees will be and when they should be paid. It will give other details such as whether pets or smoking are allowed, and the rules about visitors, and so on. Your contract will explain what your responsibilities are to your employer and the service users you work with.

Codes of Practice

If you work in a social care setting, you should have a copy of your Care Council's Code of Practice. This describes what is expected of you and your employer when working in social care. People who work in social care in the UK will soon be on a **public register**. You must **meet the requirements** of the Code of Practice, and agree to work to it.

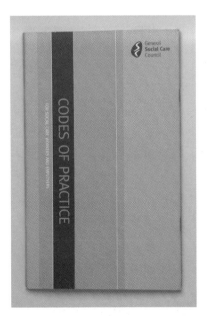

Those who work in the health care sector also have guidelines that they must work by. Nurses follow guidelines set out by the Nursing and Midwifery Council (NMC). See their website: www.nmc-uk.org.

Your Care Council's Code of Practice is available from:
England: www.gscc.org.uk
Scotland: www.sssc.uk.com
Wales: www.ccwales.org.uk
Northern Ireland: www.niscc.info

TC 001_B2

Have a go

TC 001_B2

Find your contract and Code of Practice. What do they say about your rights and responsibilities and those of the service users?

public register
a public record that everyone has the right to look at

meet the requirements
do what a code or law asks

In the workplace: Mr Flint – staff conflict

Mr Flint is new to Abbey Care Home. He is a quiet, retiring man who suffers from dementia. A few months ago he had an operation and it has taken a long time for him to recover. He has always been a fussy eater, and hates gravy and sauces on his food. He also dislikes milk and dairy products. He used to be very well built, but he has gradually lost a lot of weight. Very often he does not eat the food that is given to him.

For breakfast he likes cereal with orange juice, instead of milk. Many of the care workers say that this is not right. They give him cereal with milk because they feel that he needs the calcium.

1   *What are Mr Flint's rights?*

2   *What are the staff's concerns?*

3   *How do the workers' and Mr Flint's views differ?*

4   *What might happen if the care workers continue not to let him have his cereal with orange juice?*

5   *If you were Mr Flint's care worker, what would you do?*

Key points

o   The service user will have a contract explaining their responsibilities.

o   You will have a contract giving details of your responsibilities at work.

o   You should have a Code of Practice that you need to work to.

o   Care workers in the UK will soon be on a public register.

o   You have a responsibility to respect service users' choices.

It is very important to respect service users' choices, whatever you think of them

■ **Building a trusting relationship**

KS 2, 5, 6, 7, 14

Having a trusting relationship with the people that you care for will help you both feel valued. Be friendly, approachable and polite at all times. Get to know the service users you work with. Show them that you value them and their opinions; be sincere and show warmth. However, you should never let the relationship with a service user become too close and personal.

Think about it

Some service users can feel very vulnerable because they need someone to look after them. Imagine how you would feel if you were the service user. As a care worker you can be quite powerful and the people that you care for may feel quite helpless. You must make sure you never take advantage of, or abuse, that power.

Friendship between service users is important too

Encourage the service users you work with to be independent, so that they still have as much control over their lives as they are willing, or able, to take. Sometimes it is quicker for you to do a task for an individual. For example, it may take much longer for them to dress themselves than it would if you did it but do not be tempted to take over and do things for them. Encourage service users to be as independent as possible. You need to look at all of the person's needs – this is called holistic care, looking at the person as a 'whole person' and meeting all of their needs.

Physical, Intellectual, Emotional, Social needs (PIES)

You can remember these four areas of need if you think of PIES.

o **P**hysical needs – Food, drink, warmth, shelter
o **I**ntellectual needs – Keeping your brain active, for example, doing crosswords and Sudoku, learning new languages
o **E**motional needs – Feeling liked, loved and wanted
o **S**ocial needs – Relationships, for example, friends and neighbours.

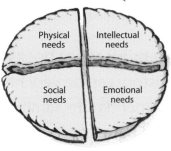

Gaining information

In order for you to give good quality care, you need to know what the needs of the service users you work with are. It is very important that they trust you. They may feel nervous and unsure about telling you **sensitive** things, so building a trusting relationship will help you both. Some service users may wish to have family or friends with them when you are getting information. Others will not. Always check with the individual first that they are happy to have family or friends present, because you need to respect the service user's confidentiality.

TC 003_A1_aiii

sensitive
embarrassing or difficult

Reminiscence is very useful when caring for someone who has dementia

Reminiscence books that tell a story of the individual's life history can be very helpful, especially for people with dementia. The family could help to put together a family tree and use photographs, cards and newspaper articles of important things and events to build up a story of the service user's life. This can help you to find out more about the person you are looking after. It can also be helpful, comforting and reassuring for them.

reminiscence
remembering things from the past

These points will help you to gain information about service users:

o be approachable

o treat each person as an individual

o answer the service user's questions honestly

o report anything you cannot deal with

o check that information you have been given is accurate
– reflect back if necessary

o   make sure the area is quiet

o   provide communication aids if necessary, e.g. hearing aids, pictures, pens, paper, an advocate

o   make sure the environment is private and relaxed

o   make sure the client can understand what you are saying – speak clearly and avoid terms service users might not understand.

Evidence *PC 1, 2; KS 5, 6*

Think about a service user that you care for. Explain what their needs are. (You may wish to look back to the section about Meeting individual needs, pages xvi–xvii.)

How do you work in a way that helps to meet their needs?

In the workplace: Paulo's problem

Paulo has a mental health problem. He is suffering from depression. Paulo is Portuguese and speaks very little English. There are no members of staff who can speak his language. Paulo appears to be very distressed and worried and spends the day sitting on his bed.

1   *What are Paulo's rights?*

2   *What problems might there be getting information about Paulo?*

3   *How could you try to build a trusting relationship with Paulo?*

Key points

o   Try to make service users feel valued.

o   A trusting relationship is very important in care work.

o   Encourage service users to be independent.

o   Get to know the service users you work with.

o   Service users may feel nervous about giving information.

■ Conflicts or difficulties in care work
KS 20

You may come up against **conflicts** or difficulties from time to time. It is important that these are dealt with properly and professionally. How you approach the situation can make all the difference.

When groups of people live and work together, it is very likely that there will be difficulties and differences of opinions from time to time. We are all individuals with different ideas, thoughts, wishes and priorities. We all go about our lives in different ways. A good care setting will try to **accommodate** all of these differences, but conflicts may still occur. Ideally, it is better to be a step ahead and prevent difficulties from happening in the first place.

conflicts
disagreements or different viewpoints

accommodate
fit in

Mr Harrup wants a male carer to help him get washed and dressed in the morning but there isn't one on duty

Jessie wants to go into the town. She needs a carer with her but all the carers are busy helping others to get up

Residents in the sitting room want to watch different TV programmes

Examples of conflicts and difficulties

Mrs Meacham has dementia and keeps shouting out in the middle of the night. Other residents are getting cross and are unable to sleep

Mr Eve smokes and is a resident in a care home which has a no smoking policy

Examples of conflict

Have a go

Check the HSE website, www.hse.gov.uk. What does it say about reducing stress at work?

How to deal with conflict

How the worker deals with conflict is very important. Listen to the individuals concerned. Value each person's opinion and do not take sides. Stay calm and make sure that your body language and tone of voice are not giving out the wrong

TC 002_E2
TC 003_A1_bi

message. For example, folded arms and raising your voice are not helpful. (Look again at communication skills in Unit 21.) Some conflicts are easily sorted out, but if not, you must always get support and advice from your supervisor.

Try to make sure that you do not become stressed. It can be very bad for your health and can affect others.

Remember

Be aware of your and others' safety. An angry person can become **aggressive**. Find your workplace policy for dealing with aggression.

aggressive
angry, forceful and may become violent

diarrhoea
liquid faeces

commode
a portable toilet

In the workplace: Joseph's personal care

Joseph has learning disabilities. He also has ulcerative colitis. This is a painful bowel condition which can cause frequent **diarrhoea**. Joseph gets scared when he is on his own. His condition is particularly bad at the moment. He is unable to walk over to the toilet, as he has drips attached to him. At night he needs to ask for the **commode** about two or three times an hour. Sometimes it smells very unpleasant. The residents in nearby rooms are getting tired and fed up. They do not talk to Joseph and complain to the staff.

1   *What are Joseph's rights?*

2   *What are the other patients' rights?*

3   *What might happen if this situation continues?*

4   *If you were looking after the residents, what would you do?*

Evidence
PC 6; KS 20

Think about a time when you have helped to resolve a conflict. Write a self-reflective account to show how you dealt with it. Did you go to anyone for advice? If so, what did they do?

Key points

o   Differences of opinion can happen when many people live and work together.

o   A good care setting will try to cater for people's differences.

o   It is better to prevent difficulties from happening in the first place.

o   You must get help if conflicts cannot be easily sorted out.

In care work you will come across many people from backgrounds that are different from yours. This includes the people you work with. It is important to respect people's differences; their culture, language and ways of doing things. Sometimes people from different backgrounds or different ages, gender or sexuality are discriminated against. As a care worker, you must make sure that this does not happen, and that the people you are working with are treated fairly and with dignity.

In this element you will cover:

- What is discrimination?
- Individuals' values
- Respecting diversity
- Cultural differences
- Difficulties in supporting equality and diversity.

It is important to treat everyone fairly and with dignity

Discrimination means treating someone unfairly, for example, because of their age, race or **gender**. You need to protect the people in your care from discrimination.

gender
whether someone is male or female

TC 002_C

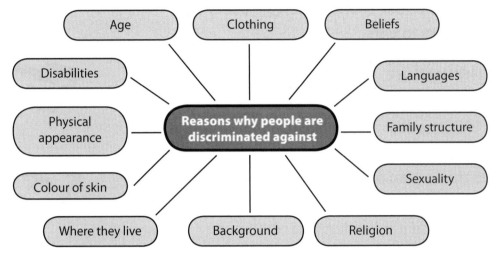

Age · Clothing · Beliefs · Disabilities · Languages · Physical appearance · **Reasons why people are discriminated against** · Family structure · Colour of skin · Sexuality · Where they live · Background · Religion

These are some of the reasons people may be discriminated against

When someone discriminates against another person it may be because they have a **stereotyped idea** of what that person is like. They do not see the person as an individual but only as a member of a group, for example, based on their age, clothing or language. They make assumptions about the individual based on what they think they know, for example, assuming that all elderly people are frail. We say they have a **prejudiced attitude**.

stereotyped idea
a simplified idea about a group of people

prejudiced attitude
a point of view based on stereotyped ideas

In childhood we learn from the people around us. If those people have prejudiced attitudes, then we may grow up believing that those attitudes are right. Often we are unaware of our prejudiced attitudes, but they can make us act in ways which discriminate against other people.

As a health and social care worker, you need to think about your own attitudes and ensure that they do not make you act in ways which discriminate.

Service users should be encouraged to feel valued as individuals and you need to show that you respect them as well as their background, culture and values. Remember that service users have **civil rights**. These rights include full access to the NHS, welfare benefits and public services. Service users should also have the opportunity to vote.

Overt and covert discrimination

Most **overt** discrimination is now illegal in the UK. For example, the Race Relations Act of 1976 made it an offence to discriminate on the grounds of race. The Disability Discrimination Act of 1995 made it an offence to discriminate on the grounds of disability. **Covert** discrimination is much more difficult to deal with because it is hidden and often not recognised. Examples of covert discrimination might be:

○ Residents who are put to bed and got up at specific times to fit in with staff shifts
○ Adults with learning disabilities who are prevented from doing things that other adults take for granted such as socialising, choosing their own clothes or forming relationships
○ Cinemas or clubs that do not have access for people with physical disabilities

civil rights
rights belonging to people born and resident in the country

overt
obvious

covert
hidden or disguised

TC 002_B1_b

Have a go

What do your Care Council's Code of Practice and Statement of Purpose say about treating individuals with respect and dignity? You may wish to go through these with your supervisor or assessor.

In the workplace: Tom's discrimination

Tom has learning disabilities. He lives in a care home. A minibus collects him every day to take him to the day centre where he works. His friend goes on the bus. Tom could meet him at the bus stop or they could even walk but he would have to leave half an hour earlier and breakfast is not ready in time. He would like to make his own breakfast so he could catch the bus but the home's policy does not allow this.

1 *How is Tom being discriminated against?*
2 *What could be the effect on Tom?*
3 *What would you do if faced with this situation?*

Care workers can be discriminated against as well, for example, because of their sexuality, where they come from or their gender. Care workers have the right to be respected too.

Think about it

Think of a time when you have felt that you were treated differently or unfairly. For example, have you been treated differently because of your gender, how you speak, the clothes you wear or the colour of your skin?

In the workplace: Gary is gay

Gary is a care worker in a care home. He loves his work and gives lots of time to the residents; he even spends his own time arranging outings and activities for them. Gary is gay. His boyfriend sometimes meets him from work at the end of his shift; he waits in his car outside.

Mrs Marshall found out about Gary's sexuality. She told several other residents about Gary and suggested that they 'stick together' and refuse to let Gary look after them. They then complained to the care worker in charge. Mrs Marshall made it clear that she pays a lot of money for her care and has stated that she will not have 'someone like him' looking after her.

1   *How is Gary being discriminated against?*

2   *What might be the effect on Gary?*

3   *If Mrs Marshall complained to you, what would you do?*

Evidence   *PC 1, 2, 3, 4; KS 1, 2, 7*

Look at your Care Council's Code of Practice and Statement of Purpose, and write a case study about a person you care for. Explain how you respect their differences and do not discriminate against them. (You may wish to choose someone who is very different from yourself.).

Key points

o   Discrimination is treating someone differently or unfairly.

o   Service users may not be able to speak up for themselves.

o   Individuals may be discriminated against in various ways.

o   The people that you care for should feel valued.

o   Help service users to use their civil rights.

We all have our own individual values. They may be quite different from other people's. Sometimes you may need to work with people who have different values from you, but you must make sure that you still care for them in a fair way. Make sure service users can express their values without fear of discrimination.

Some of our values can be influenced by how we were brought up and the people we are with. Values can also change as we move through different life stages.

TC 002_E1

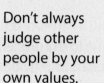

Remember

Don't always judge other people by your own values.

In the workplace: Pearl's values

Pearl works in a care home for older people. One day, as she walked past the open door of a resident's room, she saw two residents kissing. Pearl felt embarrassed and uncomfortable. She didn't believe it was appropriate behaviour. She told them to go back to the lounge and said that she would report them if they did it again.

1   *Were the residents treated with respect and dignity?*

2   *How would you have reacted?*

3   *What advice would you give to Pearl?*

4   *How should care workers make sure that they do not impose their own values on the individuals they work with?*

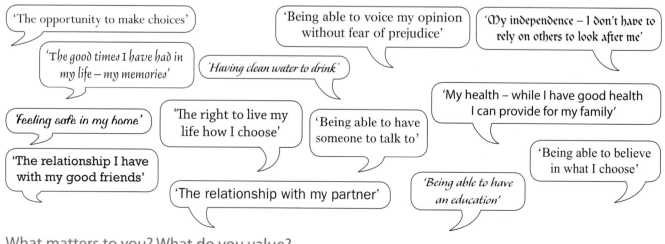

'The opportunity to make choices'

'The good times I have had in my life – my memories'

'Having clean water to drink'

'Being able to voice my opinion without fear of prejudice'

'My independence – I don't have to rely on others to look after me'

'Feeling safe in my home'

'The right to live my life how I choose'

'Being able to have someone to talk to'

'My health – while I have good health I can provide for my family'

'The relationship I have with my good friends'

'The relationship with my partner'

'Being able to have an education'

'Being able to believe in what I choose'

What matters to you? What do you value?

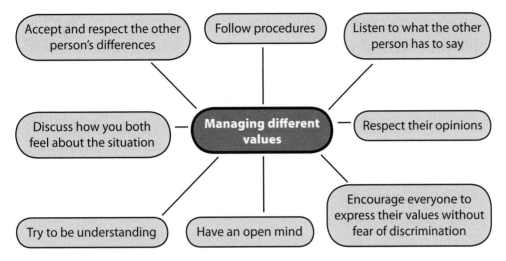

It can be difficult to manage differences sometimes

Think about it

What difficulties might you have if you are looking after someone with different values from your own?

Evidence KS 4, 7

Write a list of health and social care values. Explain how they differ from some of the values of the service users you work with.

Key points

- o Your values may be quite different from other people's.
- o You will sometimes work with and care for people with different values from your own.
- o Values can change as we move through different life stages.
- o Treat people in a fair way and don't discriminate against someone because of their values.

■ **Respecting diversity** *KS 1, 2, 7*

It is important to recognise and respect people's differences, or **diversity**. We are all valuable members of society with something positive to contribute.

We all have our own individual likes and dislikes. Think about the food you like and the clothes you wear. Do you smoke, drink alcohol, follow a particular religion – or not? What is important to you? What really irritates you?

Having different values does not have to be a problem. Look at your list from the Have a go activity. You probably found quite a lot of differences between yourself and your friend, even if you thought you were very similar. Your values may be different in some areas too, but you still get along.

Health care values may be different from service users' values. For example, health care professionals would prefer it if people did not smoke, drink too much alcohol and that they exercised more, and some expect others to follow advice they may not follow themselves! Service users may choose not to follow these health and social care values. You need to respect this. You can give advice, but you cannot insist they take it.

Diversity enriches life

Think about the good things that people from other countries have brought to us. For example, different food, fashion, music and technology, to name just a few. Do you enjoy trying different food if you go on holiday abroad? Do you like seeing different places or experiencing different cultures? It is healthy for us to open our minds – we can learn a lot from each other.

diversity
differences in race, religion and lifestyle

Have a go

Talk to your friend about your likes and dislikes. Think about what you both value. Make a list of your similarities and your differences.

Remember

What one person considers important, another may not.

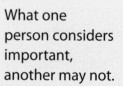

In the workplace: Maureen's opinions

Jane has just started a new job as a care assistant in a care home. She has never been a care worker before. There are many members of staff and residents from different ethnic backgrounds. Maureen has been working in the care home for 25 years and she has seen many changes in this time. When she first started, most care workers and residents were British.

Maureen is helping Jane to settle in to her new job. On their break Maureen says to Jane, 'All these foreign workers are taking our jobs and the foreign residents are taking advantage of our health service. It would be better if they all went home.'

1   *How might Maureen's opinions affect how she cares for residents?*

2   *What effect might her views have on Jane's work?*

3   *What are the benefits of having different ethnic backgrounds in the work force at this care home?*

4   *If you were Jane, what would you say?*

Key points

o   We must respect other people's differences.

o   We all have our own likes and dislikes.

o   Variety can be good; it would be very boring if we were all the same.

o   We all have something positive to contribute to society.

o   It is good for us to open our minds – we can learn a lot from each other.

We live in a multicultural society. It is important that you think about and respect the service user's cultural needs. How you care for a person from a different cultural background may be quite different from how you do things for yourself. Raising awareness of differences, such as cultural differences, can help to combat discrimination.

It would be impossible to go into detail about the preferences of each different cultural group here, but there is a lot of information available. We will look at some of these in the other units, including Unit 21 Communication, Unit 214 Eating and drinking and Unit 218 Helping people with their personal care. You must remember not to 'label' the person you are caring for. For example, you must not presume that all Muslims need to be cared for in the same way. Involve the individual in their care by asking them what they would like. If you cannot ask them, ask their family or friends. Having an idea of what some of their preferences are will help to build a professional relationship.

TC 002_C

Have a go

Have a look at www.ethnicityonline.net to find out about different cultures.

In the workplace: Cultural respect

Madhavi is a health care worker in a small hospital. She works on a busy ward. Benjamin was admitted to the ward. He is Jewish.

Madhavi spoke to Benjamin and then asked her supervisor if she could contact the kitchen to make sure that **kosher** meat was available. She also offered to contact the local **rabbi**.

1   *How did Madhavi show respect for Benjamin?*

2   *If Madhavi was not sure about Benjamin's cultural needs, where could she find out about them?*

kosher
prepared according to Jewish law

rabbi
Jewish religious leader

Different types of people can share enjoyment of the same event

Evidence *KS 1, 2, 7*

Think about a person that you have cared for with different values and beliefs from your own. For example, the person may have been a Jehovah's Witness or a Muslim. Explain how you have respected their rights and choices.

Key points

o People from different cultures may have different needs and preferences.

o Involve the service user by asking them what they would like.

o If you cannot ask the service user about their preferences, ask their family or friends.

o You must not 'label' people by expecting them to behave in a certain way.

o Knowing an individual's preferences helps to build a trusting relationship.

Even though you may try very hard to protect the people that you care for, they may still experience discrimination. If this does happen, it is important that you know what you can do to help them. You will also need to know about the laws to protect people from discrimination.

Have a go

There are many laws to protect individuals from discrimination. Can you think of any? Have a look at www.hmso.gov.uk to keep up to date.

People depend on you

TC 002_C

There may be times when you feel that the people you care for are being discriminated against by other people or systems. The service user may rely on you to be 'their voice' so it is important that you help support them. Even if you cannot do anything about the discrimination yourself, you must never ignore it. Report it to your supervisor or manager. Your inspection team can also offer advice. Remember that your local **Citizens Advice Bureau** will always help too. You can also sometimes challenge discrimination by raising awareness of differences between people.

Citizens Advice Bureau
a free service that advises people

In the workplace: Rashid's diet

Rashid is Muslim. He is a resident in a care home for individuals with physical disabilities. He is the only Muslim there. His family do not visit very often. Other residents have a wide range of food to choose from.

The chef provides food for Rashid, but there is often either very little, or no, choice. He has vegetable curry four or five times every week. He eats very little and is losing weight. You have tried talking to the chef but things do not change.

1 *How is Rashid being discriminated against?*

2 *What effect might this have on Rashid?*

3 *If you were looking after Rashid what would you do?*

'Not vegetable curry again!'

Think about it

Do you always think about the service user's cultural needs and preferences?

Evidence *PC 6, 7*

Give an example of when someone was discriminated against. Write a self-reflective account to explain how you supported them. Did you ask anyone for advice and support for them?

Commenting on care

Care providers try to look after the people they care for well. However, if a service user or his or her family do have a complaint it is important to get it sorted out as quickly as possible. Under the Care Standards Act individuals must be able to comment on the care and the service they receive. Each workplace must show the procedure for making comments or complaints. This should be written in a way that is easy to understand. For example, it may be in large print, picture form, Braille or audio if individuals need help to understand their rights.

Compliments count!

It is not just complaints that should be reported. Compliments should be recorded too! Many of the people you care for, and their families, are very happy about the care you give, so it is important for the managers to know what is going well.

Encouraging people to comment on their care can help to show what is good. It also shows what work is needed on areas that are not so good. You can help by encouraging individuals, families and friends to have their say.

Greenacres Care Home

What you think is important to us. If you wish to make a comment please fill in this form.
Use black ink if possible.

The name and address of the person who wishes to make the comment

Name:	Maria Mc Intyre	Telephone:	01609 783129
Address:	31 Handfield Road	Mobile:	07845 898499
	Trowely		
	Norfolk		
Postcode:	NR29 6XQ		

I would like to make a   comment ☐   compliment ☑   complaint ☐

Please write the details below

I would like to say how pleased I am with the care that my mother is receiving. She and I were worried about her moving from her own home into Greenacres. The care staff have been really kind to her and helped her to settle in. Her key worker Carol is brilliant. Thank you.

Print name: Maria Mc Intyre   Sign: Maria Mc Intyre   Date: 25.11.06

If you are filling this form in for someone else please write your name and contact details below.
Signed:
Name: Telephone:
Address: Postcode:

Please send the completed form to the Manager

The comments procedure should be available for everyone to refer to

> **Remember**
>
> Your views matter as well. Your comments and suggestions can help to improve things too.

Have a go

TC 002_D1

Find and read the policy on reporting comments and complaints where you work.

In the workplace: Unhappy Mrs Scott

Mrs Scott is a resident in a care home. She cannot see well and she uses a wheelchair. She feels that she does not have equal access to the services that are provided for the other residents. For example, the notice board shows some of the outings that are planned, but Mrs Scott cannot read them because the board is too high. She has missed the opportunity of taking part in a lot of activities.

Mrs Scott has mentioned this several times to various people. Now she is fed up and wishes to complain. She asks Milly, a care worker, how she can make a formal complaint. Milly gives her the complaints procedure (in small print) and a pen.

1   *How is Mrs Scott being discriminated against?*

2   *How could this be avoided?*

3   *Will she be able to complain, now that Milly has given her the complaints procedure?*

4   *What would you do?*

Evidence *KS 9*   TC 002_D1

Explain how you would let a service user know about how to comment on their care. (You may need to find your procedures at work to refer to.)

Key points

o   Individuals may be discriminated against by other people or systems.

o   The people you care for may rely on you to be 'their voice' to help them.

o   Always report discriminatory behaviour to your supervisor or manager.

o   There are laws to protect individuals from discrimination.

o   It is a requirement under the Care Standards Act that individuals can comment on the care and the service they receive.

Assist in the protection of individuals

Abuse can take many forms. It can be physical, mental, financial, sexual or neglect. The signs may not always be obvious, so you need to be alert so that you can protect the people you care for. You need to know what to do if you know or suspect that someone is being abused. There are laws and policies to protect people. You will need to know about these. Remember also – it is not just service users who are at risk of abuse – you are too.

TC 002_F1_a,b,c

In this element you will cover:

○ What is abuse?
○ Why abuse may happen
○ What to do if you suspect abuse.

Think about it

How often are service users alone with someone? How easy would it be for them to tell someone if they were being treated badly?

Abuse always affects the person being abused in some way

To protect individuals from abuse you need to know what abuse is. Abuse is taking advantage of someone by treating them unfairly and being cruel to them. A person who needs to rely on someone else to help care for them is at risk of abuse. You need to be able to recognise the signs and symptoms. Sometimes it is not obvious that abuse is happening, but it can have very serious effects on the person being abused. You will need to keep a look out to protect service users.

There are many types of abuse

Type of abuse	An individual could be abused by
Physical	hitting, pulling, pushing, holding down, handling roughly
Emotional (psychological)	bullying, calling names, threatening, making the individual feel bad about themselves
Sexual	touching in private places, making suggestive comments, showing sexually related materials, such as pictures and videos
Financial	spending their money, taking things that belong to the person
Neglect	not giving the person enough food, personal care or attention
Institutional	the routine of the workplace based around what works best for the care workers, not the service users

Evidence *KS 17*

Write an account explaining what might make you think that an individual is being abused. Give as many examples as you can.

In the workplace: What's going on?

Caron is a domiciliary care worker and she has been caring for Mr Jarvis for 5 weeks, going in every Monday to Friday to cook and help with some personal care. Caron has noticed that Mr Jarvis seems very quiet lately and some things are making her question if Mr Jarvis is suffering some kind of abuse. Mr Jarvis' son David and daughter-in-law Julia help him at the weekend.

Caron is worried about Mr Jarvis. To be on the safe side she tells her supervisor about her concerns. Her supervisor said that symptoms on their own do not always indicate abuse and that you have to look at the whole picture. Her supervisor asked why Caron is suspicious.

Why do you think that Caron was suspicious?

Symptoms on their own do not always indicate abuse. You need to look at the whole picture. For example, an individual with bruises could have fallen recently but unexplained bruises would make you suspicious. Several signs together would strongly suggest abuse.

Remember

It is important to recognise the signs and symptoms of abuse so that you can protect people.

In the workplace: Why won't Kirsty join in? TC 002_F1

Cairngorm View is a day centre for individuals with learning disabilities. Kirsty is 22 years old and she lives with her parents and two brothers. She attends the centre twice a week, where she does lots of activities.

One day Aileen was working at the day centre and Kirsty was very quiet. She sat in a corner on her own and would not sit with the others. Aileen spent some time with Kirsty, who then agreed to join in a cookery activity.

Kirsty spilled a jug of milk on her trousers so Aileen took her to the bathroom to help to change into clean ones. When Aileen was helping Kirsty in the bathroom, she suspected that Kirsty was being abused.

1   *What might make Aileen think that Kirsty was being abused?*

2   *What type of abuse may she have experienced?*

3   *What should Aileen do next?*

Abuse can happen anywhere

It is possible for anyone to abuse another person, even someone you think is very trustworthy. It could be a partner, relative, friend, neighbour, volunteer or care worker. We sometimes read about such cases in the newspaper.

Abuse can happen anywhere. It could happen in the individual's own home, in a day centre, a care setting or in a hospital.

If you work with vulnerable people you must have training on how to recognise if someone is being abused and what to do if you suspect it is happening. Everyone has a legal right to be protected from harm and abuse.

Remember

We all have a legal right to be protected from abuse.

Remember

It is important to recognise the signs and symptoms of abuse so that you can protect people.

Evidence *PC 1, 4; KS 17*

Write a self-reflective account or collect a witness testimony to show how you have protected a service user from harm and abuse. Explain how you looked for signs of harm and abuse.

Key points

o Abuse can sometimes be obvious, but often it is not.
o Service users are vulnerable, so they are at risk of abuse.
o Abuse can occur anywhere.
o Care workers should have training to protect service users from abuse.
o We all have a legal right to be protected from abuse.

There are many reasons why abuse can happen. The person who is abusing may not even realise that what they are doing is wrong. Having an understanding of why abuse happens might help to prevent it.

TC 002_F1_d

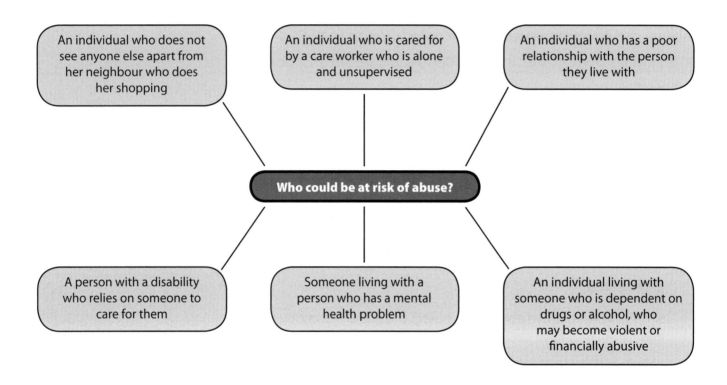

An individual who does not see anyone else apart from her neighbour who does her shopping

An individual who is cared for by a care worker who is alone and unsupervised

An individual who has a poor relationship with the person they live with

Who could be at risk of abuse?

A person with a disability who relies on someone to care for them

Someone living with a person who has a mental health problem

An individual living with someone who is dependent on drugs or alcohol, who may become violent or financially abusive

Workplaces that are poorly run may have poor practices. Staff shortages sometimes put pressure on the existing staff. This could lead to hurrying the service user, rough handling or **neglect**. You should always report staff shortages to your manager. Staff shortages may also mean you have to work alone, putting you at risk of abuse. Make sure that people know where you are working if you are working alone. Workers who are not properly trained may abuse an individual – sometimes without even realising it. For example, they may use old-fashioned practices, such as moving and handling or restraint techniques that are now banned.

neglect
not caring for someone properly

In the workplace: Don't move Mrs Lang like that!

Mrs Lang has had an operation and is recovering in a care home. It is lunch time and she asks to be sat up. Jane is a new care worker. She knows that she cannot do this on her own and calls on another care worker, Alison, to help her.

Jane has just attended a moving and handling course and goes to get equipment to lift Mrs Lang. Alison calls her back and goes to one side of Mrs Lang. She hooks an arm under Mrs Lang's armpit, obviously expecting Jane to do the same. Jane knows this is wrong, but goes along with Alison's method. Mrs Lang suffers a dislocated shoulder.

1   *How is this abusive to Mrs Lang?*

2   *Why do you think that Alison did not follow the proper guidelines?*

3   *What would you do if you were Jane?*

Remember

Rough handling is abusive to the service users.

Evidence *KS 15*

Write an account giving some reasons why abuse could happen.

Sometimes care workers may not realise they are abusing an individual when they use old-fashioned practices

Key points

o   There are many reasons why an individual may be abused.

o   Poorly run workplaces may lead to abuse.

o   The more dependent an individual is, the more at risk of abuse they are.

o   The abuser may not be aware that what they are doing is wrong.

o   Workers who are not trained correctly may abuse service users without realising it.

If you suspect abuse, it is very important that you know what to do and do not ignore it. You have a responsibility to protect service users from danger, harm and abuse. Never promise to keep information or secrets to yourself; make it clear that you will have to share information with your manager or someone more senior about behaviour that might be harmful. Explain that you will only tell the people who have to know.

TC 002_F1_e, f

Each workplace will have a procedure to explain what to do if you suspect someone is being abused. If you cannot speak to your manager or another senior manager at work, then you could contact your inspection team. Each region has guidelines to explain what you need to do if you know or suspect that a vulnerable person is being abused.

It is important to record events and conversations you have. Your records must be written clearly and be accurate and factual. You must not write your opinions or presume something has happened. You must only write exactly what you have seen, or heard from the person reporting the incident.

Remember

You must always report suspected danger, harm and abuse.

Never probe the individual to give you more information. Disclosure of abuse must be handled very carefully.

Have a go

TC 002_F1,F2

Find your local policy on protecting vulnerable individuals; then check your workplace policy on reporting danger, harm and abuse.

Evidence *KS 8*

TC 002_F1,F2

Explain in your own words what your Care Council's Code of Practice says about protecting individuals from danger, harm and abuse.

In the workplace: Mrs Jefferies' terrible experience

James is a care worker in the community. One day he went to visit Mrs Jefferies as usual. James let himself in and found Mrs Jefferies lying on the floor in the hall, crying. He helped her to sit up and Mrs Jefferies told him that she had had an intruder.

A young man had knocked on the door and said that he needed to come in to check the gas meter. Mrs Jefferies let him in. Then the man started to be verbally abusive to her and demanded money. She was so frightened that she gave him money from her purse which was on the table. The man pushed her down on the floor and left.

James helped Mrs Jefferies to a chair in the lounge and comforted her.

1   *How was Mrs Jefferies abused?*

2   *What effect has this had on Mrs Jefferies?*

3   *What should James do in this situation?*

Key points

o   Service users have the right to be protected from abuse.

o   You must always report suspected or actual abuse.

o   Each workplace will have a policy about what to do if you suspect abuse.

o   You could ask your inspection team for advice if you suspect abuse.

o   Always complete records relating to abuse accurately and clearly.

It is important to stay calm when individuals are upset

What have I learned?

1 Give five examples of how the Human Rights Act protects individuals' rights.

2 How does the Care Standards Act promote the rights of service users?

3 Explain how you can build a trusting relationship with service users.

4 Give three examples of conflicts you may face at work and how you should deal with them.

5 Give three examples of how individuals may be discriminated against.

6 Give three examples of laws and policies in place to protect individuals from discrimination.

7 Give three examples of signs, symptoms and effects of abuse on individuals.

8 Explain what you should do if you suspect abuse.

9 What does your Care Council's Code of Practice say about protecting individuals from abuse?

Any questions?

Q *I do not look after anyone from a different culture and will probably not need to. My assessor has asked me to do a project about how to care for people from different cultures. Do I need to do this?*

A Your assessor is right to test your knowledge about how to care for people from different cultures because you are working towards a national qualification. They will need to feel satisfied that you would be able to care for someone from a different culture if needed to. Try looking at the link given in Unit 24b www.ethnicityonline. net.

Q *I am finding Unit 24c very difficult. All of the service users are well looked after and not abused. I will not be able to get assessor observation for this element.*

A Read through Unit 24c. Not all abuse is obvious. Assessor observation is needed in each element. Do you look for signs of abuse, or assess the possibility of abuse with the people you care for?

Q *I was recently involved in an incident when a carer that I work with was accused of abuse. I was asked to write a statement. Can I photocopy this and put it in my portfolio to use it for evidence?*

A No, do not photocopy the statement. Confidential records should never be kept in your portfolio. Talk to your assessor about this.

Any questions? (continued…)

Q *I was in my local shopping centre recently with a service user who was shopping for clothes. The ladies section was upstairs and there was no lift. I felt that the service user was being discriminated against because she is a wheelchair user. I spoke to the manager on her behalf. My assessor was not with me. How can I use this for evidence for my NVQ?*

A Well done, you were right to stand up for your service user. Discuss this with your assessor and look at Unit 24b. You could ask your supervisor for a witness statement.

Q *Do I need observations to finish this unit, or can I just complete the activities given?*

A *You need to have observations in each element of this unit. Your assessor should see you covering some of the Performance Criteria while being observed in other units. That evidence can be cross-referenced to this unit.*

Case study

The carers who really cared

Mrs Brown, aged 86, had lived in The Larches Care Home for about two years after having a stroke. She had no family with whom she had any contact but her friends did visit sometimes. She liked living at The Larches and got on well with the staff and other residents. She thought of them as her family now.

Mrs Brown became ill and she knew that she did not have much longer to live. All the staff in the care home gave her the best of care. Towards the end, she could not talk and wrote shaky notes instead. Once, when asked if her shoulder hurt, she wrote 'ouch'.

The staff, friends and sometimes other residents, who were her friends too, took it in turns to sit with Mrs Brown. One lady who was nearly blind but who still loved to knit made her a scarf to keep her neck warm. It had holes in but it gave Mrs Brown great comfort.

After a peaceful death, she was laid out by the manager and her key worker. They put make-up on her just as she had always liked it. Some staff and residents chose to visit her to say goodbye. As she was taken from The Larches they all lined up at the door with their heads bowed, and curtains were closed as a mark of respect.

The funeral arrangements were made by the care home. Mrs Brown's key worker spoke at the service about Mrs Brown. She used the life story from her care plan which they had written together.

At the wake held at the care home, a table was set with champagne, glasses, nice food and a picture of Mrs Brown – just as she had wanted. They all toasted the memory of a good friend.

1 *How did the care staff show respect for Mrs Brown?*

2 *How were the other residents' wishes respected?*

HSC214

Help individuals to eat and drink

This is an optional unit. It links with Unit 213 Provide food and drink for individuals, but you cannot choose to do both of these units together. If you have chosen to do Unit 213, there is a lot of information here that you can use.

For these units, you need to show that you can meet service users' individual needs and encourage them to be as independent as possible.

You will need to know what a healthy and balanced diet is, so you can help to keep the people you care for healthy. You will also need to know what to do if someone has an allergic reaction to something they eat or drink.

Infection control is important when helping individuals to eat and drink. You will need to show that you can handle food hygienically. Read through Unit 22 to find out more about infection control.

How you will be assessed

Your assessor will need to observe you for most of this unit. He or she may also ask you to collect witness testimonies and self-reflective accounts.

This unit covers the following elements:

o **214a** Make preparations to support individuals to eat and drink

o **214b** Support individuals to get ready to eat and drink

o **214c** Help individuals to eat and drink.

A well-balanced diet is very important if we are to be healthy. We all have our own preferences when it comes to food and drink choice. Sometimes religious and cultural needs can affect our choice. You must also be able to prepare and handle food safely. Food poisoning can make someone very ill and put their life at risk.

In this element you will cover:

- What is a healthy and balanced diet?
- What is an unhealthy diet?
- Finding information about what a service user likes and dislikes
- Religious, cultural needs and diet choice
- Handling food safely.

A nutritious diet will help to keep a service user fit and healthy

It is important for you to know what a healthy and balanced diet is. Encouraging service users to make good choices about what they eat is a very important part of supporting them. Some individuals may need to have a special diet for medical reasons, such as diabetes. Check the service users' care plans to find out about their dietary needs.

A healthy balanced diet

A healthy balanced diet gives individuals all the **nutrients** in the right amounts for their age and sex. The amount of food taken in by an individual needs to balance with the energy they use. If these are not balanced, the individual will lose or gain weight. For example, an energetic teenager needs to eat more than an older person who is not very active, because the teenager uses more energy.

nutrients
parts of food essential for health

Remember

We can manage longer without food than water. Adults should have between 2 and 4 litres of water a day (in food and liquid).

The amount of food taken in should balance with the energy that is used

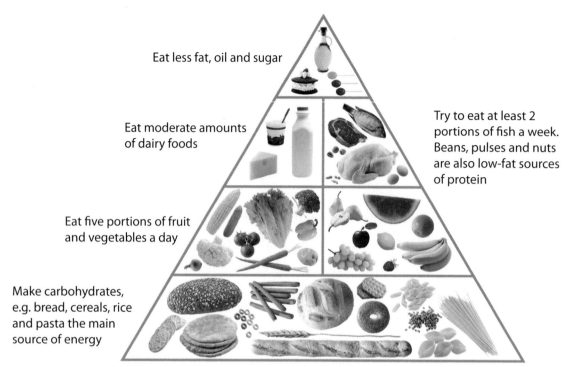

Eat less fat, oil and sugar

Eat moderate amounts of dairy foods

Try to eat at least 2 portions of fish a week. Beans, pulses and nuts are also low-fat sources of protein

Eat five portions of fruit and vegetables a day

Make carbohydrates, e.g. bread, cereals, rice and pasta the main source of energy

Use a nutrition pyramid to help service users to follow a healthy diet

Everyone should eat a variety of foods, so that our bodies get all the nutrients that we need. This is especially important if an individual is recovering from an accident or an operation. The pyramid shows the amount needed from each food group every day. Try to choose low fat dairy foods and lean meat. Eat two portions of fish each week.

Alcohol should be kept within the recommended limits or, better still, to occasional use only. The long-term effects of too much alcohol include conditions that can cause serious damage to the liver, or the stomach. It can also lead to dementia.

Remember

The nutrition pyramid is a guide. Always check the service user's care plan to see if they need a special diet. For example, they may need a low fat or high protein diet.

Have a go

Oats, kiwi fruit and apples are examples of 'superfoods'. These are thought to be especially good at helping to fight illness and to promote good health. See how many others you can find.

It is important to encourage the individuals you care for to drink on a regular basis. For example, you could offer them water, fruit squash, fruit juice and other drinks. However, they should avoid too many sugary drinks, such as colas and drinks that contain high levels of caffeine, as too much caffeine is bad for the health.

Have a go

Keep a diary of what you eat over the next few days. Compare this with the nutrition triangle. Are you getting enough of each food group?

Evidence *PC 1; KS 8*

Check a service user's care plan and write a day's menu for them, making sure it is healthy, well balanced and takes into account any special dietary needs they may have. (Make sure you explain how the menu meets the needs of the service user.)

Remember

There are many fashionable slimming diets. Some of these could lead to a person not getting enough vitamins and minerals. Always ask a care professional, such as a dietician, before suggesting any diets to service users.

Think about it

Some snacks can be very unhealthy because they contain high levels of saturated fats, sugar and salt. Look at the choice of snacks that are offered to individuals. Could you suggest a healthy option?

Key points

o   You need to know what a healthy diet is, so that you can encourage service users to choose a healthy balanced diet.

o   We need to eat a variety of foods so that our body gets all the nutrients that it needs.

o   Adults should have between 2 and 4 litres of water a day (in food and liquids).

A lot of research has been carried out about what we eat. It has shown that too much salt is bad for you because it can lead to high blood pressure and heart disease. Research has also shown that eating lots of fruit and vegetables can help to prevent some cancers.

A person who eats too much and does not exercise may become **obese**. This puts a huge strain on the body, and can lead to many other problems. Obesity has been linked to heart attacks, varicose veins and diabetes. It often leads to low self-esteem, which means that the person does not feel good about themselves. Eating too much junk food can make the person feel sluggish because it can be filling, but does not contain many nutrients.

obese
being very overweight

Obesity is becoming a major problem in the UK

Recommended daily allowances

The government has suggested the recommended daily allowance (RDA) of many nutrients, such as salt, fat, protein etc. The RDA is the amount that an average man or woman needs every day of each nutrient in order to stay healthy. A service user may not need as much if they are not very active but it is still very important that what they do eat is nutritious. If a service user has a very small appetite, it is even more important that the little that they do eat is very nutritious, and gives them what they need to stay healthy.

Why don't some people choose to eat well?

There can be many reasons why an individual does not choose a healthy, balanced diet. They may not know what a healthy diet is. Diet can also be linked to social class because poorer people may not be able to afford good quality food.

Busy lifestyles mean that some people eat a lot of processed or convenience foods, which usually contain a lot of salt and fat. Other people just do not want to follow the advice to eat well, because they feel that the unhealthy option tastes better!

Remember

Make sure that service users have enough fibre in their diets to prevent constipation

What can you do?

Make sure that you know what a healthy diet is so that you can help service users to make healthy choices. If you help service users to develop independent skills by supporting them to do their own shopping, point out the healthy options and alternatives.

Make healthy food appealing by presenting it nicely on the plate.

Think about it

If an individual is not keen on vegetables they are more likely to try some if you just give them a small portion.

What can food manufacturers do?

Manufacturers must show the nutritional value of food items on the packaging. Food manufacturers and supermarkets use labels that show nutritional information in many different ways. Some are colour-coded, while others show the amount of each ingredient as a percentage. These can be the recommended daily allowance (RDA, see page 165) or the guideline daily amount (GDA).

The Food Standards Agency's 'traffic light' system of food labelling is another system in use, and is becoming more popular. Colour-coded panels clearly show the levels of total fats, saturated fats, sugar and salt in foods such as ready meals. This can help people to make healthier choices at a glance. The colours mean:

Red: eat this once in a while

Amber: this is fine to eat most of the time

Green: a good choice at any time.

> **Have a go**
>
> Compare different types of food labels to see which system you prefer or find easiest to understand.

Nutrition information				Guidelines daily amounts		
Typical values (cooked as per instructions)	Per 100g	Per pack	% based on GDA for women	**Women**	**Men**	**Children** (5-10 years)
Energy	594 kJ	2971 kJ				
	142 kcal	709 kcal	35.5%	2000 kcal	2500 kcal	1800 kcal
Protein	4.2g	21.0g	46.7%	45g	55g	24g
Carbohydrate	16.6g	83.0g	36.1%	230g	300g	220g
of which **sugars**	1.9g	9.5g	10.6%	90g	120g	85g
of which starch	14.7g	73.5g	–	–	–	–
Fat	6.5g	32.5g	46.4%	70g	95g	70g
of which **saturates**	3.6g	18.0g	90.0%	20g	30g	20g
mono-unsaturates	2.0g	10.0g	–	–	–	–
polyunsaturates	0.9g	4.5g	–	–	–	–
Fibre	1.9g	9.5g	39.6%	24g	24g	15g
Salt	0.4g	2.0g	33.3%	6g	6g	4g
of which sodium	0.16g	0.80g	33.3%	2.4g	2.4g	1.4g

You may want to keep an eye on your **salt** intake as too much may increase your blood pressure.

It's important to watch your **calorie** intake, as without regular exercise too many may lead to weight gain.

To maintain a healthy lifestyle, we recommend aiming for at least 30 minutes of moderate exercise each day, such as brisk walking.

Some foods have an 'at a glance' chart showing how healthy the item is

Manufacturers must also list any additives that are in the food. Most of these are harmless, but some people can have an allergic reaction to certain added ingredients. Some of these are said to make children overactive. You can find out more about food and nutrition on the website www.food.gov.uk.

In the workplace: Kelly's shopping

Kelly lives in a flat with her three children. She does not work and has very little money to spend on food. She tends to buy lots of cheap, processed foods, such as pies, sausages and beef burgers which fill the children up. Kelly usually buys the children some sweets at the end of the shopping trip. She does not buy fresh fruit very often because it is too expensive.

1 *What do you think is wrong with what she buys?*

2 *How could you advise Kelly to help her to provide more healthy foods for her family?*

Remember

Make sure that service users don't fill up on food that isn't nutritious.

Evidence *KS 10*

Give three reasons why some individuals may decide not to make healthy food and drink choices. For each reason explain how you would encourage the individual to make the healthy choice.

Key points

o Not eating enough fruit and vegetables has been linked to some cancers.

o Obesity is becoming a big problem in our society.

o Eating too much junk food can make you feel sluggish.

o Busy lifestyles mean that some people eat a lot of ready-made foods that are high in salt and fat.

o Some additives have been linked to hyperactivity in children.

It is very important to find out about what a service user likes
and does not like to eat and drink. If they are given food and
drink that they do not like, they may not eat it. They could
become **malnourished** and **dehydrated**.

How can you find the information you need?

Service users should be asked what they like and don't like to
eat. This should be written clearly in their care plan, so that
anyone caring for them will have the information that they need.

malnourished
*weak due to lack of
healthy food*

dehydrated
*not enough fluid in
the body*

Mr Davies likes to have a late breakfast and enjoys
porridge. He prefers his main meal at lunch time and a
light tea late afternoon. Spicy foods should be avoided
as they give him indigestion. He does not like cold
drinks, but enjoys a plain biscuit with a cup of tea.

Care plan notes like these let everyone know Mr Davies'
food preferences

If the service user has difficulties speaking, you could use
pictures or pen and paper. Go to Unit 21 to find out more about
how to overcome communication problems. You could also ask
their family and friends. If the service user has come from
another care provider, they may be able give you the
information that you need.

Remember

Always check the
care plan because
the individual's
needs may
change.

In the workplace: Dorothy doesn't like it

Dorothy is 81 and has had a hip replacement. She is very independent and lives alone, so she will be recovering in a care home for a few weeks until she can manage again by herself.

Her family visit regularly and are alarmed to learn that she hardly eats anything, as she usually has a good appetite. Ilsa is one of the healthcare assistants caring for Dorothy. Ilsa cannot understand why Dorothy doesn't like the food. There is often lasagne, minced chicken curry or vegetable stir-fries. Dorothy doesn't like that 'new fangled stuff'. She likes meat, two veg, some potatoes and pudding. She loves jelly and instant custard but Ilsa thinks that they look horrible.

1   *How could Ilsa find out what Dorothy likes to eat?*

2   *How could Ilsa make sure that all the team knows what Dorothy likes to eat?*

3   *Are Dorothy's physical needs being met?*

4   *What other problems could Dorothy face if she doesn't eat?*

5   *What could Ilsa do to help Dorothy?*

Key points

o   Service users may not eat or drink if they are given food and drink that they do not like.

o   Ask service users what they like to eat and drink.

o   Information about preferences should be written clearly in the care plan.

o   Remember that needs and preferences can change, so check and update the care plan regularly.

o   Ask family and friends if a service user cannot tell you what they like and dislike.

'Here you are, Mrs Jackson, it's your favourite.'

'I know that I said I liked cabbage a lot – but not every day!'

Everyone likes variety sometimes!

169

Our society is changing and becoming much more multicultural. (You can look back at Unit 24 for more about this.) It is very important that you respect religious and cultural needs regarding eating and drinking. It will upset the service user you care for if you do not take these very important needs into consideration.

As a care worker, you may be faced with individuals who have different preferences to your own. For example, you may be a vegetarian, but may need to prepare meals or snacks that contain meat. It is important that you do not allow your beliefs to get in the way of the needs of the individual.

Religious, cultural and personal preferences

Knowing the types of food and drink the service user likes will help to build a trusting relationship. Some individuals choose not to eat certain foods because of religious reasons. Some vegetarians choose not to eat meat because of their concern for animals. Some people have foods that they just don't like.

It is important not to make assumptions about the choice of food and drink because of the person's culture. Some people follow cultural or religious customs more strictly than others.

Cultural food preferences

People from some groups will only eat food that has been prepared in certain ways depending on their religious laws. For example, meat from animals that have been slaughtered according to Muslim Law is halal. Meat for Sikhs must be jhatka, while some Jewish people eat only kosher food.

Remember

Some Jewish people keep milk and meat products separate. They must not be prepared or cooked together, or eaten at the same meal.

Have a go

Use the Internet to find out about other cultural dietary preferences.

Hindu
Very strict vegetarians
Will not eat food stored near meat
Check ingredients for animal-based additives such as gelatine

Muslim
No pork or pig products
No alcohol
Meat and dairy products must be halal

Vegan
No dairy foods, eggs or animal-related products

Some cultural food preferences

Sikh
Often choose vegetarian food
No beef (the cow is sacred)
Other meat only if jhatka
No alcohol

Jewish
Food must be kosher, including chicken and eggs
Meat only from animals with split hooves and that chew the cud (sheep, cows)
Fish only with fins and scales, such as cod

Christian
If Catholic, may prefer fish to meat on Wednesdays or Fridays
Others may also give up luxuries such as chocolate during Lent

A good care worker will respect other people's needs and preferences

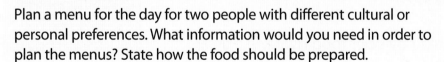

Evidence *PC 1, 3; KS 3*

Plan a menu for the day for two people with different cultural or personal preferences. What information would you need in order to plan the menus? State how the food should be prepared.

Special terms explained

Halal – Meat from animals that have been slaughtered according to Muslim Law

Jhatka – The animal has been killed with one stroke

Kosher – Animals are humanely slaughtered according to Jewish Law

Lent – The period of time from Ash Wednesday to Holy Saturday when Christian people often give up a favourite food

Ramadan – Muslims fast once a year during their holy month of Ramadan. They eat nothing between sunrise and sunset

Key points

o Society is made up of many people from different cultural backgrounds.

o It will offend the service user if you do not take their cultural needs into consideration.

o Do not make assumptions about the choice of food and drink because of the person's culture.

o It is the service user's right to have their choices respected.

Infection control is important when helping individuals to eat and drink. You will need to show that you can handle food **hygienically**. Food poisoning can spread very easily and quickly. Service users may be at risk of catching infections because they may already be unwell, and have a weak immune system. Older people can be more at risk too. Food poisoning can kill people, so you must protect service users.

Handling foods

If it is part of your job to prepare and handle food, then you need to follow some basic hygiene rules and have a Food Hygiene Certificate. This will show that you have had training in safe food handling.

Food poisoning is extremely unpleasant for the individual who gets it. They can become very ill, and even die. Signs of food poisoning can include vomiting, diarrhoea and flu-like symptoms. Food poisoning occurs when there are dangerous **bacteria** on food when it is eaten.

Food poisoning is easily spread by poor food hygiene. For example, germs can be passed into food if someone preparing and handling it has dirty hands. Other risks include eating food that has had flies on it. Never use food that is past its 'use by' date. Leaving food out of the refrigerator can make it go bad.

infection
a disease that other people can catch

hygienically
working in a clean way that reduces the risk of infection spreading

TC 004_D

bacteria
tiny living organisms that can cause disease

Unpleasant things can happen if food is left out

When preparing and serving food:
✓ make sure that you wear a tabard or an apron to control the spread of infection
✓ Use separate chopping boards and knives for raw and cooked foods
✓ Wash your hands after touching raw meat and fish
✓ Always check the 'use by' date.

Handling raw meat
When dealing with raw meat, especially chicken, it is important to use separate chopping boards and knives from those used to prepare other foods. Remember to store all raw meat at the bottom of the fridge to avoid the risk of harmful bacteria, spreading from dripping juices from the raw meat, onto cooked food. After handling raw foods, always wash your hands.

Safe storage of food

Food should be well wrapped and stored correctly to prevent the spread of bacteria.

Clean fridges regularly, using an antibacterial cleaner that will kill harmful bacteria. Defrost the fridge regularly; otherwise the temperature of the fridge may become too warm as the motor works harder to keep the correct temperature. Food needs to be arranged in a way to avoid the spread of harmful bacteria. Dairy products and cooked foods should be on the higher shelves, while raw meat should be stored on the bottom shelf. This prevents moisture or blood dripping on to other food.

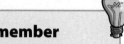

Remember

People who handle food must have food hygiene training.

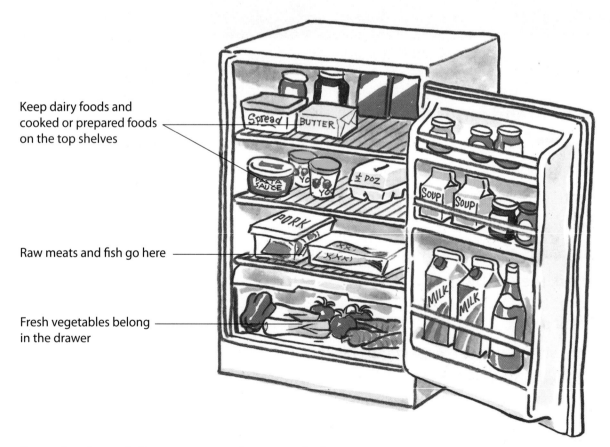

Keep dairy foods and cooked or prepared foods on the top shelves

Raw meats and fish go here

Fresh vegetables belong in the drawer

Store food carefully to prevent the spread of germs

Use-by dates

Food safety also applies to dried goods, tins and frozen foods. Before preparing or serving food you should always check the use-by date. It is surprisingly easy to miss the use-by date of food that lasts a long time, for example, tins, packets of food and frozen food. Rotate the items so that you use the oldest first. Remember to check to see how long foods can be kept after they have been opened. You could label leftover foods with the date that you opened them to avoid serving food that could harm someone.

Have a go

Check the use-by dates of food in your food cupboard and the freezer at home and at work.

Evidence *PC 6*

Collect a witness testimony from your supervisor to show how you safely and hygienically prepared food and drink for service users.

Think about it

Some bacteria that can cause serious food poisoning are *salmonella*, *campylobacter* and *e-coli*. Think of the ways these can be avoided with good hygiene.

Key points

o Food poisoning can spread very easily and quickly.
o Food poisoning can kill people.
o Signs of food poisoning include vomiting, diarrhoea and flu-like symptoms.
o Food poisoning can be spread by poor food hygiene.
o People who handle food must have food hygiene training.

There are several reasons why some individuals may need help with eating and drinking and there are many people who can help them to be independent. It is very important to encourage independence, as it helps the person feel that they have some control of their life.

Eating and drinking should be an enjoyable time. Many social events involve food and drink. Don't forget that the environment plays an important part in the enjoyment of the meal. A poor environment can often spoil what should be an enjoyable experience.

In this element you will cover:

- Helping with eating and drinking
- What makes a pleasant eating environment
- Dealing with questions and worries about eating and drinking.

We all like to eat in nice surroundings, with friends around us

Most people can eat and drink independently, but some will need you to help them. They may have a physical problem, such as a broken arm. Or there may be another reason, such as confusion or dementia. Think about the reason why a service user might need help with eating and drinking.

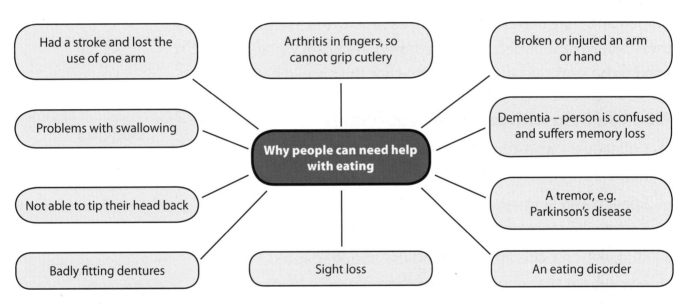

Had a stroke and lost the use of one arm	Arthritis in fingers, so cannot grip cutlery
	Broken or injured an arm or hand
Problems with swallowing	Dementia – person is confused and suffers memory loss
	Why people can need help with eating
Not able to tip their head back	A tremor, e.g. Parkinson's disease
Badly fitting dentures	Sight loss
	An eating disorder

There could be many reasons why individuals need help to eat and drink

How much help does a service user need?

Your Care Council's Code of Practice says that you must 'treat each person as an individual and promote independence'. Always check to find out how much help each service user needs. A care plan includes all of the individual's care needs; helping to eat and drink will be one part of this. Remember, though, that needs sometimes change, and the care plan must reflect this.

Remember

It is important that you get to know the service users you care for and their individual abilities and needs.

Active support

Even though some service users may have difficulties with eating and drinking, it is important that you give **active support**. This means that you help service users to be as independent as possible.

Some service users are embarrassed about needing to be helped and may therefore refuse to eat and drink. They could then lose weight or become dehydrated. As a care worker you need to be sensitive and watchful in case this should happen.

Who can help with eating and drinking?

- Colleague – who knows the client well and knows what helps

- Speech and language therapist – can help with chewing and swallowing problems

- Occupational therapist – can advise about adapted equipment that might help, for example, with helping someone to eat or drink (see page 187)

- Dietician – can give advice about general nutrition.

Support groups

There are many people who can help to advise you and the service user, for example, Parkinson's, **stroke**, or Alzheimer's societies. The Royal National Institute for the Blind (RNIB) can advise people who are blind or cannot see very well. Often members of these groups have experienced similar problems to the service user and have managed to overcome them.

There are also several Disability Living Centres around the UK. They have experts to hand, and equipment available to look at and try. They will demonstrate equipment and help make sure that the service user gets what is right for them.

active support
encourage individuals to do as much for themselves as possible

Evidence
PC 2; KS 4

Think about a service user that you care for. Explain how you actively support them with eating and drinking.

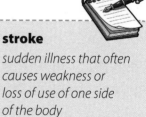

stroke
sudden illness that often causes weakness or loss of use of one side of the body

In the workplace: Sheena's stroke

Sheena is in a care home and is recovering from a stroke.

She is now getting ready to go home, but she is very nervous, because she is worried that she will not be able to manage. The right side of Sheena's body is weak. She has difficulty swallowing, and chokes easily on food and drink.

Her care assistant, Rosie, reassures Sheena that everything will be alright. She reminds Sheena that there are experts who will make sure that she has what she needs.

1   *What may Sheena find difficult about eating and drinking when she gets home?*

2   *Who can help to advise her about her eating and drinking problems?*

Think about it

Imagine how you would feel if you needed help to eat and drink. Would you feel frustrated that you had to wait to eat until someone could help you?

Key points

o   There can be many reasons why some individuals may need help with eating and drinking.

o   There are people who can help and advise about problems with eating and drinking.

o   It is very important to encourage independence, because it helps the person feel that they have some control over their life.

o   Check the care plan to find out the service user's needs with eating and drinking.

o   Some service users may be embarrassed about needing help and may refuse to eat and drink.

What makes a pleasant eating environment? *KS 11, 13, 15*

Help service users to look forward to their meals. The eating environment can make all the difference. Make sure that there are no unpleasant smells where people are eating, and that meal times are free from interruptions. Turn the television off and, if possible, have some quiet background music on. Nice table cloths, napkins and crockery with a small vase of flowers will lift service users' spirits and make them feel valued. Think about how the food is served too.

Remember

Before the meal, ask the service user if they wish to use the toilet and give them the opportunity to wash their hands to prevent the spread of infection.

Think about it

If service users enjoy meal times, they are more likely to have better appetites and make positive food choices. This will help to keep them in good health.

Where to eat

Your workplace may have a dining room where people eat in small groups. Make sure that the area is clean and tidy and free from clutter. The room should be warm, but not too hot. Remember when people are sitting still they are more likely to feel the cold, so avoid draughts.

Meal times should be a social event, so try to make sure that the service user sits next to other people that they get on with. Meal times are a good time to encourage service users to talk to each other.

Encourage service users to be independent and to eat with dignity and respect. Provide protection for their clothes. Avoid treating service users like children, for example, by using inappropriate types of 'bibs'.

Think about it

Be careful with seating arrangements. Would you choose to eat a meal with somebody you did not like?

Meal times should be an enjoyable social time for everyone

Think about it

Some residents may not be able to walk to the dining room. If they have their evening meal in their room, how can you make sure that the food is not cold when it gets to them?

If members of staff go outside to smoke, make sure they do so where the smoke cannot drift into the dining room.

Do care workers or other members of staff sometimes sit down and eat with the residents?

Have a go

Look at the meal-time environment in your organisation. Does it encourage an enjoyable eating experience for the people you care for?

In the workplace: Cherry Tree Court

Cherry Tree Court is a care home for older people. Residents who need help to walk, have their evening meals in their rooms. The food is often cold when they get to eat it. Residents who do not need help to walk, go to the dining room, which has a seating plan. The television is usually on, sometimes showing children's programmes. The room looks cluttered because there is a storage area in one corner, and the hoists are charged up in another corner. Some members of staff stand outside the patio doors and smoke after the meals have been given out. They are not allowed to smoke inside.

1 *What effect may this environment have on the residents of Cherry Tree Court?*

2 *How could meal times be made more enjoyable?*

Remember to check the eating environment before you serve food

How food is presented can make all the difference

Evidence *PC 2, 3*

Collect a witness statement from your supervisor to show how you make sure that the environment is pleasant so that the service users you care for can eat in comfort and with dignity. Show how you also support individuals with their hygiene needs.

Remember

Try to make the area as pleasant as possible when individuals are eating.

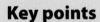

Key points

o A clean pleasant environment will make eating a meal much more enjoyable.

o How the food is served can make all the difference.

o Make sure that the area is clean and tidy and free from clutter.

o Meal times are a good time to encourage service users to talk to each other.

o Before the meal ask service users if they wish to use the toilet and give them the opportunity to wash their hands.

Service users may ask you questions about eating and drinking. For example, they may ask your advice if they are unsure what they can eat if they are on a special diet.

Evidence PC 5

Collect a witness testimony from your supervisor to show that you have passed on questions that are not within your role.

Dealing with questions

As a care worker, you may be able to answer some questions about eating and drinking, but not others. You should pass more complicated questions on to the correct person. Sometimes it is not within your role to answer a question. Even if you think that you know the answer, it is safer to pass the question to your supervisor.

Always make sure that the service user's questions are answered. Always pass on information and write in the service user's care plan when you have given advice. It could have very serious consequences if you do not pass on information or their questions.

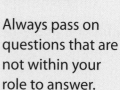

Remember

Always pass on questions that are not within your role to answer.

Evidence PC 4

Write a reflective account to show how you have answered a service user's questions about their dietary needs.

In the workplace: Alvina's advice

Alvina is new to care work and she works in the community. She has just completed her induction. Oriana is a service user who has been told that she has high **cholesterol**. She has been advised by the dietician about what to eat and what to avoid but has forgotten what she was told. She cannot fully understand the leaflet that she was given.

Oriana likes both meat and fish. She asks Alvina about the 'good' and the 'bad' cholesterol. Alvina remembers seeing a programme on television about cholesterol but is not really sure that she can answer her questions. She says that she will speak to her supervisor, who will contact Oriana soon to answer her questions.

1   *Why was Alvina right to pass the question on to her supervisor?*

2   *What could happen if care workers did not pass on questions that were not within their role to answer?*

cholesterol

an important substance that moves fats around the body; high levels can cause strokes or heart attacks

Key points

o   Some questions you may be able to answer, but others you may need to pass on.

o   It is important to pass queries on to someone if it is not within your role to answer them.

o   Ensure that a question that a service user has asked you is answered as it may have very serious consequences.

o   Always pass on information and write in the service user's plan of care when you have given advice.

Meal times should be enjoyable. You may be able to help an individual to be independent when eating and drinking by using specially designed equipment. Simple adaptations can make all the difference. If an individual has problems with eating and drinking, it is important to recognise these and know what to do. Recording and reporting problems is vital in order to pass on information.

In this element we will cover:

○ Practical help and equipment used to help individuals to eat and drink
○ Problems that individuals may have eating and drinking
○ Recording and reporting problems with eating and drinking.

Have a go

How would you feel if you needed help with eating and drinking?

Encourage individuals to be as independent as possible when eating and drinking

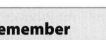

There are many people who can help to advise you and the individual about help with eating and drinking. The advice may simply be from a colleague who knows the individual well and knows what helps. There are also other people around that you could go to for advice, for example, occupational therapists. Occupational therapists can give expert advice on how to remain independent. If necessary they can recommend equipment that might help.

> **Remember**
>
> Make sure that you get expert advice before spending lots of money on expensive equipment.

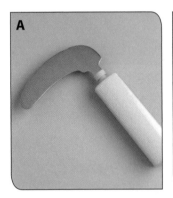

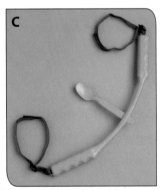

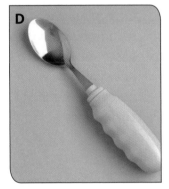

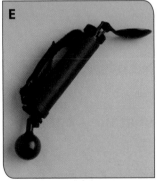

A Rocker knife
B Angled fork
C Spoon with hand straps
D Easy-grip handle
E Good-grip handle
F Weighted

What kinds of problems do you think these items could help with?

There are ways to help individuals to be independent with eating and drinking other than the use of equipment. It may be enough to just cut up the food into manageable sizes so that the individual can eat more easily.

Someone who is visually impaired may be able to imagine a clock face. The care worker can arrange the food in separate portions around the plate and tell the person where the food items are in relation to a clock face. For example, 'the tomatoes are at 6 o'clock'. This is often enough for a visually impaired person to be independent and to enjoy their meal.

Arranging food in a clock face pattern can help people with visual impairment

Practical tips to assist people who need help to eat and drink

✓ Wash your hands.

✓ Make sure that you have all that you need, for example, the meal, salt and pepper, napkin, etc.

✓ Make sure that the person is sitting up, to help with swallowing and digestion.

✓ Make sure that the service user is comfortable before you begin.

✓ Show them (or describe) the meal and ask what they would like to start with.

✓ Sit down beside the person, and slightly in front of them.

✓ Do not rush the service user; give them time to chew and swallow each mouthful.

✓ Make sure that the service user is offered a drink before, during and after the meal.

✓ Chat to the person to make the meal time relaxed, but do not ask them a question just as you place food in their mouth!

✓ Give the service user the opportunity to wipe their hands and mouth afterwards.

Evidence
PC 1, 2, 4, 5

Collect a witness testimony from your supervisor to show how you have helped someone to eat and drink.

Remember

High salt levels can be harmful. Avoid adding salt to food at the table. Always check the care plan.

In the workplace: Rose's fall

Rose had a fall and broke her wrist two weeks ago. She is right handed but now she cannot use her right arm or hand at all. The care workers are trying very hard to help Rose to maintain her independence.

1 *Why do you think the care workers are trying to help Rose to be independent?*

2 *What equipment might help Rose to be independent?*

Think about it

There are ways to help individuals to be independent with eating and drinking other than the use of equipment. It may be enough to just cut up the food into manageable sizes so that the person can eat more easily.

Have a go

Sit down and practise having a colleague help you to eat and drink. You could have a blindfold on to see what it is like to be visually impaired. Swap places and be the care worker helping the service user to eat and drink. Think about:

o **How you felt having someone help you to eat and drink?**

o **Was the speed right?**

o **Was the food given to you in the right combination?**

o **Was it the right temperature?**

Key points

o There are many people who can help to advise you and the service user about help with eating and drinking.

o A colleague who knows the individual can help advise you.

o An occupational therapist can help an individual to eat and drink independently.

o Equipment can be expensive, so get advice before you buy.

o A service user who is visually impaired may be able to imagine a clock face which may help them know where the food is.

Sometimes people have problems while they are eating and drinking. You may notice that someone is finding it difficult to chew or swallow. They may even have a serious allergic reaction to the food that they have been given.

Eating and drinking should be enjoyable, but it can soon turn into a miserable time if the service user is experiencing difficulties and pain when doing so. When you help the service user at meal times it is a good time for you to see if all is well or if they are having problems.

Remember

Service users may not tell you that they are having problems, so you will need to look for signs.

In the workplace: A sore mouth

Mrs Maxwell is a resident at Valley View, a care home for older people. She has worn dentures for many years. She enjoys her food and has a good appetite.

Her upper dentures broke and the care staff made an appointment for her to see her dentist. Mrs Maxwell had a new set of dentures made, but she found them difficult to get used to. They made her mouth very sore, and gave her mouth ulcers.

Sasha noticed that Mrs Maxwell was eating very little at lunchtime and looked as if she was in pain while eating. She also noticed that Mrs Maxwell was starting to lose weight. Sasha spoke to Mrs Maxwell and it became clear what the problem was.

Sasha reported Mrs Maxwell's problem to her supervisor who then made another appointment for her to see her dentist. Meanwhile Mrs Maxwell agreed to have her food liquidised or pureed to make it easier to eat.

1 *What might give you a clue that someone has a sore mouth when eating?*

2 *What effect could this have had on Mrs Maxwell if Sasha had not reported this to her supervisor?*

Remember

Individuals can soon become malnourished and dehydrated if they do not eat and drink.

Remember

If a person is dehydrated they can become muddled, confused and agitated because their blood chemistry is altered.

If a person is having difficulty swallowing food (dysphagia), perhaps because they have had a stroke, then serving food without lumps and giving thickened liquids may prevent them from choking and becoming malnourished and dehydrated.

Food allergies

Some people are allergic to certain foods. If any of the service users you care for are allergic to a certain food, this must be written very clearly in the care plan. Serious allergic reactions can be life threatening. A service user should be asked if they are allergic to anything when they join your care service. Usually people who have a food allergy are very good at reading food labels and being aware of what they are eating.

Some common foods that may cause an allergic reaction

Some foods that may cause an allergic reaction
Strawberries – Especially common in young children
Eggs – Usually appears in very young children, most grow out of it by the time they are five years old
Shellfish – May include both fish and shellfish. Take care not to cook shellfish in the same oil as other foods. More common in teenage years or adulthood
Nuts – There has been a great increase in recent years in the number of children suffering from nut allergies. Many foods contain nuts that we may not be aware of, e.g. salad dressings.

Signs and symptoms of a serious allergic reaction:

o redness of skin, nettle rash (hives)
o swelling of throat and mouth, difficulty in swallowing or speaking
o feeling sick, stomach pain, vomiting
o wheezing, severe asthma
o collapse and unconsciousness

Anaphylaxis is the name for a severe allergic reaction. It is very serious and needs treatment straight away because it could lead to death. Immediate medical help should be called.

As a care worker, if you know that one of the service users you care for has such an allergy, make sure that they have their medication with them at all times. Check expiry dates on their medication too. Make sure that the allergy, and what to do in the event of a reaction, are written in the care plan.

Choking in adults

This is often caused by something stuck in the back of the throat (usually a piece of food). It is very frightening for the person who is choking. As with any other emergency, try to keep the individual calm. Reassure them, so that they do not become more anxious.

What to do if someone chokes

Signs and symptoms of choking:

o red face at first, later turning grey
o coughing and distress (panicking)
o difficult to speak and breathe
o usually holds the throat or neck.

Your aims are:

o to remove the item
o to get medical help as soon as possible if it cannot be removed.

Remember

Some people are allergic to foods such as dairy products and wheat.

Remember

Individuals who know they have a serious allergy usually carry a special injection pen (sometimes called an epipen) at all times.

Remember

First aid techniques cannot be learned from a book. Arrange to have some first aid training if you do not have an up-to-date certificate.

1. If the individual is breathing, lean forward and encourage them to cough. Remove the item if it is coughed up.

2. If they become weak or stop breathing, stand beside them and slightly behind them. Support their chest and give up to five sharp back slaps between the shoulder blades. Stop if the obstruction comes out, check their mouth.

3. If this does not work, try abdominal thrusts, starting by standing behind the person. Lean the person forward. Bring your hands around the front of the person, just below the breastbone. Make a fist with one hand, and grasp this fist with your other hand. Sharply pull your joined hands in an inwards and upwards movement. The force should get rid of the obstruction.

4. If it does not clear, try steps 2 and 3 up to three times.

5. If it still does not clear then call for an ambulance straight away.

If someone chokes you must try to remove the item, and get medical help as soon as possible

Evidence *KS 17*

Explain what you need to do if someone chokes.

Remember

The abdominal thrust is a dangerous procedure which could cause severe damage if used unnecessarily.

Key points

o Eating and drinking should be enjoyable.

o You may need to look for signs to see if an individual is having problems with eating and drinking.

o There has been an increase recently in the number of children with nut allergies.

o If the service user you care for is allergic to a certain food, then it should be written clearly in the care plan.

o You need to act quickly and calmly if a person is choking.

It may be necessary for you to pass on information about how much the service users you care for are eating and drinking, or if they are having problems. It is important not to ignore problems. Accurate record keeping is vital. If records are not accurate it can have an effect on the care that the service user receives. It is a requirement that service users' needs are properly assessed and that they are given the care that they need. If a service user is having problems eating and drinking, or if they are losing weight, it may be necessary to record what they eat and drink.

In the workplace: Is Mr Lewis eating?

Mr Lewis lives in a care home for older people. He has had a stroke. He can eat independently if someone cuts the food up for him and if he has a plate guard so that the food does not fall off his plate. Mr Lewis' family are very concerned and have complained that he is losing weight. They say that food is given to him without a plate guard and taken away before he has eaten any of it.

The manager looks at Mr Lewis' food and fluid charts to check to see how much he has eaten and drunk over the last few days. There are several gaps where nothing has been filled in. There is one day when only a cup of tea is recorded at 10 am. His weight was last recorded two months ago. The manager speaks to the care team who say that Mr Lewis eats well and very rarely leaves anything.

Mr Lewis' family put forward a formal complaint which is being investigated.

1 *What records could be kept to monitor Mr Lewis?*
2 *Who is responsible for keeping these records?*
3 *Why is it important to keep records accurately?*
4 *What effect might this have on Mr Lewis, the care team and the manager?*
5 *If you were looking after Mr Lewis, what would you do?*

Food and Drink Record Chart

Name: Davina Jones .... Room: Room 1 ....
Date: 12 February 2007 .... Is resident receiving a special diet? Yes/(No)

Please record all food and drink consumed, **giving details of type and quantity eaten**.

Breakfast	Details	1/4	1/2	3/4	All	Energy	Protein
Cereal + Milk + Sugar (tsp)							
Egg					✓		✓
Bread/Toast (slices)			✓			✓	
Butter/Margarine/Jam/Marmalade		✓				✓	
Tea/Coffee + Milk + sugar (tsp)					✓		
Other (*e.g. supplement*)							
Lunch							
Soup			✓			✓	✓
Cheese/Egg/Fish/Meat/Pulses							
Vegetables							
Potato/Rice/Pasta/Bread							
Dessert				✓		✓	✓
Drink							
Other (*e.g. supplement*)							
Supper							
Soup							
Cheese/Egg/Fish/Meat/Pulses							
Vegetables							
Potato/Rice/Pasta/Bread							
Dessert							
Drink							
Other (*e.g. supplement*)							
Before bed							
Drinks							
Cake/Biscuit							
Other (*e.g. supplement*)							
					Total		

A completed diet and fluid chart is a way to ensure service users are eating and drinking the right amounts

Evidence

PC 8

Collect a witness statement from your supervisor to show how you have recorded and reported the intake of food and drink for one of your service users.

Key points

o You may need to pass on information to your supervisor about problems a service user is having with eating and drinking.

o You may need to record how much a service user is eating and drinking.

o Always report and record information accurately.

o If records are not accurate, it can have serious consequences.

o If you have problems filling in records, ask your supervisor to help you.

What have I learned?

1 What makes a healthy, balanced diet?

2 How can you find out about a service user's preferences?

3 Give three examples of how a person's cultural needs may affect their choice of food.

4 What are some causes of food poisoning?

5 How can you prevent food poisoning?

6 Why might some individuals need help with eating and drinking?

7 Give three examples of adapted cutlery and crockery and explain who might find them useful.

8 Name four foods that may cause an allergic reaction.

9 How would you deal with someone who was choking?

10 Why is it important to keep records of an individual's intake accurately?

Any questions?

Q *I prepare food for service users, but I don't have a Food Hygiene Certificate. If I do this unit will it mean that I don't have to get one?*

A If you are handling food, it is advised that you have a Food Hygiene Certificate.

Q *I am working on Unit 214 at the moment and wondered if I could do Unit 213 as well, because I prepare and serve food for service users regularly.*

A No, you cannot choose this combination of units together.

Q *I work in the evenings and only prepare light meals for service users. Will I still be able to do this unit?*

A Yes, as long as you are preparing food and drinks for service users, this will be fine.

Q *I already have a Food Hygiene Certificate; can I use this as evidence?*

A Yes, your assessor will be able to use this to support your evidence for this unit.

Case studies

Sammie

Sammie has learning difficulties. She lives in a small care home called The Firs. She eats a lot of chocolate and sweets and Sammie's parents are worried because she is becoming overweight. They give her some pocket money each week. Care workers at The Firs encourage her to choose a healthy, well-balanced diet and offer her healthy snacks instead of sweets.

Sammie attends the local college every day. At lunch time she goes to the cafeteria and usually buys a burger with chips and at break time she buys a chocolate bar.

1 *What healthy meal choices could Sammie make?*

2 *What are the risks to Sammie's health if she continues to eat unhealthy food?*

3 *If you were Sammie's care worker, what would you do?*

4 *Who could you go to for advice on the best way to guide Sammie?*

A hot summer

Maud is 79 years old and lives in a care home for older people. She is very independent and manages to do most things for herself. She has her meals in the dining room and drinks are offered mid morning, afternoon and evening.

The last few weeks have been extremely hot. The heat is making many residents and staff uncomfortable. Jenny, who is a new care assistant, noticed that Maud was a little muddled and short tempered. She thought that it must be due to her age so did not report it. As the days went on Maud became more and more confused and aggressive towards the care team. She refused any help at all, and would not eat or drink anything.

The next day, when Jenny went to see Maud, she was lying on her bed and was very weak. Jenny called for her supervisor who then called the doctor. Maud was taken to hospital and was treated for dehydration.

1 *Why do you think Maud became confused?*

2 *If you were Jenny how could you have prevented this from happening ?*

3 *Why is it important to report problems straight away?*

HSC218

Support individuals with their personal care needs

This unit links to Unit 219 Support individuals to manage continence. If you have chosen Unit 219, there is a lot of information in this chapter that will help. You cannot do both Unit 218 and Unit 219 together.

For this unit, you need to show that you can hygienically and sensitively help with the personal care and toileting needs of service users. You will need to show why some individuals need help, how to help them, and how to respect their preferences.

When working with service users, you may see changes in their condition and ability to manage their own toileting and personal care. You will need to know what these changes mean and what to do about them.

How you will be assessed

Your evidence must come from real work activities. You will need assessor observation and/or expert witness testimonies to cover some parts of each element in this unit. Your assessor may ask you to collect some self-reflective accounts

This unit covers the following elements:

o **218a** Support individuals to go to the toilet

o **218b** Enable individuals to maintain their personal hygiene

o **218c** Support individuals in personal grooming and dressing.

Support individuals to go to the toilet

Not all service users are able to take themselves to the toilet. There could be many reasons why some of the people you care for need help. Other service users just need to be reminded to go to the toilet, because they may forget to go.

Different people need different levels of help. If someone has recently had an operation, or is recovering from an accident, they may only need help for a short time. Other people may be permanently disabled. Some service users will have a long-term health problem that means they have difficulty walking. They might need to use a commode or a **bedpan**. Another person may be **incontinent** and may need more support from you.

In this element you will cover:

∘ Sensitivity when dealing with personal care
∘ Helping service users to use the toilet
∘ Recognising what is normal
∘ Reporting and recording.

bedpan
a piece of equipment used for going to the toilet in bed

incontinent
unable to control the bladder and bowels

There are many reasons why individuals may need help with their personal care

It can be very embarrassing to have someone else looking after your personal care. When going to the toilet, most of us would prefer to use our own toilet and do so in private. Unfortunately this is not always possible. It will help service users if you treat all aspects of going to the toilet in a straightforward way. You may feel embarrassed at first too, and so it may help you if you remember that getting rid of body waste is an essential and perfectly normal process. **Promoting continence** is an essential part of a care worker's role.

promote continence
provide the environment in which people are able to use the toilet appropriately and at the right time

Think about it

How would you feel if someone had to help you to go to the toilet? How would you want to be treated?

Being sensitive

Always make the activity as private as possible to maintain the service user's self-respect. Try to avoid other people hearing you when you discuss personal care and toilet issues with a service user. When giving personal care, keep the service user covered. Do not expose their 'private parts'; you can keep them covered with their clothes, a sheet or a towel.

Think about it

Imagine you are a resident in a mixed ward and you need to go to the toilet, but you cannot get out of bed. The care worker brings you a bedpan. The other residents are watching you. How would you feel?

'What was that Mrs Abbot, you've wet yourself?'

Be discreet when talking about personal care

In the workplace: Promoting continence

Miss Jaffrey lives in a care home for older people. She is a very reserved and private woman who was a school teacher in a girls' school when she was younger. Miss Jaffrey has started to wet herself at night sometimes.

When Paul, a care worker, was helping her to go to the toilet one night, he noticed that the bed was wet. He politely said that he would change the bed so that it was nice and comfortable for her when she got back. Miss Jaffrey became very angry and said that it was not her that wet the bed, it was someone else. She also asked him to send a female carer to help her back from the toilet.

1   *Why do you think that Miss Jaffrey said that it was not her who wet the bed?*

2   *What would you do if you were Paul to help promote continence for Miss Jaffrey?*

Think about it

Think of a time when you have helped a service user who wet themselves.

1   *What were their worries and concerns?*

2   *How did you deal with their feelings?*

3   *Could you have prevented them from wetting themselves in the first place?*

In the workplace: Time of the month

Tammy is 13 years old and is staying in a residential school for both boys and girls. She has two younger brothers who live at home. Tammy has just started her **periods**. An outing was planned some time ago to go to an amusement park, which she was very keen to do. She now says that she would prefer to stay behind because she does not feel well. Kristin, who is one of the carers, thinks that Tammy does not want to go because she is having her period.

1   *How can Kristin help to reassure Tammy?*

2   *What practical advice could Kristin give?*

periods
monthly flow of blood in women of child-bearing age

Some service users prefer to have someone of the same sex to help them with personal care needs, as they feel less embarrassed. If this is not always possible where you work, take the time to explain the reasons why. If you are thoughtful and caring, it will make it easier for the service users to accept.

Key points

o   It can be embarrassing to need help with personal care.

o   Most people prefer to use their own toilet facilities.

o   You can help service users by being very professional when discussing their toileting needs.

o   Make personal activities as private as possible.

o   Some service users prefer to be helped by a care worker of the same sex.

o   Promote continence by creating the right environment for the service user.

It is important that you find out how a service user lets you know that they want to go to the toilet. Always make sure that service users can call for help to let you know if they need to go to the toilet. If they have a call bell, make sure that it is within easy reach. Always respond to the call bell quickly. This can prevent the person having an accident and wetting or soiling themselves, which is embarrassing and uncomfortable for them. The care plan will tell you about the service user's needs and how to meet them.

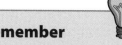

Remember

To check the care plan regularly because the service user's needs may have changed.

The Park Care Home

Name: SIOBHAN HANDLEY   Room No: 10

Care Plan: toileting needs				
Date	Description of problem	Aim of plan	Plan of action	Review date
15th Jan 07	Siobhan is sometimes incontinent of urine at night because she cannot get to the toilet quick enough. She would like to have a commode nearby at night.	To promote continence, dignity, protect her skin and maintain her hygiene.	Siobhan wears a small pad at night. Make sure that Siobhan has her call bell nearby. Respond to her calls promptly. Make sure that she has access to the commode.	22nd Jan 07

A care plan explaining how to meet an individual's toileting needs

Some individuals may be incontinent and have no control at all of their bladder and/or bowels.

Some people you care for may not be able to tell you they need to go to the toilet, for example, if they have a communication problem. They may have a learning disability, or they may have suffered a stroke. In this case, you will need to look for other signs such as wriggling and changes in behaviour. This information should be in the care plan.

Special equipment

The care plan will tell you if the individual you are caring for uses special equipment, for example a bedpan, commode or **conveen**. Some examples are given in the illustrations on page 206. If you notice that a service user is having difficulty using the equipment, let your supervisor know. Their care may need to change.

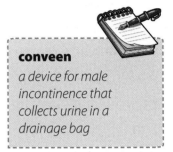

conveen
a device for male incontinence that collects urine in a drainage bag

Toileting equipment hints and tips

Going to the toilet is very private. Encourage service users to be independent. Sometimes small changes can make all the difference, for example, clothes that are easy to remove. Elasticated waistbands and Velcro instead of buttons may help.

There is also a wide range of special equipment that will help service users to be independent. Seek expert advice from a professional such as an occupational therapist, who will help you and the service users you care for to make the best choice.

Think about it

List all the different words or ways that the service users you care for use to let you know that they need to go to the toilet.

Evidence *PC 1, 2, 3, 4, 5*

Think about a service user who let you know that they wanted to use the toilet facilities. Write a self-reflective account to show how you supported them in a sensitive and safe way.

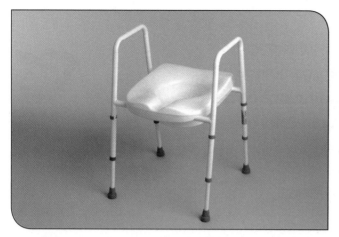

Toilet frames can make getting on and off the toilet safer and easier by giving extra support

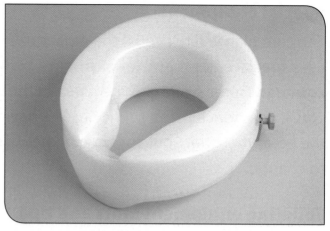

A toilet seat riser or raised toilet seat can make it easier to get on and off the toilet

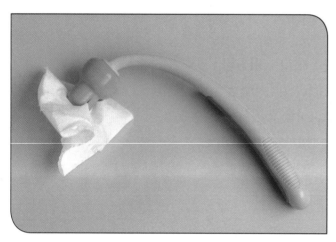

The bottom buddy is useful if an individual cannot reach to wipe themselves

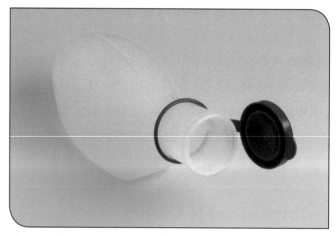

The male urinal is useful for men who are unable to use the toilet

---

Have a go

Check the care plans of the service users you care for to find out about their toileting needs.

Evidence *KS 12*

Give some examples of why some service users you support need help using toileting facilities. Describe the type of help that you need to give them.

Controlling the spread of infection

TC 004_D

When helping individuals to use toilet facilities, you need to be careful and control the spread of infection. Always wear gloves and an apron, and wash your hands thoroughly when you remove your gloves. Dispose of waste safely and correctly. We will look at controlling the spread of infection on page 226.

Help the service user to clean themselves thoroughly after using the toilet to prevent them becoming sore. Traces of faeces that have been left can lead to urinary tract infections. Always wipe in the correct way (from front to back).

Evidence *PC 6, 8, 9, 10; KS 10*

Explain how you controlled the spread of infection, for example, by using Personal Protective Equipment (PPE) and helping the service user to wash their hands. Why is it important to control the spread of infection?

Key points

o Find out how individuals communicate their need to go to the toilet.

o Some individuals may not be able to tell you that they need to go to the toilet so you need to look for signs.

o Promote continence by responding to call bells quickly so that the service user can get to the toilet in time.

o Simple changes can make all the difference, for example, replacing buttons on clothes with Velcro and elasticated waistbands.

o If necessary there is a range of equipment available to help with toileting.

Having an idea of what is normal body waste and what is not might prevent a service user from unnecessary discomfort. It may also prevent something more serious from developing.

We need to know what is normal before we can work out what is not. Each service user is an individual. What may be normal for one individual may not be normal for another. You need to be aware of any changes from what is normal for the service users you care for. Report any changes to prevent unnecessary discomfort. Sometimes these changes mean there could be something seriously wrong.

Remember

Always report any changes in the service user's body waste.

What is normal for urine?

Urine should be clear and straw coloured. However, in the morning it is usually stronger and may look more yellow or orange. There should be no pain on passing urine.

If the urine is cloudy and smells 'fishy', it may mean that the individual has an infection. Ask the service user if they have noticed any change in their urine and tell them that you will need to report this to your supervisor. Your supervisor may ask you to collect a urine sample to send off to be tested. (If you are not sure how to do this, ask your supervisor.)

You may have urine testing kits that use 'dipsticks'. These can give an early clue as to whether there is an infection or not. These sticks can also show other things that are in the urine, such as blood. When you test urine with a dipstick, always record the results on the service user's care plan. Inform your supervisor, even if the results are normal, because you still need to record and report this information. Your supervisor may want to report your findings to the doctor.

It is important to remember to keep the service user informed about what you are doing. Always ask for their permission before taking samples and testing. Remember it is their right to be involved in their care.

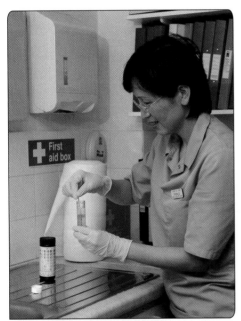 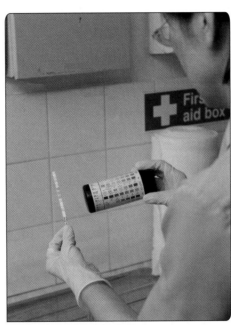

Urine 'dipsticks' testing can help to tell you if a person's urine is normal or not

---

In the workplace: Mr Sharrock's test

One morning Marina was helping Mr Sharrock with his hygiene. When she was emptying his urine bottle she noticed a change in the colour of his urine. Marina asked Mr Sharrock if she could test his urine with a dipstick.

He agreed to the test and it showed that he had some blood in his urine. Marina informed Mr Sharrock of the result and he agreed that she should tell her supervisor. Marina recorded her findings in Mr Sharrock's care notes.

1   *Why was Marina right to test Mr Sharrock's urine?*

2   *What could happen if she did not record her findings?*

3   *How did Marina show respect to Mr Sharrock?*

What is normal for faeces?

Faeces should be brown, soft and formed. Individuals will differ as to how often they pass a **motion**. As with urine, what is normal for one person may not be so for another, so it is important to find out what is right for the individual.

If faeces are hard, it may mean that the service user is **constipated**. You need to encourage individuals to drink enough fluid to prevent them becoming dehydrated and to have a diet with enough fibre to prevent constipation (see Unit 214 for more about diet).

If you suspect that the service user is constipated, report this to your supervisor. They may be prescribed laxatives. These are medicines that can help people to open their bowels. You may need to record when the service user has opened their bowels, and the texture of their faeces. You may have to record what they have eaten, when they ate and how much. This can help with early detection of constipation or to **monitor** diarrhoea. The dietician might need to recommend changes to the individual's diet.

motion
an emptying of the bowels

constipated
difficulty in passing faeces

monitor
keep an eye on

Remember

If service users need laxatives, they should be prescribed by a doctor.

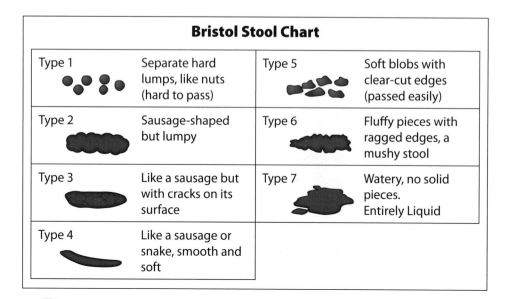

	Bristol Stool Chart		
Type 1	Separate hard lumps, like nuts (hard to pass)	Type 5	Soft blobs with clear-cut edges (passed easily)
Type 2	Sausage-shaped but lumpy	Type 6	Fluffy pieces with ragged edges, a mushy stool
Type 3	Like a sausage but with cracks on its surface	Type 7	Watery, no solid pieces. Entirely Liquid
Type 4	Like a sausage or snake, smooth and soft		

Women and menstruation

If you are looking after women of childbearing age, they may need help when they are menstruating (having their periods). You should always report any changes. Missed periods could mean a woman is pregnant, but there could also be other reasons, such as stress or **anorexia**. They may also mean that the woman is going through the **menopause**. Heavy periods could lead to the service user becoming **anaemic**. There could be other medical reasons that need investigating for heavy periods.

anorexia
an eating disorder where the person does not eat enough

menopause
when a woman's periods stop

anaemic
not enough iron in the blood

You may be asked to record what a service user passes out of their body, for example, their urine and faeces. This gives doctors and carers an idea of how the body is working. You might also be asked to record vomit or blood loss.

Recording input and output

It is very important that all recording and reporting is done accurately. For example, urine output often needs to be measured if a service user is on diuretics (water tablets) for a heart condition. If the care worker did not record all of the urine passed, doctors might think that the service user needed a higher dose of medication. This could be very serious for the service user.

FLUID BALANCE RECORD				Hospital No. 0\000641E			
				Surname Jones			
				First Names Davina			
Date	Intake				Output		
12/2/07	INTRAVENOUS			By Mouth	Urine	Other	Routes
	TYPE		Volume	Volume	Foley catheter		
Time	Record at time started		Record at time completed				
Midnight							
1	water			100			
2							
3							
4	water			100			
5							
6							
7					450		
8	tea / water			250			
9					220		
10	cranberry juice			180			
11							
12	soup / tea			360			
13					380		
14							
15							
16							
17							
TOTALS							
	24 hr. Intake				24 hr. Output		
	24 hour Balance						
	See fluid prescription sheet for drug additives						

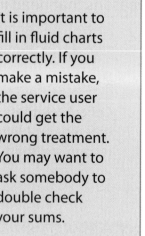

Remember

It is important to fill in fluid charts correctly. If you make a mistake, the service user could get the wrong treatment. You may want to ask somebody to double check your sums.

Input and output can be recorded on the service user's fluid balance chart

Always record accurately. If you forget to measure the amounts passed, or have difficulty in doing so, it is best to be honest and tell your supervisor. A note can then be made on the chart. If you have any difficulty measuring, ask your supervisor.

In the workplace: What should Tom do?

Tom is a care worker. He usually remembers to check to see if service users are on fluid balance charts before he takes away urinal bottles.

Tom took away Mr Peters' urinal bottle. He had not noticed that the chart was hidden underneath another one.

He had disposed of about three bottles without measuring the contents.

1   *If you were Tom what would you do?*

2   *What might happen to Mr Peters because of Tom's carelessness?*

Evidence PC 9, 11

Do you have a service user who needs to have their body waste recorded? If so, how and why do you do this?

Key points

o   It may be necessary for you to measure and record urine output, or when a service user opens their bowels.

o   You may need to record what an individual is eating and drinking.

o   Recording and reporting must be done accurately.

o   If you forget to measure output, always tell your supervisor.

o   If you have difficulty recording output, tell someone.

Individuals need help with their hygiene for many reasons. They may have had an operation and not be able to move very well, or they may have more long-term problems. It is important to give the proper help to the service user without taking away their independence. Sensitivity is essential. When you are helping people with hygiene, it is easy to spread germs. You need to be careful to prevent this.

In this element you will cover:

- Helping service users with their hygiene
- Finding out about a service users' preferences
- How we can promote independence with hygiene
- Infection control and helping individuals with their personal hygiene
- Problems and changes with hygiene.

Grab rails can help an individual to be independent with bathing

Ask the service user how much help they would like. There may be many reasons why an individual needs help with hygiene. It may be that they have arthritis, or they may have had a stroke. You may be able to think of many more reasons. The amount of help each individual needs will differ from person to person – from no help at all to complete assistance with all personal care.

Show sensitivity when helping individuals with their hygiene. Many people feel embarrassed about showing their body. If an individual has had a **mastectomy** or has a skin condition, they may feel very self-conscious. Never show that you are shocked about what you see. You may wish to refer to Unit 21 and read about non-verbal communication.

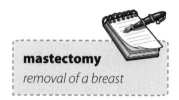

mastectomy
removal of a breast

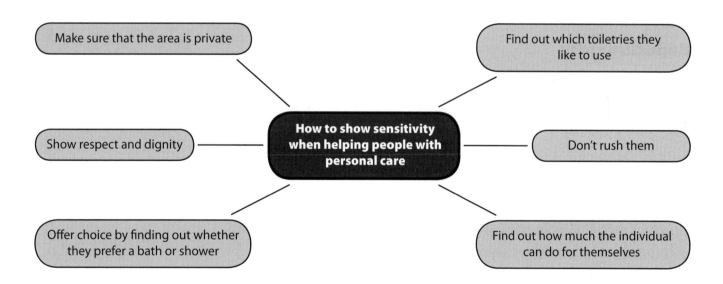

Make sure that the area is private

Find out which toiletries they like to use

Show respect and dignity

How to show sensitivity when helping people with personal care

Don't rush them

Offer choice by finding out whether they prefer a bath or shower

Find out how much the individual can do for themselves

Every service user's needs and abilities must be assessed regularly. It is their right under the Care Standards Act. It is very important that the proper help is given. Too much will take away their independence and too little help may lead to neglect. The Social Care Council Code of Practice states you must 'promote the independence of service users'. Your workplace Statement of Purpose should also reflect this.

Always refer to the care plan to see what level of help is recommended. Remember, though, that needs can change, sometimes on a daily basis. The care plan is a guide and needs to be updated regularly.

You may need to help several service users with their personal hygiene. Treat them all with equal respect and sensitivity.

Scotland

For information on how to promote the independence of service users, see the Scottish Social Services Council www.sssc.uk.com

Think about it

Think about the service users you care for. Why do some need help with hygiene? Have a look in their care plans to see what assistance is suggested. Are the care plans accurate?

Reducing risks

A frail service user choosing to bath independently may be at risk because they could slip or fall, but we must recognise that they have the right to take risks. These risks would need to be agreed between the service user and your manager.

Remember

Always check the individual's care plan.

A risk assessment should have been completed with the service user. Possible risks will have been identified and discussed, so that they can make their own choice. Always check risk assessments and be aware that service users' needs and abilities may have changed. If so, you will need to report this to your supervisor. Records will need to be updated if the condition of the individual changes.

Keeping everything tidy and to hand will make personal hygiene easier

Evidence KS 7

What does your workplace Statement of Purpose and your Care Council's Code of Practice say about risks and promoting the independence of service users?

Key points

- o A person may feel embarrassed about showing their body.
- o Levels of risk have to be assessed, agreed and managed.
- o All service users' needs and abilities must be assessed regularly.
- o Always refer to the care plan to see what level of help is recommended.
- o The Social Care Council Code of Practice states you must promote the independence of service users.

It is important to consider service users' preferences. What they would prefer may be very different to what you might like. There may be **cultural** considerations that you might need to think about too.

Individual choice

You need to be aware of any preferences that service users may have. If they are unable to communicate well, you could ask their family or friends. Some people may prefer a bath to a shower. You may think that it is more practical to have a shower, but it may not necessarily be what they like. Do not impose your views on them. Some individuals may wish to bath or shower weekly and just have a daily wash. You need to respect their choices and views.

Toiletries and timing of wash

There are many toiletries available, but a service user may like a particular brand. Bars of soap may not be as hygienic as liquid soap, but the service user may prefer to continue using their favourite soap. Check to see what products they like. When do they prefer to bathe? In the morning, in the afternoon or in the evening? If they had a restless night and did not sleep well, they may wish to sleep and wash later than normal.

Have a go

Find out which toiletries the individuals that you care for like.
Do they prefer any particular brands?

'A shower will be better for you Mrs Jones'

If a service user prefers to take a bath, you must respect their choice

Cultural needs

As well as personal preference, some people have religious or cultural needs regarding washing and cleansing. It is important that you find out about these preferences and respect them. If you do not, then you may offend the person and their family.

Think about it

Think about a time when it has been difficult to meet a service user's wishes regarding their personal hygiene.

In the workplace: Sunita's angry husband

Sunita is a 56-year-old woman who has to go to hospital for some tests. Jason is a new care worker who has been asked to help Sunita get ready. He knows that she cannot walk very well and will need some help. He asks if he should take her toiletries over to the bathroom for her. He offers to fill the bath for her so that she can bathe before she goes to the hospital. Sunita's husband comes to see her and is extremely cross about the situation. They are Muslim.

1   *Why do you think Sunita's husband is angry?*

2   *How could this have been avoided?*

3   *What might Sunita's preferences be regarding help with personal hygiene?*

Cultural preferences

Individuals from some cultures who need help with their personal care may prefer or insist on a care worker of the same gender. That means males for men and females for women. Where possible you must respect their wishes to avoid causing offence and embarrassment. For example, women from some cultures may accept help from a male care worker if necessary, but a Muslim or Hindu man would be very offended to be helped by a female care worker.

Here are some examples of cultural preferences. Remember to ask the service users you care for how they would like you to help them.

o   Many people prefer to wash in running water. If showers are not available, you should provide a basin and fresh water.

o   Members of some faiths, such as Muslims, may wish to perform special washing rituals before prayers.

o   Some people prefer to wash themselves rather than using toilet paper. If bidets are not available, provide a jug of water.

o   Sikhs may prefer to keep their hair long, and so may need help washing and combing it.

Have a go

Visit www. ethnicityonline.net for more details on how you can help people from different ethnic backgrounds with their hygiene needs.

Evidence *PC 1, 2*

Give some examples of different preferences regarding personal hygiene. Write a reflective account to show how you have shown sensitivity and respected these preferences.

'My name is Eliora, and I am Jewish. I would prefer another female to care for me, but would accept a male if necessary. If I were an orthodox Jew like my mother I would most definitely wish to have another female. I like to wash before I eat and before I pray.'

'My name is Raakin. I am Muslim. We all consider cleanliness desirable, but Islam insists on it, because a Muslim is expected to be pure physically, morally and spiritually. I cleanse my teeth and nostrils regularly. I trim my nails and remove armpit and pubic hair where dirt might collect. I must not leave my excess hair untrimmed for more than 40 nights.'

'My name is Parmita, and I am Hindu. Please may I have a female to help me with hygiene? If my husband were the patient he would be very offended if a female helped him. I am pleased that there is a bidet available because I like to use running water to cleanse myself after using the toilet. (A jug with water would also do.) While I am having a period I am considered unpure, and so I take a ritual bath when the bleeding stops. This is a very private matter and I prefer not to talk about it.'

'My name is Devin. I am Sikh. I must not cut my hair, so I like to use conditioner to keep my hair and beard smooth and glossy. I keep my turban on at all times but I may need help to change and retie it. If I need to have an operation and the operation site needs to be shaved, please return the shaved hair to me so that I can get rid of it myself.'

Key points

- o It is important to consider service users' preferences.
- o Check to see what products service users prefer.
- o Do not impose your views on others.
- o Remember the cultural considerations of service users.

There are many ways that we can help individuals to be independent with their hygiene. There are also other professional people, such as occupational therapists, who can help assess the service user and suggest equipment that can be used to help them to be independent.

How much help?

The amount of help that service users need with personal hygiene will differ between individuals. You must promote the service user's independence so they feel that they still have some control over their own life. An individual with arthritis in their hands may find turning on the taps very difficult. You could consider changes to the taps, or filling the basin for them. This small action could help the person to remain independent. If the service user can wash themselves all over, apart from their back, you could just help with what they are unable to do. Never be tempted to do more to save time.

Equipment

There are many ways of helping people to manage their own hygiene and independence. An occupational therapist is a specialist who can advise on changes and equipment to help people to be independent. They will assess the individual's needs fully and make suggestions about what will really help them to manage independently. The use of equipment is not always necessary.

Remember

To make sure that if service users are bathing on their own they have a way of calling for help.

Think about it

Think about how you would feel if you needed help with personal care. How would you like to be treated?

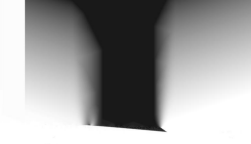

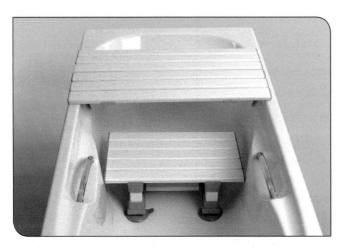

Bath seat – this can help an individual who finds getting in and out of the bath difficult

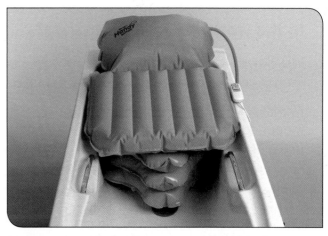

Mangar handy bather – an inflatable battery powered bath seat, which allows the user to lie down in the bath

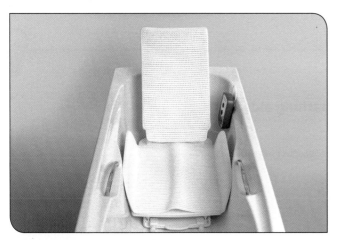

Aquajoy premier bath seat – enables independence; the individual can lower and raise themselves by using a waterproof floating battery hand control

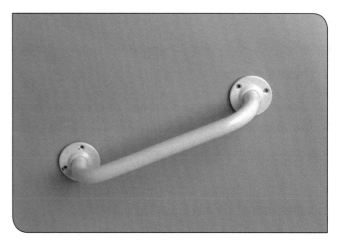

Grab rail – can give extra support when getting in and out of the bath

Individuals should be encouraged to do as much for themselves as they can, but never forced to do things. Some people are nervous about getting in and out of the bath even with special equipment. They may be scared in case they slip and have a fall. Or they may worry that powered equipment will not work properly. You will need to build the service user's confidence and let them know that you will be there to help if needed.

Think about it

How could each of the bathing aids listed above help individuals bathe? If equipment such as these were not available what effect might this have on people's lives?

Have a go

Use the Internet to find out about the range of bathing aids available to help individuals to be independent.

Remember

Make sure that the water is at a safe temperature. Older and younger people are more at risk of burns.

Some health and safety tips

o   Make sure that the room is warm and has no draughts.

o   Close windows and make sure that the area is private.

o   Use a thermometer to check the temperature of the water; it must not be too hot or cold.

o   Place toiletries, materials and equipment within easy reach. This will avoid frustration for the service user if they cannot get what they need and may prevent falls.

o   Always leave the service user with a means of calling for help.

o   If you need to go back into the room, remember to knock first.

Evidence PC 2, 4, 5, 6; KS 6

Write a reflective account to show how you have helped to support a service user with personal hygiene. Explain how you have promoted their independence and safety.

Working with other professional colleagues

It is very important that all the people who are involved in the care of the individual work as a team and communicate with each other. It is useful to know about the different job roles of others.

You might find it helpful to ask another professional, for example an occupational therapist, if you can shadow them to find out more about what they do. You will see how they support people to be as independent as possible. They may be very interested in what you do.

Key points

o   The amount of help that service users need with personal hygiene differs between individuals and can change.

o   There is a wide range of equipment to help people to be independent and hygienic.

o   Make sure that the bathroom is warm and free from draughts.

o   Use a thermometer to check the temperature of the water.

o   Make sure that the service user can call for help if they need to.

o   Always respect privacy.

Germs can spread very easily from one person to another. You must protect service users and yourself by limiting their spread. Your own hygiene also plays a big part in infection control.

Spreading infection

Germs can get on to your uniform and spread from one person to another very quickly. It is essential to use the correct precautions to stop infection from spreading.

Make sure you wash your hands and wear gloves and an apron before helping service users with their hygiene. Tell them that protective clothing will help to prevent everyone from catching infections. Remember to wash your hands when you remove your gloves and put them in the correct bin. Never put dirty laundry, such as soiled bedding or clothes, on the floor. Dispose of laundry in the correct bags.

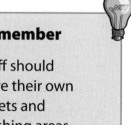

Remember

Germs can easily spread from one person to another.

Always use the service user's own toiletries and never share their personal items with others, as this could spread infection. Sharing toiletries and equipment also takes away the person's individuality.

Your own hygiene should be of a high standard. Wear a clean uniform each day which has been laundered in a hot wash. Wash uniforms separately from other household laundry. It is a good idea to have a spare uniform at work in case of spills. Tie hair back and make sure your fingernails are clean and not too long. Do not wear strong perfumes.

Remember

Staff should have their own toilets and washing areas.

Your hygiene is important to prevent the spread of infection. Jewellery can be dangerous, and germs can easily be spread if you wear rings, bracelets and necklaces. Keep make-up to a minimum

Evidence *PC 3, 8; KS 10, 17*

Write a reflective account to show how you have helped a service user with hygiene. Show how you have controlled the spread of infection and had good personal hygiene yourself. Explain why it is important to control the spread of infection and to have good personal hygiene yourself.

Key points

o   Germs can spread easily from one person to another.

o   Use the service user's own toiletries and never share their personal items with others.

o   Your own hygiene should be of a high standard.

o   Reassure service users that protective clothing will help to protect everyone from infection.

o   To help control the spread of infection, wash your uniform separately from your other household laundry.

You are more likely to see a service user on a regular basis than your manager is. You may notice changes with the service user's hygiene. It is important that you deal with these changes correctly in order to protect the individual and care for their needs properly.

Dealing with problems

You may have concerns about a service user and their hygiene. They may suffer from arthritis, which might become worse so they are unable to wash themselves as well as they did a week before. Their standard of hygiene may have become worse because they do not want to ask for help. Sometimes changes may simply mean that the individual is not feeling well – perhaps they are getting a cold.

Skin irritations can make washing painful. Make sure that you wash and dry irritated skin very carefully; pat dry – do not rub. Use prescribed toiletries as directed. Cuts and grazes can easily become infected, so ensure good hygienic practices.

Some individuals may still not want to wash even though you have encouraged them to. Never force your values and standards on to other people, nor force anyone to do anything that they do not wish to do. See if there is a reason why they don't want to wash and offer sensitive help and support if you need to. You could talk to them about the benefits of being clean, for example, it can make you feel better and prevent germs spreading. If a service user is offered help with washing and they refuse it, make sure that an accurate record is kept in their care plan.

Remember

You must always report changes or problems in the individual's personal hygiene to your supervisor. This will need to be written down in their record of care.

In the workplace: Caring for Keith

Keith lives in a small care home for people with learning disabilities. He is 30 years old. Keith refuses to wash and sometimes wets himself. Some of the other residents are unkind and refuse to sit near him. They say that he smells. Keith wishes to join in with activities, but does not understand why the other residents will not talk to him and let him join in. Keith's family are upset when they visit, especially when they see other residents are ignoring him. They think that carers should make him wash whether he wants to or not.

1 *Why do you think Keith does not want to wash?*

2 *If you were a carer looking after Keith, what would you do?*

Think about it

Sometimes people may refuse to wash, for example, if they are confused. Gentle encouragement sometimes works.

Evidence *PC 9; KS 9, 16*

Write a self-reflective account to show how you have noticed and reported a change or problem relating to a service user's hygiene.

Remember

Care plans are private so remember not to share them other people without asking the service user first.

Key points

o If you have concerns about a service user's hygiene, you should discuss this with them.

o Changes in abilities of maintaining personal hygiene may simply be that the individual is not feeling well.

o Sometimes you may need to gently persuade a service user to wash.

o Always report changes to your supervisor.

o Remember the service user's information is private – always maintain confidentiality.

If you have ever broken a bone and had a plaster cast on your arm, you will be able to understand how difficult life can be without the use of one of your arms. Dressing and undressing become very tricky. Think about fastening buttons and zips on jackets with only the use of one hand! It can be very frustrating when you cannot do things for yourself.

In this element you will cover:

- Finding out about individuals' grooming needs and preferences
- Promoting independence when helping with grooming and dressing
- Conflicts and problems with grooming and dressing.

Supporting individuals to do as much as they can for themselves, will help them to have control of their lives

All service users' needs and preferences will be different. They should be encouraged to express them. There may be cultural considerations too. Finding out about how best to help the individual will show that you value them.

Service users are individuals and may need different degrees of help from you with dressing and **grooming**. Ask them what they can do for themselves and how you can help. Look at their care plan to see what is advised, but remember that their needs can change.

Our individuality is very much expressed by the clothes we wear, our hairstyle, make-up and the jewellery and perfume we wear. Help service users to express their individuality. Find out what their preferences are. If they are unable to tell you, ask their family and friends. Your Care Council's Code of Practice says that you must respect individual's views and wishes.

Shaving

Check male service users who shave to see if they prefer a traditional wet shave or an electric shave. Female service users may like to remove excess body hair. If so, do they prefer to shave or use hair removal creams, or visit a beauty therapist?

Offering choice

It is very important to offer choice, even if the individual cannot communicate very well. It can be confusing for some individuals to be given too much choice, so you could offer two options. This way you are still respecting their right to choose.

grooming
helping people to have a tidy appearance such as brushed hair, clean teeth and being clean shaven

Remember

Check your policy on shaving; you may not be allowed to help with wet shaving.

Remember

Always use the service user's own personal items. Never share them as this is seen as an abuse of rights and could spread infection.

Nails

Don't forget to pay attention to fingernails and toenails. Great care must be taken with toenails. Your workplace may have a policy that only a **chiropodist** should care for these. If this is the case, you will need to know how you or the service users you care for can contact them.

Hair

Is there a hairdresser that service users can visit? Some care establishments have a visiting hairdresser. Find out how appointments are booked. Some service users may have a different hairdresser that they use. Make sure that all individuals have an equal chance to use these services.

Remember

Check your policy on care for toenails.

Do not impose your views on the service users you care for about choices that they have made. For example, you may think that some clothes a service user chooses to wear do not match. Remember it is their identity and their choice and you must respect this. However, if the individual chooses a thin summer dress on a cold winter day, you have a duty of care to protect them from harm. You may need to use gentle persuasion to encourage them to wear more suitable clothing.

Looking good makes people feel good!

Evidence *PC 1, 3*

Collect a witness testimony from your supervisor to show how you have respected a service user's choice and preferences with grooming and dressing.

Cultural considerations

As well as personal preferences, some individuals may have religious or cultural needs regarding how they dress. It is important that you find out about these and respect their preferences. If you do not, then you may offend the person and their family.

Have a go

Visit www. ethnicityonline.net for more details on how you can help people from different ethnic backgrounds with dressing and grooming.

In the workplace: Ethel's choices

Ethel is 80 years old and lives in a care home. She likes to be different; her family sometimes describe her as eccentric.

Ethel likes to choose what to wear, and loves bright make-up. The colours of her skirts and jumpers often clash, or she puts her tops on the wrong way round. At other times she chooses clothes that are unsuitable. For example, last week it was very cold, but Ethel wore a thin orange stripy blouse with bright purple trousers to go into town. People often turn, look and sometimes laugh at her. The care workers are very worried and have tried to advise Ethel on what to wear. One care worker even hid a dress that she thought was inappropriate. A few care workers think this is funny and laugh at Ethel.

1   *What are the carers' concerns?*

2   *Is it right for Ethel to choose what she wears?*

3   *What would you do in this situation?*

An individual's culture can affect their choice of what to wear

Key points

o   Encourage service users to express their individuality.

o   Offer choice even if the individual cannot communicate very well.

o   Sharing personal items can spread infection.

o   Do not impose your own views about choices that a service user makes.

o   Individuals may have cultural needs that might affect how they dress.

You have a responsibility to help promote service users' independence. It will make them feel that they have control over their life and feel valued. There are many professionals who can give you and the service users you care for advice on ways of working and, if necessary, on equipment that might help.

Encourage individuals (but do not force them) to do as much for themselves as possible to maintain their independence. Do not be tempted to do things for them just because it is quicker. Dressing and undressing are private, so respect this by making sure that the environment is private. Always knock before entering the room and make sure that curtains are closed. Ensure that mirrors are available so they can check their appearance.

Dressing aids

Aids are available to help with dressing and grooming. For example, long-handled brushes and combs are useful for those who cannot lift their arms high enough to reach their hair. Dressing and grooming aids can make all the difference to a service user's life. Long-handled shoe horns can be helpful for those who cannot bend down. Buttonholes can be very difficult to manage, so you could suggest replacing these with Velcro fastenings.

Have a go

Think about a service user who has difficulties with dressing and grooming. What equipment could help them to be independent?

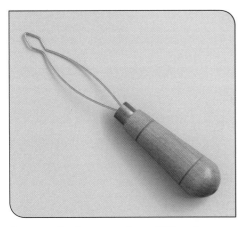

Buttonholes can be difficult to manage – a button hook like this can help

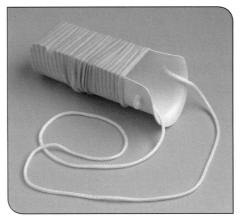

'Stockings or sock aids' can save bending down to put socks on

Have a go

Ask an occupational therapist to show you a range of dressing aids. The therapist can explain how they work and help enable individuals to dress independently.

Looking after personal belongings

When living in a care home, it is easy for clothes to get lost when sent to be washed. You can help service users avoid this by labelling clothing and equipment clearly. Encourage individuals to keep their clothes and equipment tidy and to put things away after use.

In the workplace: Saffron's new jeans

Saffron lives in a care home for teenagers with learning disabilities. She likes to spend her money on new clothes. Last month she saved her allowance and bought a new pair of jeans. Today Saffron wanted to wear her new jeans, but when she went to her cupboard they were not there. She was very upset and started to become angry.

Hannah, Saffron's key worker, had noticed that there were some clothes in the laundry room. She checked through them and found Saffron's jeans.

Saffron was very pleased that Hannah had put a name label in her jeans.

1 *Why is it important to label service users' clothes?*

2 *What might have happened if Hannah had not labelled Saffron's jeans?*

Remember

If you are responsible for washing service users' clothes, make sure that you read the labels.

When supporting service users to buy clothes, help them to choose items that can be washed and dried easily. This is especially important if the individual has problems with continence and their clothing needs frequent washing at a high temperature. Woollen clothing often needs special care, such as hand washing and dry cleaning, which would be unsuitable for frequent washing. Some items can be tumble dried and require no ironing. This can help to return clothing to individuals quickly.

Soiled clothing needs to be washed at a high enough temperature to kill germs. If you are washing clothes, make sure that the machine is set on a cycle of at least 65 degrees.

Head lice

Combs and brushes should not be shared. Head lice can be spread very easily between individuals; you need to discreetly check for these. If a service user does get head lice, they can be treated very easily and quickly with special lotion. Make sure you only use lotions ordered by a doctor; some lotions are especially for those with sensitive skin. Reassure service users that they do not have head lice because they are dirty; in fact, lice prefer clean hair.

Remember

Your clothes should be washed at a temperature of at least 65 degrees for at least ten minutes to kill germs and prevent the spread of infection.

Evidence *PC 1, 2, 3, 4, 6*

Ask a service user you care for for a witness testimony to show how you have supported them with grooming and dressing.

Head lice are becoming more resistant to chemical treatments. Keep hair free from lice by applying conditioner each time the hair is washed and using a fine-toothed comb to comb them out. A special spray available from the chemist can help to prevent head lice.

Head lice are spread easily by head-to-head contact. You can avoid spreading and getting head lice by not letting your hair get very close to other people's heads.

Have a go

Find out what natural herbal remedies are available to treat head lice to avoid the use of harsh chemicals.

Key points

o Encourage individuals (but do not force them) to do as much for themselves as possible.

o You can help service users to avoid losing their clothes by labelling them clearly.

o Do not force individuals to buy clothes just because they are easier to look after.

o Take precautions to prevent the spread of head lice. They can spread very easily between individuals.

If you come across problems and difficulties with dressing and grooming it is important that you deal with them properly. Small problems can soon turn into big ones, and can have an effect on service users.

Even though you try your best to care for service users' individual needs, you may still be faced with conflicts and problems. It may be that the clothing a service user wants to wear is not available. In many care settings there are several residents. Even if there is a good laundry service, it is not realistic to think that laundry can be dealt with immediately. Maybe the individual wishes to wear the same clothes each day, even though they are dirty and need washing. Careful handling of situations like this is very important. It can be very difficult because we have a responsibility to care for service users properly, but they also have a right to refuse help and support.

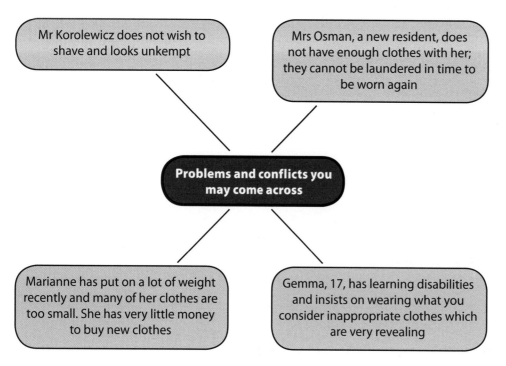

Mr Korolewicz does not wish to shave and looks unkempt

Mrs Osman, a new resident, does not have enough clothes with her; they cannot be laundered in time to be worn again

Problems and conflicts you may come across

Marianne has put on a lot of weight recently and many of her clothes are too small. She has very little money to buy new clothes

Gemma, 17, has learning disabilities and insists on wearing what you consider inappropriate clothes which are very revealing

Sometimes there are no straightforward answers. A bit of give and take may help but always let your supervisor know if you cannot resolve a problem

Have a go

Look at the four problems on page 238. Have you come across situations like these in your work? Suggest how you could resolve issues like these.

An individual's condition might get worse. For example, a person with arthritis may manage on their own by taking their time and doing things slowly. If they get flu, they may then find it difficult to manage without some help. When they have recovered and are back to their normal self, they may wish to be independent again. An individual's changing needs must be met.

Remember

That service users' needs do change from time to time.

Try to build a trusting relationship and get to know the individuals well. Remember if you do notice problems to report them to your supervisor straight away. Details will need to be written in the individual's care records.

Remember when filling in records to write clearly and accurately. Entries must be factual and not your opinions. Don't forget to date and sign the entry too.

Key points

o   You may be faced with conflicts and problems.

o   Small problems can soon turn into big ones and can have an effect on the service user and others.

o   Careful handling of difficult situations is very important.

o   Remember if you do notice problems to report them to your supervisor straight away.

o   It is important to write clearly and accurately when filling in records.

What have I learned?

1 Give five examples of when individuals may need help with their toileting and hygiene needs.

2 What toileting and bathing aids are available to help an individual to remain independent?

3 How might knowledge of a person's cultural or religious background affect the help you give them with toileting, personal hygiene and dressing?

4 What changes might you see from the norm and what might these changes mean?

5 Explain how you can prevent the spread of infection.

6 Give examples of three problems relating to personal hygiene and explain what you should do.

7 What dressing aids are available to enable service users to be independent with dressing and grooming?

8 How can you prevent the spread of head lice and how would you treat them?

Any questions?

Q *I work on my own in individuals' homes giving personal care. How can I get the evidence for this unit?*

A Perhaps you could ask your supervisor to work alongside you and ask for a witness testimony. You could ask the service user to give you a witness testimony too.

Q *The service users I care for can manage their own personal hygiene. Can I still do this unit?*

A Perhaps you need to look at the optional units again and find another one which relates more closely to the work that you do.

Q *I work in a care home for people with dementia and they need a lot of help with personal care and going to the toilet. My assessor does not work with me. I asked a few service users if it would be alright for her to come and assess me with bathing them and helping them to use the toilet, they said yes. Will this be OK?*

A No, the service users that you care for may not be able to make informed choices because they have dementia. You must always be aware of an individual's rights. Speak to your assessor about other types of evidence.

Case studies

Mrs O'Brien

Mrs O'Brien is 85 years old and has a colostomy (an opening in the abdomen for getting rid of faeces). She has managed quite well living at home until her arthritis became so bad that she was unable to use her hands properly and her mobility became poor. She agreed to go into a local care home.

Mrs O'Brien is worried and embarrassed about what the care workers might think about her colostomy.

Susan, a care worker who is 20 years old, is trying to settle Mrs O'Brien into her new home.

1 *What difficulties might Susan have in helping Mrs O'Brien?*

2 *How could Susan and other care workers help Mrs O'Brien to feel less embarrassed?*

3 *Who could help Mrs O'Brien with any difficulties with her colostomy bag?*

Mr Palfrey

Mr Palfrey lives in a small care home. In the past six months he has developed dementia and his condition is getting worse. Each morning the carers help him to have a wash. The staff have not had training in dementia, so they are not sure how to manage him.

Mr Palfrey sometimes becomes angry and usually says that he has washed and changed his clothes even if he has not. Jenny finds it difficult looking after Mr Palfrey and other care workers avoid him. Mr Palfrey's daughter has complained, saying that he is being neglected.

1 *Why do you think Mr Palfrey gets angry when the care staff try to help him?*

2 *What might happen if the situation is not resolved?*

3 *How could Jenny help Mr Palfrey with his hygiene?*

HSC215

Help individuals to maintain mobility

This unit is an optional unit, which means it is one that you can choose to work on. You can choose this unit if you work with people who have problems with their mobility. Mobility means a person's ability to move from one position or place to another.

The individuals you provide care for do not need to be wheelchair users for you to choose this unit. They could simply be people who need encouragement and support to move about their environment. Some may be recovering from an accident or an operation, so will only need temporary help.

This unit looks at how you can support or help individuals to keep the mobility they already have, and how to use mobility equipment if it is needed. It also looks at what you should do when you see that an individual's mobility has changed.

How you will be assessed

Your assessor will observe you working to cover your Performance Criteria. You will also need to answer some questions, or give explanations, to cover the knowledge specification.

This unit covers the following elements:

o **215a** Support individuals to keep mobile

o **215b** Observe changes in mobility and provide feedback

Support individuals to keep mobile

We often take it for granted that we can walk, run or move around freely without anyone's help. What effect do you think it would have on you if you were not able to move around? How do you think you would feel? It may help you understand the people you care for better if you think about the difficulties you would have, and the help you might need, if you had mobility problems.

This element looks at different ways you can support, or help, individuals to keep their mobility. It also looks at why they should be supported to keep mobile.

In this element you will cover:

- Muscles, bones and joints
- Health conditions affecting movement
- Problems caused by immobility
- The best ways to keep mobile
- The benefits of keeping mobile
- Identifying risks
- Reading and following care plans
- Mobility appliances
- Checking mobility appliances before use
- Health and safety of the environment
- Supporting the use of mobility appliances.

Imagine how you would feel if you could not move around well enough to do the things you love

The human body has over 200 different bones, and four main types of **joints**. Without bones and joints you would not be able to stand, sit, walk or run. It is your bones that give your body shape and support. Your bones and joints are connected to **muscles** by **ligaments**. Your body could not move without your muscles and ligaments.

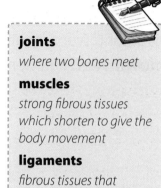

joints
where two bones meet

muscles
strong fibrous tissues which shorten to give the body movement

ligaments
fibrous tissues that connect muscle to bones

Joints

The four main types of joints in your body are:

o   hinge joints

o   pivot joints

o   ball and socket joints

o   glide joints.

Hinge joints

You have hinge joints in your knees, elbows, fingers and toes. A hinge joint lets your **limb** bend. You can think of a hinge joint as a door opening or closing. A door cannot open or close more than the hinge will let it. This is just like your knee or elbow. When you bend and straighten your leg, it bends at the knee and will only straighten so far. A hinge joint is very strong. When you walk, your knees straighten and take the weight of your body.

limb
an arm or leg

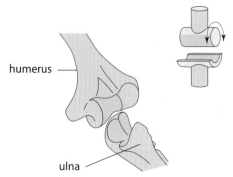

humerus

ulna

A hinge joint

Pivot joints

The joint in your neck is a pivot joint. It lets you rotate, or turn, your head. You also have a pivot joint in your elbow. This allows you to turn the lower part of your arm. You cannot turn your head or lower arm all the way around because there are muscles and ligaments that stop this.

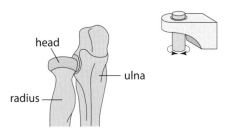

The pivot joint between the ulna and the head of the radius allows the lower arm to rotate

Ball and socket joints

This type of joint gives you the most range of movement. You have a ball and socket joint in each hip and shoulder. This type of joint lets you move your limbs up and down, from side to side and around in a full circle. A ball and socket joint is where the end of one bone sits in the hollow of another bone.

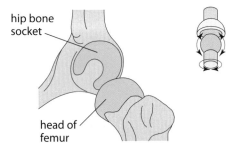

The ball and socket joint between the hip bone and the femur allows the range of movement needed for walking and other activities

Glide joints

These can be found in your spine, or backbone. They can give you a lot of movement, but not as much as the ball and socket joint. A glide joint is where bones glide or move over each other. To help the bones move over each other easily there is a disc or pad of cartilage. Cartilage is a tough **flexible** tissue, which also acts as a shock absorber between the bones in your back.

flexible
bendy, elastic

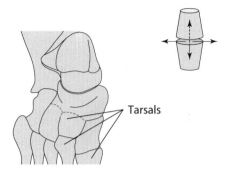

Tarsals

Glide joints between the small bones, or tarsi, are also found in the foot. They help keep the foot flexible

A special fluid called synovial fluid protects most of the joints in your body. This fluid helps your joints to move smoothly and without pain.

Think about it

Try moving the different parts of your body to see how each joint moves. Be careful not to force your limbs and joints to move any more than they should. Stop if you feel any pain.

Have a go

Look up the names of the bones referred to in these joints. See if you can find other examples of the joints mentioned here.

Evidence *KS 6*

Discuss how the body moves and the different joints you have in your body with your assessor.

Key points

o   Bones and joints help you to stand, sit, walk and run.
o   There are four main types of joints in the human body.
o   Each joint has a special way of moving.
o   Joints are supported by muscles and ligaments.

Throughout your life, the bones in your body are constantly changing. This is because they are living. Most people's bones will repair themselves by growing new bone if it is damaged. The bone will probably need to be held in place, so that it mends in the right position, which might mean wearing a plaster cast. It may take a while, but eventually the person is back to normal, doing everything they did before.

Unfortunately, some individuals develop conditions as they get older that stop, or slow down, how bones and joints repair themselves. Many older people have a condition called osteoporosis, where the bones break very easily and do not mend well.

Not all mobility problems are caused by age

Some individuals are born with health conditions that affect their mobility. Mobility can also be affected following an accident or illness. Some individuals develop conditions that affect the muscles and ligaments connecting to bones, so they cannot move around easily. They may not be able to control their movements well, or the muscles may be too weak to support their weight.

Conditions which may affect mobility:

- arthritis
- cerebral palsy
- muscular dystrophy
- brain injury
- multiple sclerosis
- stroke
- loss of a limb
- osteoarthritis
- Parkinson's disease
- rheumatoid arthritis.

Have a go

Always be aware of general conditions that may affect service users. Use the Internet to find out more about any special conditions.

Evidence *KS 6, 7, 9*

Look at the conditions on page 248 and choose one that an individual you provide care for has. Read up on the condition and write about it, saying how it can affect an individual's movement and mobility. Show what you have written to your assessor.

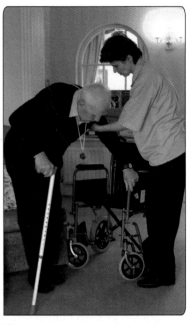

There are a number of conditions that can cause problems with mobility

In the workplace:
Understanding Parkinson's disease

Trisha works at Cove Court Day Centre, which provides support to older men and women. Trisha often works with Musquates, an older man who comes there twice a week.

Trisha has noticed that his mobility is getting worse. She knew he had a condition called Parkinson's disease so she decided to read more about it. Trisha found out that this condition affects part of the brain, and this then affects the body's movement and mobility. She also learned that the signs of Parkinson's disease include tremors (shaking), slowness of movement, rigidity (stiffness), difficulty with balance and a shuffling walk. Trisha was pleased that she had learned this new information. She felt it helped her to understand Musquates' difficulties a little better.

1 *Do you work with anyone who has Parkinson's disease?*

2 *How does this condition affect them?*

Key points

o Your bones are constantly changing.

o Usually your bones and joints will repair themselves if damaged.

o Some individuals' bones do not mend easily.

o Some individuals are born with conditions that affect their mobility.

o Some individuals' mobility can be affected by illness or disease.

Some people may have difficulty in moving around because of their age or health. Some may not want to mobilise because it causes them pain. Sometimes an individual's lack of mobility can then cause other problems.

Dangers of immobility

Not moving around can be very bad for your health. If you do not use your muscles, they can become very weak. Your joints become very stiff and painful, and you may gain weight from not exercising.

Simply by being **immobile**, the individual could face a lot more health problems. The less a person moves around, the more his or her health could be affected. The more a person's health is affected the less they will want to move around. It can become a vicious circle.

immobile

not moving – sitting or lying still

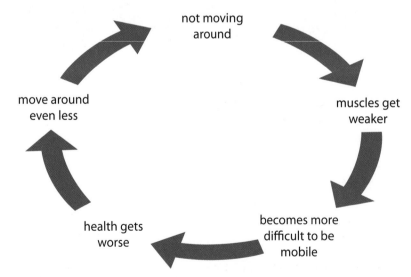

Not being mobile can create a vicious circle where it becomes even harder to be mobile

Think about it

Imagine sitting down or lying in bed all day without moving. But then imagine doing this every day. What effect would it have on you?

Here are a few more problems that can be caused by a lack of mobility:

- chest infections
- swollen feet and ankles
- incontinence
- deep vein thrombosis
- constipation

- urine infections
- loss of **independence**
- pulmonary **embolism**
- depression
- pressure sores.

independence
being able to do things on your own without anyone's help

embolism
small clot of blood

In the workplace: Moving is painful

Brian is a 78 year-old man who has arthritis. He will not move around because he says it causes him pain.

Explain what other problems his immobility could cause him.

Evidence *KS 11*

Look at the individuals you provide care for. How has immobility affected their health? Write down the effects and show this to your assessor. Why is it important to control the spread of infection?

Key points

- The more immobile an individual is, the more health problems they may get.
- Pain can be caused by not keeping mobile.
- Immobility can cause many other health problems, including chest infections, swollen feet and ankles, constipation and pressure sores.

Have a go

Look up any of the health problems from the list above that you have not heard of before, or that you do not know what they mean. See if you can understand how they can be caused by not moving around. You could speak to your manager or colleagues if you need more help.

Keeping mobile does not have to be hard work. A little activity on a regular basis can help individuals to keep mobile. Before you can help individuals to keep mobile, you need to be aware of your organisation's policies and procedures.

Policies and procedures

- Health and Safety
- Best Practice
- Human Rights

- Equal Opportunities
- Discrimination
- Organisational Requirements.

Think about it

If you ask service users what kind of activity they have enjoyed in the past, you can probably find something they would like to do now.

Have a go

Above are just a few of the policies and procedures you need to be aware of before you start helping individuals to keep mobile. Talk about them with your manager to find out what you need to know.

Ways to be mobile

The word 'exercise' can make a lot of people panic. The thought of having to puff and pant until they are soaked in sweat can put a lot of people off. It doesn't have to be this way! Even simple activities can help people to keep mobile.

Activities with a purpose can be used so that the individual does not even feel as if they are exercising. This could be as simple as walking to the shop to buy a newspaper. The individual could also weed the garden, clean their bedroom and do other forms of housework, or just walk to the dining room.

Activities are often even more enjoyable in a group. The service users you care for might be able to visit a garden, or museum with friends, or walk to a restaurant for lunch. Other activities could include dancing or movement to music, or throwing and catching a ball.

Activities for all

Not all individuals are able to walk, and some people are unsteady on their feet. This can happen to younger or older people. No matter what their age, it should not stop them from keeping mobile. The individual should still be encouraged to do some sort of activity. Activities can be changed to meet the abilities of the individual. For example, people can still move their arms or legs to music, or do some gardening while sitting in a chair or in a wheelchair. Both younger and older people can enjoy moving to music or pottering around the garden. They can play catch, using a bean bag instead of a ball, if that is easier for them.

Whatever activity the individual chooses to do, you should make it fun. If the activity feels like hard work, then the individual may soon give up on it.

Exercise does not have to be hard work – it can be enjoyable too!

Evidence *KS 1, 3, 4*

Talk to your assessor about the different policies and procedures in your workplace that relate to service users' mobility. Explain what these policies say you should do in preparation for supporting individuals with their mobility.

Remember

Whatever the activity is, encourage service users to dress in suitable clothes.

Key points

o You need to be aware of your organisation's policies and procedures on mobility before you start any activities.

o Exercise should be fun and be for a purpose.

o All individuals can keep mobile, regardless of their ability.

o Activities can be changed to meet the individual's ability.

Look again at page 251 in the section about the problems caused by lack of mobility. You can help to prevent these problems by supporting the service users you care for to stay mobile.

Body and soul

Mobility and exercise have always been thought of as being good for the body and the mind. A walk in the countryside or park can be very relaxing. You can see lots of nice things, smell different smells and hear different sounds. These things can make you feel good, and being outside can make you feel refreshed. So walking can help you to keep active, and feel good about yourself.

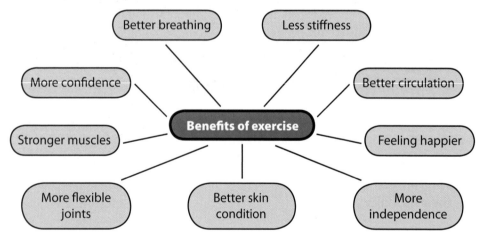

Keeping mobile is good for the mind as well as the body

You have already looked at how to keep mobile, and you have learned that there are many ways to be active and mobile. You may work with individuals who use a wheelchair because they need help to walk. Encouraging them to keep their arms or legs moving is just as important. Moving their arms and legs can help their **circulation**. It also helps to prevent joints becoming stiff and painful.

> **Have a go**
>
> Have you tried any of the activities on page 253 with the service users you care for? If not, ask your manager or the physiotherapist if it will be safe for the service users to do the activities. Watch the individuals during the activities; speak to them at the end. Did they enjoy them? Do they look happier? Find out what benefits they got from the activities.

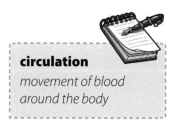

circulation
movement of blood around the body

A better social life

A person who is in pain may not want to talk very much. This can stop them from making friends and they can become lonely. Encouraging individuals to take part in fun mobility activities can help them to enjoy themselves. Working as a group may help the individuals to talk with each other, and to develop friendships.

If a person feels healthy and is not in pain, then exercise can help them to feel good about themselves. They may want to do more for themselves. This will give them more independence. Being as independent as possible makes people feel good. So you can see that keeping mobile has many benefits, not just for the body, but also for the mind.

Disability doesn't have to mean no exercise!

Key points

o Keeping mobile can help the body and mind.
o Mobility can help the muscles, joints and circulation.
o It can make the individual feel happier.
o It can help in making friends.
o It can help the individual to be independent.

The most serious risk when exercising is having a heart attack. Breathing difficulties can be serious too. Other less serious risks include **sprains and strains**. Before you support individuals to exercise you must find out if they have any health problems that could put them at risk from injury or illness.

sprains and strains
damage to the muscles or ligaments

There are many ways you can find out this information. You could read through the individual's records, speak to their physiotherapist or doctor, or simply talk to the individual and ask them. Before you can read an individual's records you need to be able to access them. You have already looked at how you access records in Unit 21. If you are unsure about this, please read it again.

Health issues to take account of

You need to find out if the individual has any heart problems. You also need to find out if they are used to exercise. Activities or exercise can make the heart beat faster. If the person is not used to exercise, it can put too much pressure on the heart and may lead to a heart attack.

Remember

Make sure service users have their inhalers with them, or any other medication they might need, when they take part in exercise.

Some of the service users you care for may have problems with their breathing. This could be because they are not used to exercise, or because of an illness. It is very important that you find out if the person has any breathing problems before they start exercising. If that individual walks up a hill, or walks too fast or too far, they may have difficulties in breathing. This is common in a condition known as asthma. Asthma sufferers often have small inhalers they can use if they have trouble breathing so make sure they have it with them, and that you know how to help them if they have difficulties. **Emphysema** is another health condition that can cause shortness of breath.

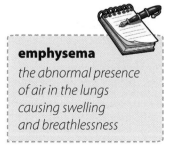

emphysema
the abnormal presence of air in the lungs causing swelling and breathlessness

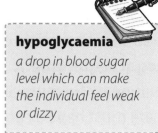

Diabetes is a serious medical condition affecting sugar levels in the blood. Too much exercise can cause **hypoglycaemia**. Make sure you would know what to do if an individual became unwell while exercising.

hypoglycaemia
a drop in blood sugar level which can make the individual feel weak or dizzy

In the workplace: Holistic needs

Ron attends a rehabilitation session each week following a heart attack. His needs are identified holistically. He is encouraged to walk in the park to meet his physical needs. He discusses his feelings with his care worker to meet his emotional needs and is encouraged to interact with others in the session to meet his social needs.

1   *What are the risks if he does not walk in the park?*

2   *What are the risks if he does not discuss his feelings with the care worker?*

3   *What are the risks if he does not interact with others?*

Evidence *KS 4, 10*

Find out what health condition or issues the individuals you work with have that could put them at risk when exercising. Read their records and speak to your manager, the physiotherapist or doctor to see what risks there might be. Tell your assessor about any individual's health condition. Say how the condition could put the individual at risk and how you found this information.

Remember

It is important to find out what risks might be involved for a service user if they exercise.

Key points

o   You can identify risks by reading reports and talking to others.

o   Risks could include heart problems, asthma and diabetes.

o   Exercise may harm individuals with heart or breathing problems.

A care plan is a detailed written document that shows you how you should provide care for an individual. Care plans are a **legal requirement** under the Care Standards Act 2000. The National Minimum Standards say that all individuals receiving care must have a care plan.

Senior members of staff should write a care plan once the individual has been assessed. This usually happens when someone first has care, but the care plan should also be updated regularly. From this assessment it is agreed with the individual how they might be able to overcome any difficulties they might have with their mobility. For example, they could be offered support to use aids, equipment, or the help of care workers and other professionals.

legal requirement
must be done by law

Have a go

Read the care plan for Daniel Baker. What could happen if you did not follow the care plan, and allowed him to walk to the bathroom without support?

CARE PLAN REQUIREMENTS

Name Daniel Baker	Date of Birth 21.12.72
Relevant Information RTA resulting in open complicated fractures to both legs	
Unit Woodrush Rehab Unit	Date of Plan 08.08.07

Planned Activity	Target Date	Nursing Requirement	Date Achieved
To minimise effects of immobility	08.08.07	1) Assess risk of pressure sores and address any issues arising from the assessment	08.08.07
To safely use crutches to mobilise with support	30.08.07	1) Arrange physiotherapist assessment and input 2) Encourage and support short walks to and from the bathroom	
To safely use crutches to mobilise without support	07.09.07	1) Reduce support whilst observing safety 2) Withdraw physical support giving only verbal support	

The care plan should say how well the individual mobilises, and what difficulties they have

Your responsibilities

Before you can give individuals support with any activity, including mobility, you must read and understand the care plan. If you do not fully understand what the care plan is asking you to do, you must speak with your manager. Once you understand the care plan you must do what it says and follow it carefully.

Remember

Never undertake any care activity with a service user without first reading the care plan.

Evidence   KS 15

Read an individual's care plan on mobility. Write a statement of what could happen to that individual if you did not follow the care plan. Show this to your assessor.

Think about it

Imagine what could happen if no one bothered reading an individual's care plan. They might end up having a lot of different treatments, which would not necessarily help their development or recovery.

Remember

To respect the service user's confidentiality when accessing their records.

Key points

o   Care plans are a legal requirement.

o   Care plans must be written following an assessment on the individual.

o   You are responsible for reading and understanding an individual's care plan.

o   You are responsible for following that care plan.

o   Ignoring a care plan can lead to serious problems for the individual.

There are many different mobility appliances or aids that can help people to move around their environment. The type of aid that an individual uses will depend on what disability they have, and the amount of support they need.

Mainly people who are not able to walk use wheelchairs. Some people who are able to walk, but not very far, may also use a wheelchair. A wheelchair can give the individual independence to go where they like without the help of another person. Unfortunately, not everyone who uses a wheelchair is strong enough to turn the wheels so they can move themselves. They may need someone to push them, or they may be able to use a motorised wheelchair.

Some people may need to use one or two walking sticks to help them balance when they are walking. Individuals who are not able to put a lot of weight on one of their legs may find a walking stick helps them to keep mobile. The weaker leg is supported by putting some of the weight on the stick. People of all ages might need to use a walking stick at some time, for example, after a sporting injury, accident or an operation.

A wheelchair can help keep people mobile

Walking sticks are a type of mobility appliance

If a person has weakness in both of their legs they may need to use a walking frame. The frame helps the person to take some of their body weight through their arms instead of their legs. Again, individuals of all ages may need to use this type of equipment to help them move around.

If an individual needs to use a stick when walking they should be encouraged and supported to use it properly. As a care worker you may be tempted to offer an individual the use of someone else's wheelchair. This may help the individual to get to the dining room quicker, but it is not helping to keep them mobile.

There are many types of walking frames

Think about it

What different mobility appliances or aids are used by the individuals you provide care for? Why do they use these aids? If you are unsure, ask your manager to explain why the service user needs their mobility aids.

Key points

o There are many different types of mobility appliances and aids.

o The type of mobility aid required by an individual will depend on his or her disability.

o A wheelchair can give the individual independence.

o A walking stick can give balance or help to take part of an individual's body weight.

o A walking frame can help an individual who has weakness in both legs.

o Individuals should only use the aid prescribed for them.

Before you support individuals to use a mobility aid, you need to check that the aid is safe and fit for use. There are three general rules you should follow for all mobility appliances. By asking yourself the following questions you are carrying out a health and safety check. For the aids to be safe and help the service user properly they should be individually measured and supplied by the hospital or physiotherapist. You can read more about health and safety in Unit 22.

You need to ask yourself these three questions:

1 Is the appliance safe?

2 Is the appliance clean?

3 Is the appliance their own?

If you answer 'no' to any of these questions, individuals should not use the aid until the problem has been sorted out.

Wheelchairs

All wheelchairs have a maximum user weight. You should never exceed this as it will break the condition of the guarantee and it can lead to the wheelchair becoming dangerous. You should also ensure the seat size, backrest height, armrest height and footrest are correct for the service user.

Remember

Never allow service users to use mobility aids that are not their own. Mobility aids are measured for one person only and may not be suitable for others to use.

Here are some things to look for when checking that a wheelchair is safe to use and the correct size for a service user:

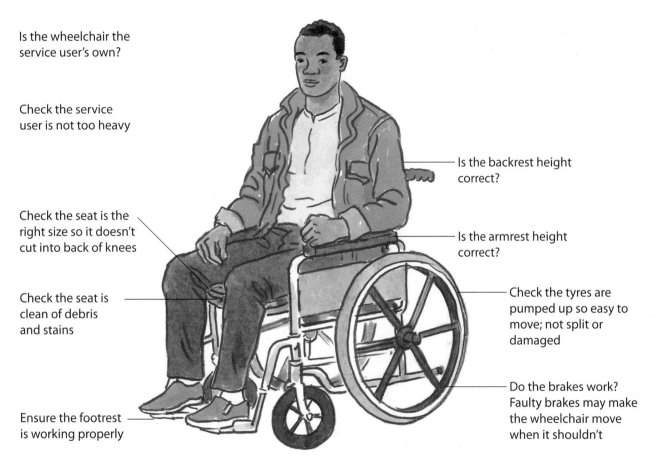

Is the wheelchair the service user's own?

Check the service user is not too heavy

Check the seat is the right size so it doesn't cut into back of knees

Check the seat is clean of debris and stains

Ensure the footrest is working properly

Is the backrest height correct?

Is the armrest height correct?

Check the tyres are pumped up so easy to move; not split or damaged

Do the brakes work? Faulty brakes may make the wheelchair move when it shouldn't

A wheelchair should be measured to fit the service user; if it is too big they may have problems moving it

Evidence *PC 3, 4; KS 14*

Check service users' mobility aids where you work. Make a list of any problems you find and report them to your manager. Ask your assessor to observe you checking the aids, or get a witness testimony from someone who sees you doing the checks. Explain why you make these checks and the problems that could arise if you did not report any problems.

Remember

Always check each appliance – is it clean, is it safe, is it their own?

Walking sticks

When being measured for a walking stick, it is important for the service user to wear their normal outdoor shoes. The individual should stand upright with their hands by their sides. Measure the distance from their wristbone to the floor – this is the correct height for the handle of the stick.

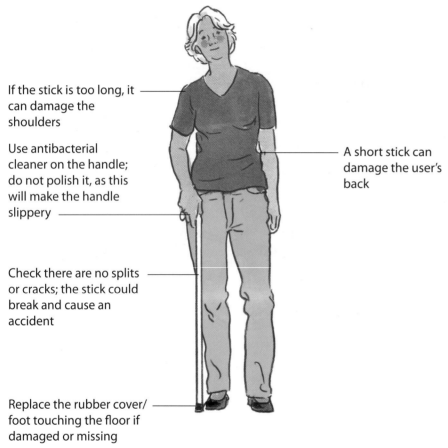

If the stick is too long, it can damage the shoulders

Use antibacterial cleaner on the handle; do not polish it, as this will make the handle slippery

Check there are no splits or cracks; the stick could break and cause an accident

Replace the rubber cover/ foot touching the floor if damaged or missing

A short stick can damage the user's back

A walking stick that is too long or too short can cause the user pain

Remember

Make sure that service users are wearing their normal outdoor shoes when they are measured for a walking stick or frame.

In the workplace: Siân's walking stick

Siân has noticed that one of the older women she visits each morning is becoming unsteady on her feet. Siân has an old walking stick that used to belong to her mother and she offers it to the woman to help her to walk.

What problems could Siân be creating for this woman?

Walking frames

The handlebars of a walking frame must be at the right height, so that the user maintains a good posture. The ideal height for the handles is level with the wristbones when the user has their hands by their sides, with elbows slightly bent.

Reporting problems

If you notice any problems with a mobility aid, you should ask the individual not to use it and report the problem to your manager. Your manager should then check the aid and get the problem fixed. If you do not report a problem with a mobility aid, it could cause the individual to have an accident.

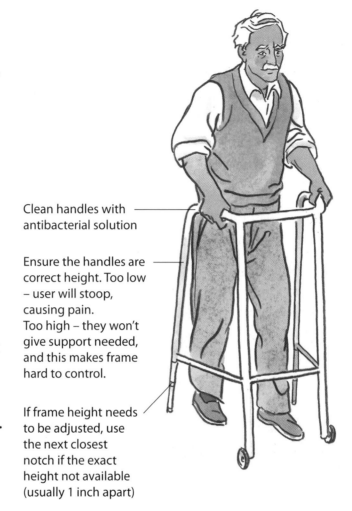

Clean handles with antibacterial solution

Ensure the handles are correct height. Too low – user will stoop, causing pain.
Too high – they won't give support needed, and this makes frame hard to control.

If frame height needs to be adjusted, use the next closest notch if the exact height not available (usually 1 inch apart)

A walking frame at the correct height gives good support and is easier to control

Key points

o Always check mobility appliances are safe and fit to use.

o Ask yourself three simple questions – is it safe, is it clean, is it their own?

o Do not use appliances that are unsafe.

o Do not use aids that are not the individual's.

o Unsafe or shared mobility aids could harm or injure the individual.

o Report any problems about mobility aids to your manager.

To make sure individuals stay safe when mobilising you need to check the environment for anything that could cause harm. These are known as hazards. A hazard is something that has the potential to cause harm, for example, loose carpets or wet floors. A risk is the likelihood that it will happen. For example, the risk of someone tripping over a loose carpet is high.

TC 004_A1

A hazard may not always be very obvious. Some things may be hazardous to one individual, but not others. You may need to look around the environment very carefully to see any possible problems.

The table below shows some of the possible hazards and how to deal with them. You may also want to read Unit 22 on health and safety again.

Removing hazards

Hazard	For:		How to remove the hazard
	Person walking	**Person in a wheelchair**	
Wet floor, spillages on the floor	✓	✓	Clean up spillages, put out wet floor sign
Objects on the floor	✓	✓	Tidy objects away
Loose or torn carpet	✓	✓	Report, place hazard sign over hazardous area
Slope	✓	✓	Use non-slip flooring, fit hand rails
Narrow doorway		✓	Widen all doorways to fit wheelchairs
Stairs or steps		✓	Fit a hand rail, provide a slope

Think about it

Look at the environment where you work. What hazards, or possible hazards can you see that could cause difficulties for individuals trying to mobilise?

Evidence *PC 5; KS 18 and HSC22*

Think of a time when you removed or reduced hazards in the environment. Write an account of what you did, why you did it, and how. Show this to your assessor.

Putting out a 'wet floor' sign can help to remove the risk of someone slipping

In the workplace: The wet floors

Shinbagavalli works in a care home. The cleaner has just finished mopping the floors and the residents are due in at any moment. Shinbagavalli needs to stop them from walking on the floors.

1   *Why should the residents be stopped from walking on the floors?*

2   *Can you identify the hazard and the risks?*

Key points

o   A hazard is something that could cause harm.
o   A risk is the chance of harm that could be caused by the hazard.
o   Something may be hazardous to one person, but not another.
o   There is usually a way to avoid the risk caused by hazards.

You have learned about muscles, bones and joints, and about health conditions that can affect movement. You now know the problems that are caused by immobility and the best ways to keep mobile. You have identified the risks, read the care plan, and checked the appliances. The environment is safe. Now you need to learn how to support individuals to use mobility appliances. There is a lot of preparation needed to support individuals with their mobility. The preparation is just as important as the support that you give.

Verbal support

You can give support to individuals both verbally and physically. The best support is always given verbally through talking to the individual. This is known as feedback. To have someone next to them telling them how well they are doing, giving them **encouragement** to carry on, can help the individual to achieve independence. Encouragement can make the individual feel good about themselves and what they are doing. This is a type of active support, which means that you are supporting the individual to do as much as they can themselves.

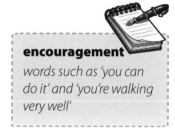

encouragement
words such as 'you can do it' and 'you're walking very well'

Physical support

Some individuals may need more than verbal support. If they are very nervous or unsure of themselves they may also need physical support. They may need you to help them to mobilise by you holding onto their arm. If you do this, you are supporting them physically.

> **Think about it**
>
> Think of a time when you had encouragement from someone. Why did they give you that encouragement? How did it make you feel?

It is very important that you do not let the individual hold onto your arm. If the person fell to the floor, they would pull you down with them. This could seriously injure you and you would be unable to help. When you are physically supporting an individual to mobilise, put one hand gently under the person's elbow. Hold out your other hand so that the person can put their hand on top of yours. This way if the individual falls, you can let go quickly to stop yourself from getting hurt.

Moving and handling techniques must be learned in a practical course. You should not try a manoeuvre until you are confident that you have the necessary skills.

Holding the individual correctly keeps you both safe

Evidence PC 1, 3, 5, 8, 9, 10, 12

Ask your assessor to watch you supporting a service user to mobilise. Before you give support, encourage the individual by telling them how keeping mobile will help them. Check the mobility appliance is safe to use. Remove any hazards and check the care plan. When supporting the individual to mobilise, make sure they are using the appliance correctly and give verbal and physical support where needed.

Key points

o Preparation is just as important as the support you give.
o You can support individuals both verbally and physically.
o Verbal support can help the individual feel good about themselves.
o Physical support may be needed if the individual is unsure of themselves.
o Never let an individual hold your arm, always hold theirs.

Remember

Never let someone hold onto your arm when you are helping them to walk.

When you work with individuals who need health or social care it is important that you observe carefully. Take notice of any change in the individual's physical or emotional condition. You are not always looking to see if the individual's condition is getting worse. You also need to look for changes that the individual is getting better.

You will need to record, or write down, what you see when you work with individuals. You will also need to tell certain people what you see.

This element looks at how you can observe any changes in the individual's mobility, and how you report changes to the appropriate people.

In this element you will cover:

- How and what to observe
- Adverse reactions in mobility activities
- Monitoring individuals' progress
- How to report changes in mobility.

It is important to notice any changes in a service user's mobility

When you work with an individual to maintain their mobility you will need to observe, or watch, how that person moves around their environment. You need to see how the individual:

o walks – with or without a walking stick or frame

o uses a wheelchair

o climbs up or down stairs or steps

o sits down or stands up.

You can use this tick chart to remind you what to look for when you are observing an individual's mobility.

✓ Does the person look as though they may fall?

✓ How far can the person walk?

✓ Are they getting tired?

✓ Can the person move around without anyone's help?

✓ Does the person hold on to furniture to help them move around?

✓ Does the person look as though they are in pain when they walk?

✓ Does walking cause the person to become short of breath?

✓ If the person uses a mobility aid such as a walking stick or frame, are they using it properly?

You can observe or watch an individual in two ways:

o when the individual knows you are watching them

o when the individual does not know you are watching.

By using both of these ways you may see different things.

The individual knows you are observing

If you observe an individual walking when they know you are watching them, you might see:

Remember

If the individual knows that you are watching them, they may act differently to how they normally act.

o   The person appears to be mobilising very well. This could be because the person wants to make you happy and so is trying harder. It could also be because they feel more confident with someone watching them.

o   The person is mobilising with a lot of difficulty. This might be because they are pretending. This could be to get your attention or sympathy. They may also mobilise with more difficulty because they are nervous about being watched.

Think about it

People may act differently if they know they are being watched. How do you think you would feel or behave if you knew someone was watching you do something?

The individual does not know you are watching

You might see the person mobilise differently when they do not know you are watching them. You might see:

o   The person mobilising well. This could be because they are not nervous about being watched. It may also be because they are not pretending anymore.

o   The person has difficulty mobilising. This could be because they do not have your attention to give them confidence. It could also be that they are not trying so hard.

We all have good days and bad days. This will be the same for the service users you work with when they mobilise. The individual may be tired or unwell. You need to observe an individual's mobility on different days and times, both when they know and don't know that you are observing them. This will help you to get a more accurate picture of the individual's mobility.

Have a go

Observe the individuals you work with on different days and times, both when they know and don't know that you are doing so. What differences do you see in their mobility?

In the workplace: Gloriose is found out!

Gloriose has used a walking stick for the past eight weeks after injuring her ankle. She says it still hurts and causes her problems when she walks. One day Lawrence, her care worker, watches her getting off the bus. Gloriose does not know she is being observed and walks down the road with her walking stick under her arm. Lawrence realises that Gloriose does not need her stick after all.

If Gloriose knew she was being observed what do you think she may have done?

Key points

o   You need to observe how an individual mobilises with or without aids.

o   You should observe an individual with and without them knowing that you are watching them.

o   You should observe an individual at different times and on different days.

Sometimes when people take part in activities they may experience an **adverse reaction**. In mobility activities, the reaction will depend on the individual's health or physical condition.

adverse reaction
a problem that can occur, e.g. pain

> **Think about it**
>
> Think of a time when you did not do any exercise for a while. How did you feel after you exercised?

Aches and pains

Many people who do not exercise regularly may ache after doing exercise. The person's joints and muscles may hurt them for a day or so. This is because the joints or muscles are not used to the exercise. This may be the same for the individuals you care for. If the individual does not exercise or mobilise very much, his or her muscles and joints may hurt them during and after the activity.

> **Remember**
>
> When you support individuals with mobility activities, you need to observe them for any adverse reactions, such as pain.

Blisters

Other adverse reactions could be blisters on the individual's hands. These may be caused if the individual is using a walking stick or frame for the first time. The skin rubbing on the handle of the mobility aid as it is held tightly can cause the blister. Blisters can be painful. How many times have you had a blister on your foot after wearing new shoes, or on your hands after digging in the garden?

Tiredness

Tiredness is an adverse reaction that happens to everyone when they exercise or mobilise. Some people get tired more quickly than others. This could be because of their age, health or ability. When people get tired, their muscles can become weaker. If you are supporting an individual to mobilise you need to stop as soon as they become tired. Let the person rest a little before they carry on. If you do not stop and rest, the individual could fall and hurt themselves.

In the workplace: Betty's fall

Simon is supporting Betty to mobilise using her walking frame. After walking halfway down the corridor Betty tells Simon that she is tired. Simon tells Betty she is doing really well and is nearly at the dining room. Betty carries on walking but then feels very dizzy. She falls to the floor and bangs her head.

1   *How could this accident have been avoided?*

2   *How else could Simon have recognised that Betty was getting tired?*

Remember

Always listen when a service user says they are tired when they are mobilising.

Key points

o   Adverse reactions are unwanted or harmful.

o   Aches and pains are adverse reactions in mobility activities.

o   You should stop mobilising if a service user is tired.

Progress means the improvements that have been made. To monitor improvements means to check or record the improvements that have been made. In order to do this, you need to know what the individual was like in the past.

A baseline is the point the individual started from. You measure their progress from this baseline to see how much the person has improved.

Monitoring a person's progress is very important. If the individual is on a training programme, you need to see if it is working. You might find that the individual is not progressing, or making any improvements. This could be because the training programme is wrong, or that the programme is not being followed properly.

Baseline
Unable to stand

Baseline	Unable to stand
Progress 1	Stands with 2 members of staff
Progress 2	Stands with 1 member of staff
Progress 3	Stands with walking frame or walking stick
Progress 4	Stands unaided

Progress 3
Stands with aid

Always measure the service user's progress from a baseline point

Think about it

Think about the progress or improvements you have made. Before reading this book you may not have known a lot about caring for individuals. Since reading this book, your knowledge will have increased – you have made progress in the amount of knowledge you have about health and social care.

In the workplace: Lillian's lack of progress

Lillian had a stroke four weeks ago which left her with weakness in her right arm and leg. She has been shown some exercises to do to help build up her strength in her arm and leg. Lillian does the exercises every day on her own, but does not seem to be making much progress. Her arm and leg are still very weak.

1 *Why do you think Lillian is not making much progress?*

2 *Read Supporting the use of mobility appliances (pages 268–269) again to help you with this.*

You can monitor an individual's progress by:

o observing them

o asking them questions

o reading their care plan

o talking to their family or friends

o speaking with colleagues or other professionals.

Evidence *PC 1, 2, 5; KS 8*

Write about a service user you work with. Describe the progress they have made with their mobility activities. Say how you monitored the progress made by the service user.

Key points

o You need to find the individual's baseline before you can monitor their progress.

o Monitoring progress is very important to identify if training programmes are working.

o Poor progress could be because the training programme is not being used properly.

You should report any changes in the way a person mobilises as soon as you notice them. This is so that the correct action can be taken.

Changes in mobility can be positive or negative. The following table gives some examples of positive and negative changes for an individual who mobilises by walking.

Changes in mobility	
✓ **Positive changes**	✗ **Negative changes**
✓ Able to walk without pain	✗ Pain increases when walking
✓ Able to walk further	✗ Distance able to walk has reduced
✓ Able to walk without support	✗ Now needs support to walk

Recording and reporting changes

It is important to record any changes that you see. You should do this straight away so that you do not forget it. You may need to find out what reporting forms your organisation uses to record mobility changes.

When you write in a record you need to be **factual**. You should write what you see or hear but not what you think. What you write should also be **legible** and signed and dated.

factual
true

legible
easy to read

To find out more about writing records, read Unit 21d (pages 44–51).

Mobility Record Form

All staff should complete this report form after each mobility activity.

Name:
Date of activity:
Brief details of activity:
Outcome of the activity; positive and negative:
Suggestions/comments from service user or staff:
Signed: Date:

An example of a mobility record form

There may be a time when you need to report or tell someone what you see straight away. You will still need to record it or make a written record. Reporting a problem on a service user's mobility will help that person to get any treatment they need straight away. The change in their mobility could be caused by a serious illness.

Have a go

Find out what form your organisation uses to record any mobility changes that you see in service users. Go through the form with your manager to make sure you understand it.

In the workplace: Dragging his feet

Gaynor is a support worker at Isle View Care Home. She notices one of the service users is walking differently. He is not picking up his left foot and is dragging it along the floor.

1 *What should Gaynor do?*

2 *What could happen if Gaynor did nothing?*

Evidence *KS 16*

Using the In the workplace text write a report that you think Gaynor should write. Explain to your assessor why you need to write reports and how you should write them correctly.

Key points

o You need to record and report changes in mobility straight away.

o Changes in mobility can be positive or negative.

o Records should be factual, legible and signed and dated.

What have I learned?

1 What are muscles, bones and joints?
2 What health conditions can affect movement?
3 What problems are caused by immobility?
4 Describe the best ways to keep mobile.
5 What are the benefits of keeping mobile?
6 How can you identify risks in mobilising?
7 Why should you read and follow care plans?
8 What do you need to check on appliances before you use them?
9 How can you support the use of mobility appliances?
10 How can you observe individuals when they are mobilising?
11 What are adverse reactions?
12 Why do you need to monitor individuals' progress?
13 Why should you report and record changes in mobility?

Any questions?

Q *The individuals I work with do not speak. How can I support them to communicate their preferences about keeping mobile?*

A Just because a person does not speak does not mean they cannot communicate. Everyone communicates in some way. Look at their facial expressions; do they look happy when they are doing mobility activities? Do they looked bored, or in pain? The individual's facial expressions and body language will 'speak' to you if that person can't.

Q *The service users I care for only do mobility activities with the physiotherapist. As a support worker I do not get involved.*

A Mobility activities are only a small part of this unit. The service users you work with still need to mobilise throughout the day and you may need to support them. Ask the physiotherapist if you could get involved with some of the activities. This will help you to provide more evidence.

Case study

Norman

Norman is 69 and is a retired head teacher. He has always kept fit by running and playing sports. He lives at home with his partner and their dog, Whiskey. Norman enjoys taking Whiskey for long walks, but has started to get terrible pain in his knees and hips. His doctor has diagnosed arthritis and has told him to keep mobile.

1 *What is arthritis and how can it affect individuals?*

2 *What benefits may Norman get from taking his dog for a walk?*

3 *What might happen to Norman if he does not keep mobile?*

A year has passed since Norman was diagnosed with arthritis. The pain in his knees and hips is becoming unbearable. Norman does not take his dog for a walk anymore because he is in too much pain. You have been asked to visit Norman each morning to help him with his personal care. Norman has always been a very able man and is not happy about having someone to help him.

4 *What information do you need to provide care to Norman?*

5 *What do you have to remember when accessing records and information?*

6 *Why must you follow his care plan?*

Norman has recently had a hip replacement and is back at home. He says he is not in any more pain and is looking forward to taking his dog for a walk again. The physiotherapist has shown him some exercises he must do to help him recover. You have been asked to support him with his exercises each morning.

7 *How are you going to encourage Norman to do his exercises and why is this important?*

8 *How can you make sure the environment is safe to mobilise in?*

9 *What should you do at the end of each exercise session?*

10 *Why is it important to keep records after each exercise session?*

11 *What would you do if you noticed Norman's mobility was improving or getting worse?*

12 *What legislation, policies and procedures will you be following when you support Norman to keep mobile?*

HSC223

Contribute to moving and handling individuals

This unit is an optional unit, one that you can choose to work on if you want to. For this unit you will need to move, handle and reposition individuals who have difficulties moving on their own.

Some individuals may only need help with moving for a short time. For example, they might be recovering from an operation or an accident, and will gradually get better. Other people might have a long-term condition. This could be a disability that they have lived with all their lives. Or it could be a more recent condition, such as multiple sclerosis or a stroke.

How you will be assessed

For this unit your assessor will observe you during work activities to cover the Performance Criteria. The Knowledge Specifications can be covered by discussion with your assessor. Your assessor may also ask you questions while you are working, or afterwards, to confirm that you know why you are doing certain things.

This unit covers the following elements:

o **223a** Prepare individuals, environments and equipment for moving and handling

o **223b** Enable individuals to move from one position to another.

Before you can begin to move individuals you need to get
them, yourself and the environment ready, or prepared.
In this element you will learn why it is important to
prepare yourself, the individual and the environment.
You will also learn how you can do this.

In this element you will cover:

o Preparing yourself
o Reading the care plan
o Checking risk assessments
o Assessing risks
o Preparing the individual
o Dealing with conflicts
o Types of moving and handling equipment
o Checking the safety of the equipment
o Preparing the environment.

Preparation of the individual is very important if they are to be
happy and comfortable

It is very important to prepare yourself before moving and **handling** individuals. This is so that you do not hurt yourself or the individual.

handling
touching or holding the individual

To prepare yourself you need to be wearing clothes and footwear that are safe.

Safe clothing

For your clothes to be safe, they need to be loose-fitting, but not baggy. Tight clothing can make it difficult to move properly. Baggy clothing can get caught in the moving and handling equipment. This could cause you injury.

Wearing appropriate clothes enables you to support service users more easily

Safe footwear

The shoes you wear should:

o be flat

o have a good grip on the sole

o cover your toes.

Your shoes should be flat to help you keep your balance. The soles, or bottom of your shoes, should grip well so that you do not slip. Your toes and heels should be covered to protect your feet.

> **Remember**
>
> Always wear flat shoes that cover your toes and have a good grip on the sole when you are moving and handling individuals.

> **In the workplace: Waheeda's clothes**
>
> Waheeda is new to care work. She is starting a new job in a day centre where she will be moving and handling individuals. On her first day she wears a long flowing skirt, wedge shoes, a big baggy jumper and a long scarf.
>
> 1 *Is Waheeda dressed safely?*
>
> 2 *What problems do you think she might have?*

Safe hygiene

Before you work with or handle individuals you need to wash your hands. You should do this to remove any bacteria or infection. You should also wash your hands when you have finished moving someone. Your hands touch a lot of things when you are working. By washing your hands frequently you can help to stop the spread of germs to other people. Look back at Unit 22 for more information about this.

Think about it

What clothes and footwear are you wearing today? Are they safe for moving and handling individuals? Ask your manager or colleagues if you are unsure.

Evidence *KS 20*

Describe to your assessor how you prepare yourself before moving and handling individuals; include your clothing, footwear and personal hygiene.

In the workplace: Ansul's lunch break

Ansul has just finished his lunch of fish and chips when he is asked by his supervisor to support a service user to walk to the bathroom.

1 *What should Ansul do first?*

2 *Why should he do this?*

3 *What effect could it have on the service user if he did not do this?*

Key points

o Always wear loose, but not baggy, clothing at work.

o Wear flat shoes that cover your feet and have non-slip soles.

o Always wash your hands before and after moving or handling individuals.

A care plan is a written report of how care should be given to the individual.

Before you read the individual's care plan you will need to access it. A care plan is **confidential** and should be kept in a locked filing cabinet. This is a requirement under the Data Protection Act. Under this Act you must get permission to access the individual's confidential records. You should get this permission from your manager.

confidential
a secret, or private information

To prepare yourself for moving and handling someone it is very important that you read their care plan. You should read the care plan each time you are at work to make sure it has not changed. The care plan will tell you how to move and handle that person safely. If you do not read the care plan, you could hurt yourself or the individual.

In the workplace: Daniel's care plan

Graham has worked as a care assistant at St Thomas' Care Home for over a year. He always reads Daniel's care plan before preparing to move him from his bed to his wheelchair.

When Graham was on holiday for two weeks, Daniel's health became worse. His care plan was changed to meet his new needs. When Graham returned to work he read Daniel's care plan and found it had been changed. Graham followed the new care plan, which stopped him hurting himself and Daniel.

1   *Look at the two care plans on page 289 and note any changes about moving and handling this service user.*

2   *What could have happened if Graham had not read the care plan?*

Remember

Never prepare to move or handle the individual without reading the care plan first.

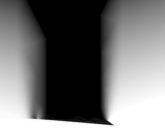

CARE PLAN REQUIREMENTS

Name Daniel Baker		Date of Birth 21.12.72	
Relevant information RTA resulting in open complicated fractures to both legs			
Unit Woodrush Rehab Unit		Date of Plan 08.08.07	

Planned Activity	Target Date	Nursing Requirement	Date Achieved
To minimise effects of immobility	08.08.07	1) Assess risk of pressure sores and address any issues arising from the assessment.	08.08.07
To safely use crutches to mobilise with support	30.08.07	1) Arrange physiotherapist assessment and input. 2) Encourage and support short walks to and from the bathroom.	
To safely use crutches to mobilise without support	07.09.07	1) Reduce support whilst observing safety. 2) Withdraw physical support giving only verbal support.	

CARE PLAN REQUIREMENTS

Name Daniel Baker		Date of Birth 21. 12. 72	
Relevant information RTA resulting in open complicated fractures to both legs. Subsequent infection at sight of wound on right leg.			
Unit Woodrush Rehab Unit		Date of Plan 01.09.07	

Planned Activity	Target Date	Nursing Requirement	Date Achieved
To safely use crutches to mobilise without support	14.09.07	1) Due to an infection of the wound full mobility has been delayed. Continue reducing support whilst observing safety.	
To exercise leg muscles whilst lying in bed		1) Encourage lifting of legs from the bed, individually, to a height of 12 (twelve) centimetres measured from the heels to exercise thigh muscles three times daily. 2) Encourage movement of toes to increase blood flow throughout the day.	

The care plan should be reviewed and changed appropriately to meet the individual's needs

Evidence *PC 2; KS 13*

Ask your assessor to watch you looking at an individual's care plan. Read the plan and explain to your assessor what you should do when moving and handling the individual. Explain why you should follow the care plan properly and the possible problems that could happen if you did not.

Key points

- A care plan is confidential.
- Always get permission before accessing an individual's care plan.
- The care plan will tell you how to move and handle the individual safely.
- Care plans can change. Read the care plan again every time before you move and handle individuals.

Have a go

Ask your manager for permission to look at some care plans. Read through the ones that are about moving and handling. See if you can find any that have changed recently.

■ **Checking risk assessments** *KS 8, 13*

You have learned about risks and risk assessments from Units 22 and 215. A risk assessment is a record of the different risks involved in moving and handling an individual, and what you should do to avoid the risks.

You can see some of this equipment illustrated on pages 298–300.

> **Remember**
>
> It is important to prepare yourself before moving and handling individuals by reading the risk assessment. You should do this each time you are at work to make sure it has not changed.

MANUAL HANDLING RISK ASSESSMENT

NAME Samantha Franks   **DATE OF ASSESSMENT** 17.9.07

WEIGHT 6st 4lb   **HEIGHT** 4ft 5"

PLEASE CIRCLE THE APPROPRIATE ANSWER

ACTIVITY	ANSWER		
Mobility	Good	Fair	(Poor)
History of falls	Yes		(No)
Able to weight bear	(Yes)	No	Sometimes
Level of understanding	Good	Fair	Poor
Uses walking aids	(Yes)	No	(N/A)
Is the individual unsteady?	Yes	No	(Sometimes)
Use of equipment	Hoist	Transfer board	(Handling belt)
Is equipment available?	(Yes)		No

OUTCOME

Samantha is able to weight bear and has a good level of understanding. She can therefore be transferred from her wheelchair to an armchair with one member of staff using a handling belt.

DUE REVIEW DATE (17.12.07)

Signed A Whithers   (Manager)

You can check that a risk assessment is up-to-date by looking at when it was last completed and when it is due for review

---

Have a go

Look at some risk assessments for the individuals you work with. Check to see if they are up-to-date. If you are unsure about this, speak with your manager.

How will reading risk assessments help you?

Risk assessments show you what problems could happen when you move and handle individuals. They also show you how you can stop these problems from happening. If you do not read and follow these assessments you could hurt yourself and the individual.

In the workplace: Jasmine and Samantha

Jasmine looks after a young girl named Samantha when she comes home from school every day. Jasmine helps Samantha to move from her wheelchair to her armchair. Before Jasmine moves Samantha, she always reads the care plan and risk assessment. On the risk assessment it says Samantha is able to weight bear. This means that she can put weight through her legs and feet.

Jasmine has not seen Samantha for a while, as she has been in **respite care** while her mother recovered from a minor operation. Samantha's mother tells Jasmine that Samantha can no longer weight bear. The risk assessment is no longer up-to-date.

1   *What should Jasmine do?*

2   *What could have happened if Samantha's mother had not told Jasmine about the change in Samantha's condition?*

respite care
when a service user stays in a special care home for a short time, while their usual carer has a rest or is unwell

---

Key points

o   Always prepare yourself for moving and handling by reading the risk assessment.

o   Risk assessments show you possible problems and how to avoid them.

o   Risk assessments can help to stop you hurting yourself and the individual.

o   Always check that the assessment is up-to-date.

As well as checking the care plan and risk assessments, you need to do your own risk assessment before moving and handling individuals. This is a requirement under the Manual Handling Operations Regulations.

Before you move or handle individuals, you need to ask yourself some simple questions. These can be seen in the checklist below. We have already looked at some of the questions. You will look at the others in more detail later.

Risk assessment checklist

✓ Am I wearing the right clothes and shoes?

✓ Is the floor dry and not slippery?

✓ Is the area around me clear and free from things I might trip over?

✓ Is the equipment clean, safe and ready to use?

✓ Am I trained to do this move safely?

✓ Am I fit enough to do this move?

✓ Can I move and handle this individual on my own?

If you answer 'yes' to all of these questions, your assessment is good and you can continue with the move. For example, what would you do if you answered 'no' to the first two questions? Would you go ahead anyway to save time? If you answer 'no' to any of the questions, your assessment shows that there might be a problem. You should not go ahead with the move until you have sorted out the problem.

Have a go

Read your organisation's policy on manual handling.

In the workplace: Too risky

Geraint is a care worker in an independent care home for older people with physical disabilities. Geraint has just returned to work following an operation on his knee. He is still having a bit of pain in his knee and cannot put all his weight on it.

Geraint has been asked to support Louis to walk from the dining room to his bedroom. Geraint has done this many times before, without any problems. Geraint assesses the risk using the checklist of questions. He answers 'no' to the question about his own fitness. Geraint explains to his manager that he is putting himself and Louis at risk of harm if he supports him to walk because of his knee. Geraint's manager agrees and asks another care worker to support Louis instead.

What harm could Geraint have caused to himself or Louis if he had supported the walk?

Evidence *KS 7, 13, 14*

Explain to your assessor the problems that can happen to yourself, the individual and others if you do not assess the risks involved in a move before doing it.

Key points

o You need to do your own risk assessment before moving and handling.

o Ask yourself a checklist of questions.

o You need to answer 'yes' to all the questions for the move to be safe.

o If you answer 'no' to any of the questions, there is a problem.

o You should not do the move until you have sorted out the problem.

The Human Rights Act 1998 says that everyone has a right to choice. This is covered in more detail in Unit 24. The right to choice also includes moving and handling. The individual has a right to choose, as much as possible, how they prefer to be moved and handled.

The service user should be involved with decisions about how they should be moved and handled. This section of their care plan should have been written only after talking and agreeing with the individual.

Before you move or handle the service user, you need to prepare them. You can do this by:

o describing what you are going to do

o explaining why you are doing it

o talking to them about how they can help.

Work with individuals when planning moving and handling

In the workplace: Getting consent

Manjit is an older man, who has had an operation on his leg. Faruke is helping him to get ready to move up the bed. She talks to Manjit, explaining what she is going to do and why. She asks Manjit to help her during the move, again explaining how and why he is being moved. Faruke checks that Manjit is happy with what is going to happen and gets his **consent** for the move.

Why is it important to get Manjit's consent?

consent
agreement

Even when the section on moving in the care plan has been discussed and agreed with the service user, you should always check that they are still happy to be moved in the agreed way. The individual may have changed their mind since the care plan was written. Or they may not be feeling very well that day.

Dignity and respect

Explaining what you are going to do, and why, is a way of treating the individual with dignity and respect. You should always explain what is going to happen, even if the person does not appear to understand, or is **unconscious**. People can still sometimes hear what is being said around them when they are unconscious.

unconscious
in a deep sleep

Encouraging the person to help in the move can make it easier for you. It also gives the person a bit more independence.

Think about it

How would you feel if you were lying in bed and a care worker suddenly started moving or handling you without telling you? How would you prefer to be treated?

Remember

Moving or handling an individual without their consent could be seen as a form of abuse. Look at Unit 24 for more information on this.

Evidence *KS 1, 3*

Explain to your assessor the rights a service user has regarding being moved and handled.

Key points

o The individual has a right to choose how they prefer to be moved and handled.
o Check that they are still happy with this before you start.
o Always tell the individual what you are going to do.
o Always explain to the individual why you are doing it.
o Always ask the individual to help if they can.

There may be times when you face conflicts or difficulties when preparing the individual for moving and handling.

A conflict can happen when the individual's choice goes against safe practice, risk assessment or the care plan. The following In the workplace may help you to understand this in more detail.

In the workplace: Moving Blossom

Blossom is an older woman, whose health has been getting worse over the last few months. Blossom is no longer able to stand up on her own. She does not have the strength in her legs to take her weight. A risk assessment has been done and the care plan has been changed. It would not be safe for staff to move Blossom, because she cannot put any weight on her legs.

The care plan now includes moving Blossom using mechanical equipment, such as a hoist. Blossom is not happy and insists she only wants to move herself, with the help of staff, not with the equipment. She says she does not want to lose her independence. She is also frightened of the equipment. Blossom's wishes are conflicting with safe practice, the risk assessment and her care plan.

1   *What do you think is the real reason Blossom does not want to use the equipment?*

2   *If you were Blossom's care worker, what would you do?*

An individual's choice may come from:

o   Personal beliefs – what they believe. For example, a Muslim woman may not allow a male care worker to support her.

o   Preferences – what they prefer. A service user may prefer to be moved by a care worker, rather than by equipment.

o   Fear – what they are frightened of. A service user may be afraid of heights, or a loss of control.

You may want to look at Unit 24 again to remind you about personal beliefs and preferences.

The service user may be frightened because they do not understand properly. It is very important that you explain everything fully to help them understand. This will help the service user to make a safe choice. If the individual's choice continues to conflict with the care plan, you must report this straight away to your manager. You should not move or handle the individual until your manager gives you further advice.

Evidence *KS 2, 3, 4, 5*

Explain to your assessor how an individual's personal beliefs or preferences could affect the way they are moved and handled. Also explain the different types of conflict you may face and how you can deal with these.

Key points

o Conflict can happen when the individual's choice goes against safe practice.
o Choice can arise from personal beliefs, preferences or fear.
o You should not move or handle an individual if their choice conflicts with the care plan.
o Always report conflicts to your manager straight away.

There are three main types of moving and handling equipment:

o   equipment that takes all of the person's weight
o   equipment that takes some of the person's weight
o   equipment that helps the individual to move on their own.

The type of equipment that is used depends on the individual's ability. The following chart looks at this in more detail.

Ability of individual	Type of equipment	Examples of equipment
Unable to help themselves	takes all of the person's weight	hoists, slings, slide sheets
Can help themselves a little	takes some of the person's weight	slide boards, slide sheets
Can help themselves, just needs support	helps the individual to move on their own	grab handles, lifting handles, handling belts

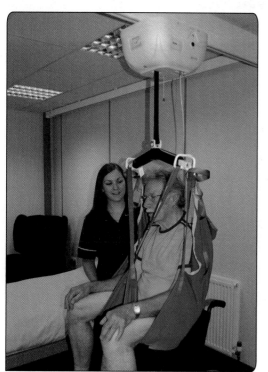

Hoist

There are two main types of hoist: portable hoists and track or ceiling hoists. You need to know how to use the hoist in your environment, as all hoists are different.

Ceiling hoists like this take up less room, but portable hoists can be moved from one room to another

Portable and track or ceiling hoists use a sling to hold the individual. The individual sits in the **sling**, which is then attached to the hoist. The hoist lifts the individual as they sit in the sling.

Slide sheet

A slide sheet is a thin, shiny piece of material that helps the individual to move. The person sits or lies on the sheet. The care worker can move the individual forwards or backwards more easily, because the sheet they are sitting on slides more easily up or down the bed.

It is important that individuals do not share slide sheets. Each person should have his or her own. Some slide sheets are disposable and are thrown away after they are used. This can prevent infection.

A slide sheet can help move an individual more easily

Slide board

A slide board is a shaped piece of wood. It is put between two chairs, or a bed and a chair. The individual then slides across the board from one piece of furniture to the other.

Long one-way glide anti-slip sheet

The long one-way glide is a single sheet with a handle at one end that helps a person to maintain a good sitting position. It allows an individual to be repositioned in a chair or wheelchair between five and seven times in a day.

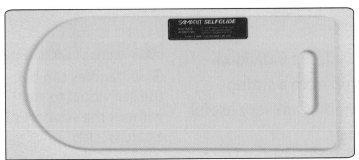

Slide boards come in different sizes, shapes and colours

Lifting handle

A lifting handle is usually put over a person's bed. The handle hangs down so that the individual can grab hold of it to pull themselves up. A lifting handle helps the individual to be more independent.

Handling belt

This is a broad, thick belt that goes around the individual's waist. The belt has handles on it that the care worker holds onto when helping the user to stand up or walk. A handling belt stops the individual being held by the arms. It helps to prevent the individual being hurt or bruised when being moved or handled.

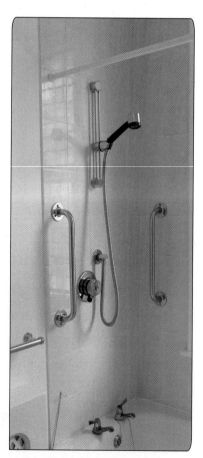

Grab handles can help the individual to stand without the support of a care worker

Handling belts prevent you harming the individual when supporting mobility

Grab handles

These are metal bars that are fixed to the wall. The individual can hold onto the bars to pull themselves up from a sitting position, or to help them sit down. Grab handles are very useful by the side of a toilet or a bath or in a shower.

There are many different types of moving and handling equipment, such as different types of hoists. Each piece of equipment works differently. It is important you understand how mobility equipment works and how to use it appropriately.

In the workplace: Hayley

Hayley is 14 years old. She has cerebral palsy and lives at home with her parents. She has a care worker who comes every morning and evening to help her with her with personal care. Hayley is unable to stand or walk and uses a wheelchair to get around. She is unable to help herself.

1   *What equipment do you think the care worker uses to help Hayley in and out of bed?*

2   *Why do you think these pieces of equipment are the most suitable?*

Think about it

What types of moving and handling equipment are used where you work? Do you know how to use all of them?

Evidence   *KS 10*

Describe the different types of moving and handling equipment used in your workplace to your assessor. Explain why each one is used for each individual.

Key points

o   There are three main types of moving and handling equipment.

o   The type of equipment used will depend on the individual's ability.

o   Moving and handling equipment includes hoists, slide boards, slide sheets, lifting handles, grab handles and handling belts.

Before you begin to use moving and handling equipment, you need to prepare it. You can do this by making sure it is clean and in good working order.

The Health and Safety Act (1974) says that all **employees** must 'care for their own safety and that of others'. By checking that the equipment is clean, you will be preventing **cross-infection**. This will help to keep you and the individual safe.

When cleaning the moving and handling equipment you use, you need to make sure you are doing it properly. Read the manufacturer's instructions to find out what chemicals can or cannot be used. Some organisations use disposable equipment; this prevents the spread of infection and saves on washing.

employees
people who work for an organisation

cross-infection
transferring infection, bacteria or disease from one person or thing to another

Have a go

Find the manufacturer's instructions for the moving and handling equipment that you use in your workplace. You may need to ask your manager where they are kept. Read the instructions on how to keep the equipment clean.

Remember

Always wash a slide sheet before using it on each service user.

All mechanical pieces of equipment also need to be checked by a qualified person. An electrician should check electrical items. He or she will make sure the equipment is safe. If it is, he or she will put a label on the item showing when it had a safety check and when the next one is due. Hoists should be checked and serviced by the company they were bought from. The hoist will also have a safety check label showing the date it is next due to be serviced.

Is it time for a test?

Always follow this simple checklist when preparing moving and handling equipment:

Safety checklist

✓ Is it clean?

✓ Is the safety check label still in date? (mechanical equipment)

✓ Are there any rips or tears? (slings or slide sheets)

✓ Has any of the stitching come undone? (slings, slide sheets, handling belts)

✓ Are there any sharp edges? (slide boards, hoists)

✓ Are there any loose or exposed wires? (electrical equipment)

✓ Has the battery been charged? (electric hoists)

Key points

o Checking the safety of equipment is a requirement under the Health and Safety Act 1974.

o You need to check that equipment is clean to prevent cross-infection.

o Always follow the manufacturer's instructions when cleaning equipment.

o You need to check that equipment has a safety check label that is still in date.

o Always check equipment before use for loose wires, rips, tears or sharp edges.

TC 004_A2

The environment in which you work can often be very busy, with lots of pieces of equipment and furniture around. Before you move and handle individuals, you need to prepare the environment.

To make sure that you and the individual are safe when moving and handling, you may need to move some pieces of equipment or furniture. This is to stop you tripping over or walking into items.

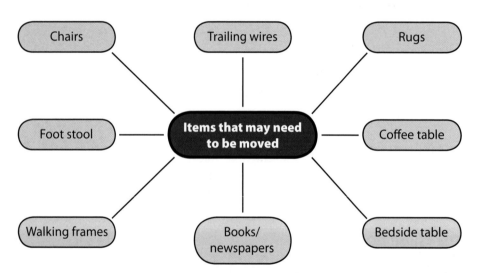

When you are moving someone, the area needs to be clear of any obstacles

When preparing the environment, you also need to get the moving and handling equipment ready. You need to make sure everything you will need during or immediately after the move is in place or at hand.

Think about it

What harm could you cause yourself and the individual if you tripped over a rug on the floor when moving and handling?

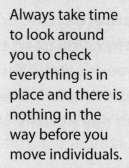

In the workplace: Joan's fall

Gayle had been very busy all morning helping individuals with their personal care. Joan, one of the service users, called over to Gayle saying she needed to go to the toilet. Joan is fairly able and moves around with a walking frame, but she finds it difficult to get out of the armchair on her own and to stand without help.

Gayle helped Joan to stand up with the use of the handling belt. However, Gayle had forgotten to get Joan's walking frame ready in front of her. The cleaner had moved it to the side of the room when she was vacuuming. Gayle turned away to reach for the frame, letting go of Joan's handling belt. Joan fell to the floor with a bang.

1 *What should Gayle have done to prepare the environment properly?*

2 *If Gayle identified she had not prepared the environment properly, what alternatives could she have done when supporting Joan to stand?*

Remember

Always take time to look around you to check everything is in place and there is nothing in the way before you move individuals.

Evidence KS 12, 14

Explain to your assessor how you prepare the environment where you work ready for moving and handling. Explain the importance of doing this, and the possible things that can happen if you do not. Give an example of when you have done this.

Key points

o Make sure the area is free from obstacles that you might fall over, so that you do not hurt yourself or the individual.

o Prepare the moving and handling equipment so that everything is ready for the move and is within easy reach.

An individual who is not able to move themselves on their own needs help to do so. They may need help from another person, or equipment might be needed. As a care worker, you need to make sure that you help individuals to move safely. You must also look after your own safety by getting help if equipment should be used by more than one person.

In this element you will learn how to encourage individuals to do as much for themselves as possible.

In this element you will cover:

- Why individuals need to change position
- How to help individuals to change position
- How to provide active support
- Minimising pain when moving individuals
- Restoring the environment
- Observing and recording changes.

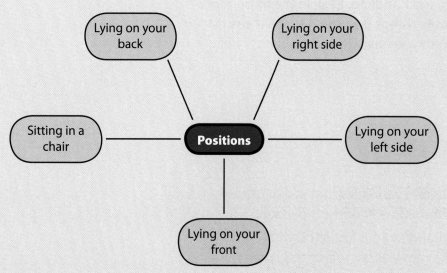

It is important to notice any changes in a service user's mobility

Have you ever been sitting or lying in one position for too long? How did it make you feel? For a lot of people sitting or lying in the same position for a long time can become very uncomfortable. It can cause pain, discomfort and even make them bad tempered.

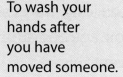

Remember

To wash your hands after you have moved someone.

If the way you were sitting or lying was causing you pain or discomfort, what would you do? You would move yourself to change your position and make yourself more comfortable. Not everyone is able to do this for themselves. This could be because they are ill, or because they have a disability.

The way you sit or lie depends on what you are doing and how you are feeling. This is the same for the individuals you care for.

There are all kinds of reasons why people want or need to change position, whether they are in bed, or up and about.

Think about it

Think about the different ways you sit or lie down and why you choose these positions.

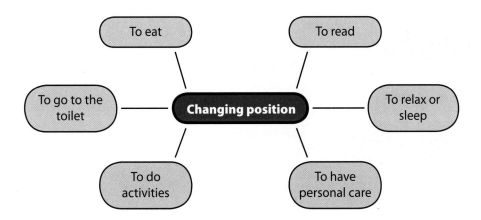

These are a few reasons why an individual's position may need to change. Can you think of any others?

Some individuals need to have their position changed regularly for medical reasons. If someone sits or lies in the same position for too long, they can develop pressure sores. You need to encourage and support them to change position regularly to prevent this.

A pressure sore is when the skin gets sore from sitting or lying on it. The skin gets very red and, if not treated, can start to break and open. Over a short time, again, if not treated, the skin starts to die and a hole develops. This can lead to pain and infection. It can also cause the individual embarrassment. The type of sore a person has is described in 'stages'.

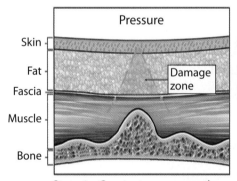

Stage 1 – Constant pressure on the skin causes damage. The surface of the skin becomes red and the area feels warm to touch.

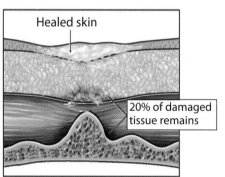

Stage 2 – The skin begins to blister and a small shallow pit may appear, which starts to weep. The damage beneath the surface of the skin is greater than you can see.

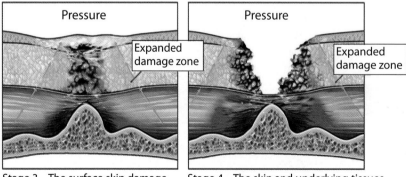

Stage 3 – The surface skin damage goes deeper into the underlying tissues and is likely to become infected.

Stage 4 – The skin and underlying tissues are deeply damaged, down to the bone. This can cause a serious illness known as septicaemia, or blood poisoning.

The four stages of pressure sore development

Other reasons for pressure sores developing can be as a result of a poor diet, lack of fluids, being underweight or overweight and wet or damp skin. If you work with individuals who have these factors it is very important that you encourage them to move or change position regularly to help avoid the risk of a pressure sore developing.

Have a go

Get some more information on pressure sores and learn about how to prevent them. Speak to your manager or colleagues if you need more help.

In the workplace: Looking after Petula's skin

Petula was admitted to hospital after being in a car accident. She is unconscious and unable to move herself. The staff change her position every hour to help prevent her from getting pressure sores. At 2.30pm she is moved onto her left side. At 3.30pm she is moved onto her back. At 4.30pm she is moved onto her right side. At 5.30pm she is moved back onto her left side, and so the cycle continues.

What could happen if Petula was left in the same position for a few hours?

Evidence KS 16

Talk to your assessor about the reasons why the individuals you provide care for need to change positions. Give an example of when you have helped to do this.

Key points

- People need to move positions to stop pain, discomfort and irritability.
- People change position to help them to sleep, eat, relax and undertake activities.
- Changing position helps to prevent pressure sores.

It is very important that all care workers involved in moving and handling individuals get the proper training. This is part of the Manual Handling Operations Regulations 1992. If you have not received training in your workplace, you must speak to your manager before you start moving and handling individuals.

Care workers should never lift or hold the whole of an individual's weight. You should use the appropriate equipment, as provided by your employer. Make sure you have someone helping you if the equipment should not be used by one person on their own.

When helping individuals to change position, the first thing you need to ask yourself is: 'Is the individual happy to be moved by this method or way?'. This is covered in the topic Preparing the individual in the first element of this unit, on pages 294–95. Look at it again if you are unsure. The next thing you should do is to check the risk assessment and care plan.

Remember

Never move or handle individuals without the proper training.

Using a hoist

A hoist is usually used when the individual cannot move themselves. Each hoist is used a little bit differently. Make sure you have read the instruction book that comes with the hoist. You should also have had training on how to use the hoist. In general there are things you should always do when you change an individual's position using a hoist.

o   Use the right sling.

o   Make sure you use the sling with the seam facing away from the individual. This is so the seam does not scratch their skin.

o   Attach the sling to the hoist.

o   Reassure the individual as they are being lifted.

- Only lift the individual high enough to clear the furniture they are sitting or lying on.
- Use the steering handles to move the hoist to the new position.
- Use the handles to guide the sling as it is lowered.
- Make sure the individual is happy and comfortable in their new position.

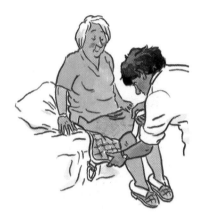

Is the seam facing away from the skin?

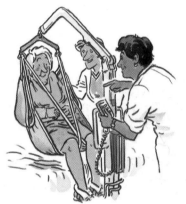

Don't lift too high!

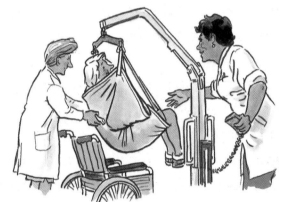

Guide the sling carefully

Supporting a move

If an individual is sitting down and they would like to move up the chair, or to a bed or different chair you can support them with the use of equipment. To do this the individual needs to be able to put their weight through their arms and/or legs. You can support the change of position using:

- a slide board
- a slide sheet
- a handling belt
- a one-way glide sheet.

Is the person comfortable?

These pieces of equipment are described on pages 298–301, in the first element in this unit. You can see how to help someone push themselves up in a chair on page 315 in the section on active support.

Moving in bed

If an individual is very ill, unconscious or cannot move themselves at all, you will need to change the position they are lying in. You can do this by using a slide sheet. To move the individual safely you should:

o have at least two care workers to make the move

o tell the individual what you are doing at all times

o put the slide sheet under the individual

o use the slide sheet to roll the individual (make sure a care worker is standing on the side they are being rolled onto, so that they do not fall out of bed)

o remove the slide sheet after repositioning

o put pillows around the individual to stop them rolling back over

o leave the individual safe and comfortable.

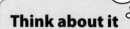

Think about it

Each time you carry out moving and handling, imagine how it would feel to be moved in that way.

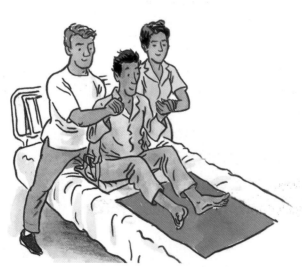

A slide sheet can also be used to move an individual who can help themselves a little

Team work

There will be times when the individual's risk assessment says that they should be moved and handled by two or more staff. This means you will be working as part of a team. As a team you need to work together and move the individual at the same time as each other. You can do this by:

o   deciding who will lead the move
o   the leader checks that everyone is ready, including the person to be moved
o   the leader says, 'Ready, steady, move'
o   on the word 'move' everyone moves the individual.

These steps are known as coordinating the move. If the move is not coordinated, you could seriously hurt yourself and/or the individual.

Evidence
KS 1, 7, 13, 17

Explain to your assessor in detail how and why you move and handle individuals using two different pieces of equipment.

In the workplace: Coordinating the move

Kieran, Valli and Bethany are helping George, a rather large man, turn over in bed. Kieran and Valli stand by one side of the bed, and Bethany on the other. Kieran says that he will coordinate the move. He checks everyone is ready and says, 'One, two, three, move.'

Unfortunately, Valli thought they would move George when Kieran said 'three' and so starts the move when she hears the number three. She suddenly gets a sharp pain in her shoulder and chest. She has hurt herself because no one was helping with the move when she started it.

What should Kieran have done as leader to avoid any confusion?

Key points

o   Make sure you have the proper training in moving and handling.
o   Use the right equipment to help you.
o   When working as a team, always coordinate the move correctly.

Active support is the help that you give individuals to encourage them to do as much as they can for themselves.

You can actively support individuals by:

o   giving them choice

o   showing them how they can help you and themselves

o   providing them with the right equipment.

Encouraging individuals to help themselves

Some individuals may be able to do more for themselves if you encourage them. The person will need to be physically able to do this and someone experienced in this area should assess the individual's ability. This could be a physiotherapist.

Getting out of bed

1   Encourage the individual to roll to the edge of the bed, but not too close to the edge, as you do not want them to fall out. Their hand should be up by their shoulder, and facing down on the mattress

2   Encourage the individual to swing their legs over the side of the bed

3   Finally, the individual should sit up, with their hands pushing down on the mattress, before moving their feet towards the floor

Turning over in bed

You can encourage the individual to turn over in bed by following these steps.

1   Ask the individual to turn their head in the direction they want to turn.
2   Get them to bend their outer leg, and put their foot flat on to the mattress.
3   Ask them to reach across their body with their outer arm. Doing this helps the upper body to turn into the roll. They should then be able to turn over by pushing down with their foot.

Pushing back up in a chair

Some people slip down when sitting in a chair. A one-way glide sheet, or an anti-slip sheet can help them push themselves up into a more comfortable sitting position. The individuals needs to:

1   Place their hands on the arms of the chair.
2   Lean forward in the seat.
3   Slightly raise their bottom.
4   Push with their feet on the floor.

In the workplace: Sam is slipping

Sam is a boy who has a condition that affects his muscles. He always slips down when sitting in his chair. It is uncomfortable, but Sam does not like to keep asking for help to sit back up.

Sheenagh, a care worker, has noticed that he looks uncomfortable and realises that he does not like to ask for help. Sheenagh speaks to the manager who arranges for Sam to have an anti-slip sheet put on his chair. Sam is very happy.

Why is Sam happy?

Key points

o   Active support can help develop independence.
o   Showing the individual what to do is active support.
o   Providing equipment for the individual is actively supporting them.

A one-way glide sheet can help stop an individual slipping down in a chair

If you move and handle individuals correctly you can help to **minimise** any pain they might have during the move. There are three main ways to do this.

You

If you know what you are doing because you have had the proper training, you should not have accidents or make mistakes that could cause the individual pain.

Involvement

Tell the individual what you are going to do before you start the move. This can help to minimise pain because they are **cooperating** and not struggling. For example, they could move their hands out of harm's way, or do other things that you ask that will stop them from getting hurt.

Environment

Make sure that furniture is out of the way so that you do not trip over it while supporting the service user. If you fell, you could both be hurt.

When you move or handle individuals you need to be very careful not to damage their skin. This could happen in the following types of move:

○ Moving up or down the bed or up a chair. The individual's bottom, heels or elbows could be dragged on the mattress or bedclothes. Lifting the individual clear of the bed can prevent this. Individuals whose skin is damaged in this way could develop a pressure sore

o   Supporting an individual to walk or stand. Holding onto the individual's arm can cause them to have bruises, especially if they bruise very easily. Use a handling belt to avoid causing pain and bruising

o   Supporting individuals to stand. Standing up too quickly can make the service user feel very giddy. They may fall over and hurt themselves. They may also be very stiff from sitting. You need to support the individual to stand up slowly to minimise any pain.

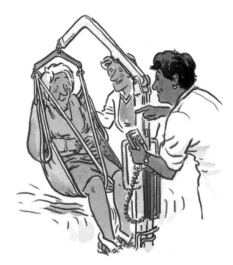

Make sure the person is clear of the bed before moving

Have a go

Practise these methods with your work colleagues. Take it in turns to be the person being moved so that you understand what it feels like. See if there is anything that you are doing that could cause the service user pain or discomfort.

Evidence *KS 14, 18*

Explain to your assessor the problems that can be caused when moving and handling are not carried out properly.

Remember

Never let an individual be dragged up a bed or chair. This can lead to them developing pressure sores.

Key points

o   Always use the correct way to move and handle individuals.
o   Get the individual's cooperation before you start.
o   Prepare the environment so that no one trips over things.
o   Be careful not to damage the service user's skin.

After moving and handling individuals, you should restore the environment. This means:

o putting back any equipment that has been used

o putting the furniture back to where it was.

Putting back equipment

Think about what your own home would look like if you did not put things back where they should be after you had finished using them. It would look very messy. Apart from the mess, it would also be very unsafe. You could trip over objects lying on the floor, or bump into things. Do you think the individuals you provide care for would be safe in this sort of environment?

Many small care environments only have one or two portable hoists. If you did not return a hoist back to where it should be, other members of staff would not know where to find it. A lot of time could be wasted finding out where pieces of equipment had been left.

Putting back the furniture

When you move a coffee table, chair or rug in preparation for moving and handling, don't forget to put it back! People usually have their furniture where they prefer it to be. It is in those positions for a reason – so that the person can get to it, reach it or use it.

For some people it is extremely important to have the furniture returned exactly where it was. For example, people who cannot see are able to move around their living environment safely by remembering where things are. If you move a piece of furniture, and do not put it back exactly where it was, the individual may trip over it. This is because they cannot see it and did not remember it being there when they last walked in

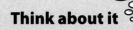

Think about it

If you were blindfolded do you think you could move around your own home by remembering where each piece of furniture is?

that area. Just imagine the difficulties you would have if any of the furniture in your house was moved and not returned to its proper position.

In the workplace: Out of reach

Melissa lives on her own and has a care worker, Judith, to help her get up in the morning and to go to bed at night. One evening Judith uses the hoist as usual to help Melissa get into bed. Judith returns the bedside table, but not quite in its usual place. On the table are a lamp, a jug of water and a glass.

Before leaving the house Judith checks with Melissa that she has everything she needs. Melissa looks around; the lamp light is on and the jug of water is full. 'Yes, thank you,' she replies. 'See you in the morning.' Judith leaves the house. Melissa decides to pour herself a glass of water. When she reaches over to the bedside table she realises it is too far away. It has not been put back exactly where it should be. Melissa cannot reach the water, nor can she turn off the light. Melissa has to try to sleep through the night with the light on and without a drink.

Before leaving what checks should Judith have made?

Key points

o   Always put equipment away where it should be stored.
o   Leaving equipment out can be very unsafe, and waste other people's time.
o   Return furniture to where it originally was so individuals know where it is and can reach what they need.

When you are working with individuals you should be observing, or watching them. You should notice any changes that affect their moving and handling.

The changes could be positive changes, or improvements. It could be that the individual is able to move without as much help as before. They may not have as much pain as previously when they move.

The changes could also be negative changes, or deterioration. For example, the individual could be in more pain when moved, or they are not able to help themselves as much as they could.

Any changes, positive or negative, should be reported to your manager and recorded in the individual's care plan. Any changes in the way an individual is moved or handled also needs to be written in their care plan. A more senior care worker or staff member will usually do this.

Daily Record Sheet	**Page No** 4

NAME Harry Frederickson

21.7.07 – Harry found it very difficult to get out of the chair this morning, even with a member of staff supporting him. He is also saying he has pains in his knees. Problem reported to the Centre Manager who will refer Harry to the Occupational Therapist.

Signed DJ Singh _____ Davinda Singh (DCO)

You must record any changes, positive or negative, so that the individual's care plan can be updated

In the workplace: Supporting Harry

Davinda has been working with Harry for two months. Harry started coming to the day centre where Davinda works after his wife passed away. Harry is unsteady on his feet and needs to be helped in and out of a chair.

Today, Davinda noticed that, even with support, Harry was finding it very difficult to get out of the chair. Harry was also complaining of pains in his knees. Davinda reported this change to her manager and recorded it in Harry's care plan. Harry was reassessed and his care plan was changed. Harry now sits in a raised chair and is supported by two staff to stand up from the chair.

If this problem had not been reported what difficulties would Harry have had?

Remember

- o When you access the individual's notes remember the Data Protection Act 1998 and ask for permission from your manager.
- o Always complete the record clearly, so that everyone can read it and understand it properly.
- o Always remember to keep the notes confidential. When you have finished with them put them back in the filing cabinet and lock it.
- o Maintain confidentiality, report any changes only to those that need to know.

Key points

- o Changes can be positive changes, or improvements.
- o Changes can be negative changes, or deterioration.
- o Always report and record any changes in an individual.
- o Changes need to be reported so that the care plan can be updated.

What have I learned?

1 How can you prepare yourself, the individual and the environment for moving and handling?

2 Why is it important to read an individual's care plan before you move or handle them?

3 What do risk assessments tell you?

4 What conflicts might you come across, and how can you deal with them?

5 How do you check moving and handling equipment is safe to use?

6 How can you help individuals to change position?

7 How can you encourage active support?

8 How can you minimise pain when moving individuals?

9 Why is it important to restore the environment after moving and handling?

10 Why do you need to observe and record changes in an individual's moving and handling?

Any questions?

Q *In the first element it says that you need to ensure that the individual understands why they are being moved and handled, and how they can cooperate. I work with individuals who cannot understand or cooperate. How can I get evidence for this?*

A Your assessor will still need to observe you working with individuals, regardless of whether they can understand or not. You will still need to explain to the individual what you are doing. Your assessor may ask you questions to cover the second part on cooperation.

Q *I work on my own in the community with people in their own home. How can I get evidence for HSC223a PC 10?*

A If you work on your own it would be difficult to get help straight away. You would need to explain to your assessor in what circumstances you think you may need assistance and how you could get it.

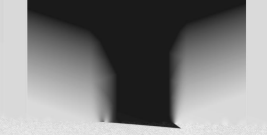

Case studies

Suki

Suki is 24 years old and lives at home with her parents. As a result of cerebral palsy, she has learning difficulties, and her arms and legs are affected.

Her care worker, Annette, visits the house every morning to help get Suki ready for the day centre. Annette also visits on a Saturday afternoon to give Suki's parents time to go out shopping. Suki is not able to stand and is transferred from her bed to her wheelchair using a hoist. At weekends, Suki sits in a specially adapted armchair, rather than in her wheelchair.

1   *What legislation should Annette follow when she moves Suki using the hoist?*

2   *What checks should Annette make before moving and handling?*

3   *Why is it important for Annette to follow the risk assessment and care plan?*

Suki is upset

One morning Annette notices that Suki is not very happy when she hoists her from her bed to the wheelchair. Suki is crying, but as she cannot speak, she cannot say what is wrong. Annette tells Suki's mother, who says Suki also cried the night before when she was hoisted to her bed. Annette records Suki's reaction in her notes for the night worker to read.

The following morning Annette learns from the night worker's notes that Suki had cried again when she was being hoisted. Annette checks the sling very closely and notices a small amount of stitching has come undone on the part of the sling that goes under Suki's legs. When Annette asks Suki if the sling is hurting her, Suki smiles, which means 'yes'.

Annette tells Suki's mother, who finds the spare sling to use instead. When Annette uses the spare sling, Suki smiles when she is hoisted. Annette records this in the notes and asks Suki's mother to send away the damaged sling and get a replacement. Annette also informs her manager of the problems.

1   *If the family did not have a spare sling, and Suki's mother insisted Annette use the sling to get her out of bed, what action should Annette have taken?*

2   *Once Annette has finished hoisting Suki out of bed, what should she do?*

Element	Links to the following units and Learning Outcomes (LO) of the City and Guilds Certificate in Health and Social Care (Technical Certificate)
21a	001. LO2 002. LO1 003. LO1, 2, 3
21b	002. LO1 003. LO1, 2
21c	002. LO1 003. LO1, 2
21d	002. LO1 003. LO3 004. LO1
22a	004. LO1, 2, 3
22b	004. LO2, 3
22c	004. LO1, 2, 3
23a	001. LO1, 2, 3, 4
23b	001. LO1, 2, 3, 4 002. LO4
24a	002. LO1, 2, 3 003. LO1
24b	002. LO1, 2, 3
24c	002. LO4
223a	004. LO1, 2, 3
223b	002. LO1*, 003. LO3, 004. LO1, 3
215a	002. LO2, 003. LO3, 004. LO1, 2, 3
215b	002. LO2, 003. LO3.3 004. LO1, 2, 3

Summary of Acts within the care sector

Throughout this book you will have read about many different laws. These laws are referred to as Acts when they are passed by parliament. This section will help you to learn a little more about them. To learn more, you may want to speak to your manager or look on the Internet. Checking on the Internet for summaries can help you to understand an Act better.

In Scotland, Health and Social Care are the responsibility of the Scottish Parliament, so legislation and policy differ from the rest of the UK. These variations are shown in blue, like this, below.

Human Rights Act 1998

- There are 16 basic human rights. They cover everyday things, such as what a person can say and do and their beliefs, as well as the more serious issues of life and death.
- Human rights are rights and freedoms that all people living in the UK have, regardless of their nationality or citizenship.
- The Human Rights Act came into effect in October 2000, letting people take their complaints about how they have been treated to a UK court.
- Although everyone has these rights they can be taken away from a person if that person does not respect other people's rights.

Care Standards Act 2000
(England, Northern Ireland, Wales)

- The Care Standards Act set up an organisation called the National Care Standards Commission. This has now been renamed the Commission for Social Care Inspection.
- The Act sets standards that all social care workers must meet. These can be found in the booklet 'General Social Care Council Code of Practice'. The Act also ensures all care provision meets with the National Minimum Standards.
- It also sets standards of the level of care given to individuals requiring social care.

o The Act requires that all staff have a thorough police check before they begin working with children and adults.

o It also requires that a list is kept of individuals who are unsuitable to work with vulnerable adults.

Regulation of Care (Scotland) Act 2001

o In Scotland, the Care Commission regulates and inspects all care services in Scotland. It uses National Care Standards to ensure that service users receive the same standard of care wherever they live in Scotland.

o In Scotland, the *Codes of Practice for Social Service Workers and Employers* sets out the standards that all social care workers in Scotland must meet.

o Social service workers and those working in social care will be registered with the Scottish Social Services Council.

Health and Safety at Work Act (1974)

This Act is regularly updated to reflect changing working conditions.

o This Act is the main one within the workplace. In this Act both the employer and employee have responsibilities.

o The employer must:
  o provide a safe place to work
  o provide Health and Safety training
  o do risk assessments for all possible hazards.

o The employee must:
  o take care of their own safety and that of others as much as possible
  o cooperate or work with the employer on Health and Safety matters
  o not, on purpose, damage any Health and Safety equipment.

Community Care and Health (Scotland) Act 2002

On 1 July 2002 free nursing and personal care for the elderly was introduced in Scotland. Elderly people who qualify receive payments of between £145 and £210 per week, depending on their needs.

Control of Substances Hazardous to Health 2002 (amended) (COSHH)

- This Act relates to you working with any substances that could cause you harm. This could include cleaning chemicals or medication.
- The employer must carry out a risk assessment of any potentially harmful substances you could come into contact with in the workplace.
- The employer must advise its employees on the correct usage of COSHH substances and provide suitable protection, e.g. gloves, aprons.
- The employee must follow the given guidelines and wear any protective clothing required.
- The employer must provide a lockable cupboard in which to store substances mentioned under the COSHH regulations.

Reporting of Illnesses, Diseases, and Dangerous Occurrences Regulations 1995 (RIDDOR)

- This Act requires the reporting of accidents, diseases and dangerous occurrences that happen in the workplace.
- This includes deaths, major injuries, accidents resulting in over 3 days off work, diseases and dangerous occurrences (such as walls collapsing).

Mental Capacity Act 2005

- This Act empowers and protects vulnerable people who are not able to make their own decisions.
- It deals with the assessment of a person's capacity and protects those who lack capacity.
- The Act created two new public bodies: a new Court of Protection and a new Public Guardian.

- It includes three further key provisions to protect vulnerable people: an Independent Mental Capacity Advocate (IMCA), advance decisions to refuse treatment and it being a criminal offence to ill treat or neglect a person who lacks capacity.

Mental Health (Care and Treatment) Act Scotland 2003

Data Protection (Amendment) Act 2003

- The purpose of this Act is to protect the individual's right to privacy.
- When you are collecting information you must let the person know who you are, the reason for collecting the information and whom you will share the information with.
- You must keep the information safe and secure so that no one without the right can access it.
- An individual has a right to see information that is kept about them. For this reason you should not include in a record anything that you would not want that individual to see.

Access to Medical Reports Act 1988

Freedom of Information (Scotland) Act 2002

This Act established the office of Scottish Information Commissioner, who is responsible for ensuring public authorities maximise access to information.

Disability Discrimination Act 2005

- This Act first came into force in 1995 and was amended in 2005.
- It requires the providers of public transport to reduce the amount of discrimination on its buses and trains towards people with disabilities.
- The Act requires public facilities and buildings to be made accessible to those who have disabilities.
- It requires employers to make reasonable adjustments to allow an individual with a disability to gain employment.

ability being able to do something

abuse physical harm or cruelty towards someone

access to get to

accommodate fit in

active support encourage individuals to do as much for themselves as possible

adapt change

adverse reaction a problem that can occur, e.g. pain

advocate someone who represents, or speaks, for someone else

aggressive angry, forceful and may become violent

allergy a bad reaction by the body to a substance

anaemic not enough iron in the blood

anaesthetic drug that puts someone into a deep sleep for an operation

anorexia an eating disorder where the person does not eat enough

appendicitis emergency when an organ called the appendix might burst

appraisal review of your work

appropriate suitable for the occasion or use

assess look at and judge

bacteria tiny living organisms that can cause disease

barrier something that gets in the way or stops you from doing something

bedpan a piece of equipment used for going to the toilet in bed

body language movements of the body communicating how someone feels

chiropodist a trained person who cares for feet

cholesterol an important substance that moves fats around the body; high levels can cause strokes or heart attacks

circulation movement of blood around the body

Citizens Advice Bureau a free service that advises people

civil rights rights belonging to people born and resident in the country

colleague person you work with

commode a portable toilet

communicate show or tell someone what you mean

confidential a secret, or private information

confidentiality keeping information secret

conflicts disagreements or different viewpoints

consent agreement

constipated difficulty in passing faeces

constructive feedback feedback that helps you to improve your practice

conveen a device for male incontinence that collects urine in a drainage bag

cooperating doing what is asked of you

covert hidden or disguised

cross-infection transferring infection, bacteria or disease from one person or thing to another

cultural customs, beliefs and ways of thinking; these can be linked to religion

culture customs, ideas and behaviour of a group of people

dehydrated not enough fluid in the body

dementia disease that affects the brain, especially the memory

depressed feeling of great sadness and hopelessness

developed improved

diabetes a serious medical condition affecting the levels of sugar in the blood

diarrhoea liquid faeces

discriminate treat unfairly, e.g. because of age, race or gender

dispose get rid of

diversity differences in race, religion and lifestyle

embolism small clot of blood

emphysema the abnormal presence of air in the lungs causing swelling and breathlessness

employees people who work for an organisation

encouragement words such as 'you can do it' and 'you're walking very well'

evacuation way to move people away from danger

factual true

faeces waste matter discharged from the bowels

failings serious problems or weaknesses

feedback telling someone how well or badly they are doing

flexible bendy, elastic

focus pay full attention to

formal official

gender whether someone is male or female

germs tiny organisms which cause disease

grooming helping people to have a tidy appearance such as brushed hair, clean teeth and being clean shaven

handling touching or holding the individual

hazard anything that can cause harm, e.g. chemicals, body fluids, slippery floors

hygienically working in a clean way that reduces the risk of infection spreading

hypoglycaemia a drop in blood sugar level which can make the individual feel weak or dizzy

immobile not moving – sitting or lying still

inappropriate not suitable for the occasion

incontinent unable to control the bladder and bowels

indelible ink ink that cannot be rubbed out

identify find out

independence being able to do things on your own without anyone's help

individual a single human being as distinct from a group

individuality being treated according to your own likes and dislikes

infection a disease that other people can catch

informal not official

intruders people who break in

joints where two bones meet

key people people who are important in an individual's life, such as parents, friends, carers, relatives

knowledge something you know and understand

kosher prepared according to Jewish law

legal requirement must be done by law

legible easy to read

ligaments fibrous tissues that connect muscle to bones

limb an arm or leg

malnourished weak due to lack of healthy food

mandatory what workers must have

mastectomy removal of a breast

meet the requirements do what a code or law asks

menopause when a woman's periods stop

minimise reduce, make smaller

mobility ability to move around, or from one position to another

monitor keep an eye on

motion an emptying of the bowels

muscles strong, fibrous tissues which shorten to give the body movement

needs things that a person cannot do without

neglect not caring for someone properly

non-verbal communication passing on or receiving information without speaking, e.g. looking bored or crying

nutrients parts of food essential for health

nutritious full of nutrients; nourishing

obese being very overweight

objectives goals or plans for the future

observe watch

opportunity having the chance to do something

overt obvious

periods monthly flow of blood in women of child-bearing age

position the way we sit or stand

prejudiced attitude a point of view based on stereotyped ideas

procedure the proper, official way to do something

professional specialists such as doctors, speech therapists, occupational therapists

promote continence provide the environment in which people are able to use the toilet appropriately and at the right time

promotion a better job, with more responsibility

public register a public record that everyone has the right to look at

qualifications exams a person has passed

rabbi Jewish religious leader

regulated made rules about

reminiscence remembering things from the past

respite care when a service user stays in a special care home for a short time, while their usual carer has a rest or is unwell

respond answer or communicate back to someone

responsibility something it is your duty to do

resuscitation special techniques used for reviving people

right something an individual is legally able to do

risk the chance that somebody will be harmed by a hazard

risk assessment a report that shows the likelihood of harm

seizure a sudden attack of illness, e.g. a stroke or an epileptic fit

sensitive embarrassing or difficult

sign language using your hands to make signs, e.g. British Sign Language or Makaton

skills something that you can do

sling a piece of thick, strong material, that attaches to a hoist

slurred the sounds of the words run into one another

sprains and strains damage to the muscles or ligaments

sputum coughed-up saliva or phlegm

stereotyped idea a simplified idea about a group of people

strength something you are good at

stroke sudden illness that often causes weakness or loss of use of one side of the body

unauthorised people those that do not have permission

unconscious in a deep sleep

valued of importance to other people

verbal spoken

vomit what is brought up when someone is sick

vulnerable at risk of harm or abuse

weakness something you are not very good at

Books and publications

S/NVQ Level 2 Health and Social Care , Yvonne Nolan (Heinemann, 2005)
Full support for your learning programme at S/NVQ Level 2

Core Themes in Health and Social Care, editor Beryl Stretch (Heinemann, 2007)
Essential underpinning of knowledge for students of Health and Social Care

Knowledge Sets, Pat Ayling, Caroline Bartle, Debby Ralilton (Heinemann, 2007)
The essential training package for care workers includes:
Knowledge Sets in Infection Prevention and Control
Knowledge Sets in Dementia
Knowledge Sets in Medication

Social Care and the Law in Scotland: An SVQ-related Reference Guide for Care Staff, (Kirwin MacLean Associates, 2005).
This useful guide also contains an SVQ unit index which lists the SVQ units that refer to legislation in their knowledge specifications

Nursing Standard (RCN Publishing Company); *Community Care* (Reed Business Information Ltd.)
These publications cover up to date practices and issues on Health and Social Care.

National Care Councils and Codes of Practice

England: General Social Care Council www.gscc.org.uk
The General Social Care Council Code of Practice for Social Workers (2002)

Northern Ireland: Northern Ireland Social Care Council www.niscc.info/
Codes of Practice for Social Care Workers and Employers of Social Care Workers

Scotland: Scottish Social Services Council www.sssc.uk.com
Codes of Practice for Social Service Workers and Employers

Wales: Care Council for Wales www.ccwales.org.uk
Code of Practice for Employers of Social Care Workers

More useful websites

www.aliveandthrive.org.uk
Action and information packs for people with disabilities

www.citizensadvice.org.uk/ Citizens Advice Bureau
The Citizens Advice service helps people by providing free,
independent and confidential advice on legal, money and
other problems

www.csci.org.uk Commission for Social Care Inspection
Independent Inspectors of care services in England

www.dh.gov.uk Department of Health
Provides public health and social care policy, guidance
and publications

www.direct.gov.uk
Information about public services all in one place

www.ethnicityonline.net
Information about the views and needs of different cultural
groups

www.hse.gov.uk Health and Safety Executive for Health and
Safety publications
There is also a useful Health and Safety in health and social care
services section

http://www.nmc-uk.org/ The Nursing and Midwifery Council
An organisation set up by Parliament to ensure that nurses and
midwives provide high standards of care to their patients and
clients. It has a register of all nurses and midwives.
NHS Education for Scotland acts as agents for the UK NMC

www.opsi.gov.uk/ Office of Public Sector Information
Access to UK legislation 1987–2007 to print out or read online

www.sqa.org.uk Scottish Qualification Authority
The Care Scotland/Health and Social Care sections have
information and evidence-gathering forms for SVQ, as well as
specimen blank documentation, information sheets, unit
downloads, assessment strategy and guidance.

Healthy living
www.eatwell.gov.uk Food Standards Agency 'Eat well, be
well' site
Includes healthy diets for different ages and stages of life,
keeping food safe, food labels and other health issues

www.nice.org.uk National Institute for Health and
Clinical Excellence
Provides national guidance for promoting good health and
preventing and treating ill-health

www.healthyliving.gov.uk an NHS Scotland site to promote
Scotland's healthy living programme

abuse 148
    people at risk of 152–3
    recognising 149–51
    reporting 154–5
accident forms 87
action plans 114–15
alcohol hand rub 73–4
appraisals 95, 106–7
aprons, wearing 71
assessing your work *see* evaluating
    your work

balanced diet 161–3
bathing 214–29
beliefs 102–3
body language 6–9, 24

care plans 204, 258–9, 288–9
Care Standards Act 123–4, 325–326
careers in health and social care vi–vii
choking, dealing with 192–3
Codes of Practice xiii, 126–7
commenting on care 145–7
communication 4–7
    adapting 40–3
    cultural differences in 10–11
    effect of disability 8–9
    extra support 16–17
    means of 33–5
    and personality 10
    rights 36–7
    seeking information 12–13
    sharing your findings 18–19
    skills needed 14–15
    supporting people 38–9
complaints 145–7
confidentiality 12, 45–7, 49
conflicts in care work 132–3
consent, importance of getting 294–5
COSHH (Control of Substances
    Hazardous to Health
    Regulations) 67, 326
cultural differences
    communication 10–11
    food preferences 170–1
    personal hygiene 219–21
    respecting 142–3

Data Protection Act 12, 45, 50, 324
diet
    cultural/religious 170–1
    healthy and balanced 161–3
    unhealthy 164–5
dignity, treating people with 134–47
Disability Discrimination Act 328
discrimination 135–7, 144
diversity, respecting 134–47
drinking 162–3

eating and drinking
    choking, dealing with 192–3
    environment/presentation 180–3
    equipment for 187
    help with 177–9
    practical help with 186–9
    problems with 190–3
    questions/worries about 184–5
    recording/reporting 194–5
emergencies, dealing with 80–9
equipment
    for bathing 222–4
    for eating 187
    handling 298–302
    for moving people 298–302
    for toileting 205–6
evaluating your work 94
    beliefs and values 102–3
    getting feedback 95–7
    knowledge and skills 104–7
    reflection/reflective cycle 98–101

facial expressions 5, 8
feedback, importance of 95–7
fires, dealing with 84–5
first aid 86, 192–3
first aid box, contents of 88–9
food allergies 191–2
food labelling 166–7
food preferences 168–71
food safety 172–5

gloves, wearing 74–5

hand washing 72–4
hazards 57–9

health and safety 55
    bathing 224
    disposing of waste 67–71
    emergencies 80–9
    equipment handling 302–3
    hand washing 72–4
    hazards 57–9
    infection control 72–5, 207, 226–7
    laws and policies 64–7
    mobility hazards 266–7
    personal health 76–9
    records, completing 62–3
    risks 60–1
Health and Safety at Work Act 64–5,
    328
health emergencies 86–9
hoists 298–9, 310–11
holistic care 129
Human Rights Act 17, 37, 325
hygiene
    care worker's personal 76, 226–7
    helping service users 214–29

infection control 72–5, 207, 226–7
information
    about service users, gaining
        129–31
    sharing with other professionals
        18–19

jobs in health and social care vi–vii

knowledge, developing 108–17

laws and policies
    Care Standards Act 123–4, 325–6
    Data Protection Act 12, 45, 50, 327
    health and safety 64–7, 328
    Human Rights Act 17, 37, 325
listening skills 20
    demonstrating 24–5
    positioning yourself 21–3
    responding appropriately 26–9
    seeking advice and support 30–1
mobility 244
    adverse reactions to 274–5
    appliances 260–5

benefits of exercise 254–5
care plans 258–9
dangers of immobility 250–1
hazards 250–1
health conditions affecting 248–9
and health risks 256–7
monitoring progress 276–7
muscles, bones and joints 245–7
observing changes in 270–3
physical and verbal support 268–9
reporting changes 278–9
ways to be mobile 252–3
moving and handling individuals
active support, providing 314–15
assessing risks 292–3
checking risk assessments 290–2
conflicts, dealing with 296–8
equipment safety 302–3
equipment types 298–302
helping people change position 310–13
minimising pain 316–17
preparing the environment 304–5
preparing the individual 294–6
preparing yourself 285–7
reading the care plan 288–9
reasons for changing position 307–9
recording changes 320–2
restoring the environment 318–19

National Minimum Standards 37
non-verbal communication 5–6, 8–9
nutrition pyramid 162
NVQs vi–xi
differences in England, Scotland, Wales and Northern Ireland xii-xiii

obesity 164

personal care needs
bathing equipment 222–4
dealing with problems 228–9
faeces, recognising normal 210
infection control 207, 226–7
menstruation 211
preferences of user 218–21
promoting independence 216, 222–4
recording/reporting 212–13
sensitivity to user's needs 201–3, 215–16
support with toileting 200, 204–5
toileting equipment 205–6
urine, recognising normal 208–9
personal development plans (PDPs) 109–10
personal health 76–9
PIES (Physical, Intellectual, Emotional, Social) needs xvi–xvii, 129
position during communication 20–4
positive feedback sandwich 96–7
pressure sores 308–9
protection of service users 112–13
see also abuse

recommended daily allowances (RDAs) 165
records and reports
accessing 44, 48
completing 50–1
confidentiality of 45–7, 49
eating and drinking 194–5
getting permission 48
health and safety 62–3
moving and handling 320–2
personal care 212–13
reflection 98–9
reflective cycle 100–1

relationships with service users, building 128–31
reminiscence books 130
respect, treating people with 134–7
responsibilities 126–7
reviewing practice 116–17
RIDDOR (Reporting of Injuries, Diseases and Dangerous Occurrences Regulations) 65–6, 326
rights 17, 102–3
of care workers 102–3
communication 36–7
of service users 123–5
risk assessment 60, 216, 290–3
risks 60–1

security issues 81–3
self-reflective accounts 100–1
sign language 13, 35
skills, developing 108–17
Social Care Councils, websites for xiii
spillages, dealing with 69
SVQs (Scottish Vocational Qualifications) xiii
SWOB (Strengths, Weaknesses, Opportunities, Barriers) assessments 105–6

toileting needs 200–13
training 103–104
formal 110–11
informal 105

values 102, 138–9

walking frames 261, 265
walking sticks 260, 264
waste disposal 68–71
wheelchairs 260, 262–3